# Building High-Speed Networks

Tere' Parnell

Osborne/**McGraw-Hill**

Berkeley   New York   St. Louis   San Francisco
Auckland   Bogotá   Hamburg   London   Madrid
Mexico City   Milan   Montreal   New Delhi   Panama City
Paris   São Paulo   Singapore   Sydney
Tokyo   Toronto

Osborne/**McGraw-Hill**
2600 Tenth Street
Berkeley, California 94710
U.S.A.

For information on translations or book distributors outside the U.S.A., or to arrange bulk purchase discounts for sales promotions, premiums, or fund-raisers, please contact Osborne/**McGraw-Hill** at the above address.

### Building High-Speed Networks

1234567890 DOC DOC 90198765432109

ISBN 0-07-211858-X

| | |
|---|---|
| **Publisher** | **Proofreaders** |
| Brandon A. Nordin | Tom Barash |
| **Editor in Chief** | Pat Mannion |
| Scott Rogers | **Indexer** |
| **Acquisitions Editor** | Irv Hershman |
| Gareth Hancock | **Computer Designers** |
| **Project Editor** | Michelle Galicia |
| Ron Hull | Michelle Zmijewski |
| **Editorial Assistant** | Ann Sellers |
| Stephane Thomas | **Illustrator** |
| **Technical Editor** | Brian Wells |
| Joe Moran | **Series Design** |
| **Copy Editor** | Peter Hancik |
| Dennis Weaver | |

For 1Lt Jeffrey Bracco, HHT/FSE, 4/7 Cavalry,
whose combat training inadequately prepared him
to deal with an author
under deadline.

# CONTENTS

**Part II**

**How to Speed Up: Local Area Solutions**

## Part IV

### Network Construction Ahead

## Part V

## Appendixes

# ACKNOWLEDGMENTS

To anyone considering writing a book, let me offer one piece of advice: don't do it. To those of you who ignore my wisdom and write one, let me urge you to surround yourselves with supportive friends and competent professionals. And thank them profusely in the "Acknowledgments" section of your books. That's the only way I've been able to survive as an author—and that's what I intend to do here.

First, I'd like to thank my good friend and colleague, Christopher Null, for contributing material in Chapter 18 on extranets and security. Chris is not only an insightful technologist, but also a gifted writer who has helped me immeasurably.

Gareth Hancock, my acquisition editor at Osborne/McGraw-Hill, somehow instinctively knew how to deal with me when deadline pressure and faithless writers brought out the worst in me. Always cheerful and upbeat, even while I was threatening his property and well being, Gareth is a model for all who hope to thrive in the publishing business. The same is true of Debbie Escobedo, editorial assistant at Osborne/McGraw-Hill. She was always poised, polite, and professional, no matter how irascible I was. She can and will have a great career in either publishing or daycare.

As always, my children, Claire and Elliot, amaze me with the understanding and patience they have with their crazed mother. Now, when I'm irritable, they ask, "Mom, are you working on another book, or are you just in a bad mood?" Their insight and acceptance constantly delight me.

Finally, I want to thank the United States Army for its amazing foresight in stationing 1Lt Jeffrey Bracco in another hemisphere for the past 12 months. Had they not done so, this book surely would not have been written.

# INTRODUCTION

Every network manager I know has asked me how fast is fast enough. Most of them have well designed, well managed networks that have been optimized to make the most of their resources. Yet nearly all of them are receiving performance complaints from some sector of the network and pressure from managers to "speed up the network." As well, nearly all of them have at least one "project from hell" haunting their pasts and making them wake up in a cold sweat after nightmares about implementing a new network protocol. This book is for them—and for you.

Truth is, there is no such thing as "fast enough" when it comes to networks. The minute you have your network zipping along, someone will demand a new multimedia application that will gobble all your bandwidth. The trick is to know precisely what new protocol or access method to implement, where to begin implementing it, how to integrate it into your existing network, and what kind of performance boost you can realistically expect from it.

To that end, I've organized this book not only by type of high-speed protocol, but also by its appropriate location. Furthermore, each chapter discusses not only how the protocol works, but also the specific implementation issues surrounding it, along with its strengths and weaknesses, and my recommendations for where it should—and should not—be used.

Part I, "Identifying the Bottlenecks" consists of six chapters.

Chapter 1, "Do You Really Need a High-Speed Network?" discusses the general issues surrounding the implementation of a high-speed network.

Chapter 2, "The Backbone is Connected to the . . ." explains how backbones work and why they are usually the first place a high-speed network is needed. It describes how to diagnose some of the major problems of insufficient bandwidth. In this chapter we also discuss some of the issues involved in selecting a network protocol for the backbone.

Chapter 3, "Down on the Farm," defines that elusive entity, the server farm, and explains why and how they have come to be. It also gives hints on how to identify throughput problems in a server farm, as well as what you need to alleviate them.

Chapter 4, "Closer to Home," deals with power workgroups—those clusters of tough customers who use every PC and network resource within login distance, and still demand more. It describes the causes and cures of a bandwidth shortage within the workgroup.

Chapter 5, "The Wide Area," takes on just that. Although this area is technical beyond the boundaries of the enterprise network, it is becoming increasingly integrated with it. As a result, a shortage of bandwidth on the wide area becomes a problem for the enterprise network manager.

Chapter 6, "The Cost of Converting to High Speed," is devoted to building a framework for planning your protocol selection and implementation. It provides worksheets and procedures for determining exactly how much building a high-speed network or segment will cost in terms of both money and time.

In Part II, "How to Speed Up: Local Area Solutions," Chapters 7 through 12 deal with high-speed local area protocols. Respectively, these are Fiber Distributed Data Interface, 100VG-AnyLAN, 100Base-T, Gigabit Ethernet, Fibre Channel, and isoEthernet. Each protocol is discussed in technical detail, including frame composition and operation, access method, manageability, scalability, media support, cabling considerations, and fault tolerance. Each of these chapters ends with a summary of the strengths and weaknesses of the protocol in question, along with my recommendations for its best deployment.

In Part III, "How to Speed Up: Wide Area Solutions," Chapters 13 through 17 discuss the high-speed wide area protocol choices available today. These are Integrated Services

Digital Network, Switched Multimegabit Data Services, Frame Relay, and Digital Subscriber Line services. Again, the technical details of the operation of the protocols are explained, along with implementation issues, strengths, weaknesses, and my recommendations. Chapter 16 is devoted to Asynchronous Transfer Mode, that local- and/or wide-area-protocol-miracle that everyone has been hearing about—and waiting for—for so long. The technical issues surrounding implementing ATM are covered in detail, as well as the issues of standardization and integration that have kept people waiting for lo these many years.

Part IV of this book deals with the management issues of the new breed of high-speed network, the intranet/extranet. Chapter 18, "How to Build Fast, Secure Intranets and Extranets," discusses the technologies that define intranets and extranets, and offers tips on how to design infrastructures to accommodate them with good performance. The information on security for extranets was developed and written by my good friend and colleague, Christopher Null, former Managing Reviews Editor for *LAN Times*. And Chapter 19, "Management Systems for High-Speed Networks," talks about the different tools and techniques available for managing your network and keeping it running smoothly.

Finally, for the brave of heart who are ready to set forth implementing a new high-speed protocol, Chapter 20, "Speed Kills: Avoiding a Crash," gives some guidance in preparing for the great undertaking. It also includes, as the title suggests, some words of warning to heed before beginning a high-speed networking project.

Most technical books begin with a rather lengthy—and by now repetitive—chapter on the International Standards Organization's Open Systems Interconnectivity Reference Model. I decided not to. Because most network managers can recite the OSI Model's layers by heart, and generally only need to refer to the Model occasionally, I've put a concise explanation and discussion of the model, compliments of Tom Sheldon's wonderful *LAN Times Encyclopedia of Networking* (if you don't have a copy, get one), in Appendix A.

For those of you who may wonder exactly who and what all the standards organizations are and how they fit together in the Pantheon of Networking Standards, I've included a brief explanation in Appendix B.

Most people don't have the good fortune that I do to have a job that lets them spend hours talking to developers, vendors, analysts, and end users about a new and emerging technology, then spend days on end testing products based on that technology. I still can't believe I get paid to do this. I can't give you the transcripts of my ream of lab notes and countless interviews, but I can give you Appendix C, a bibliography of those reference works that I have found most helpful in building a foundation knowledge of high-speed networking.

I hope that you find this book not only useful, but fun to read. I certainly had fun writing it—most of the time.

# PART I

## Identifying the Bottlenecks

# CHAPTER 1

## Do You Really Need a High-Speed Network?

Most network managers need more of everything. They need more time, more money, more equipment, more people, more patience, and more performance. Most of them have been doing the high-tech equivalent of making a silk purse out of a sow's ear for so long that they work under the automatic assumption that they won't have the resources they need, so they have made improvisation a way of life. They spend hours kludging together network patches and fixes, dreaming of a world in which they could have the latest hot products they read about in glossy networking trade magazines. Under these circumstances, it's often easy to assume that nearly every network problem is the result of not having the latest, newest, and/or fastest technology.

And so it is with network performance. When your network slows to a crawl, your users are wailing, and your boss is threatening, your first thought might be to convert your network—or at least the slow segments of your network—to one of the 100Mbps-and-faster protocols. After all, you figure that increasing the throughput ten times or greater has to improve your network's performance, even if excessive network traffic isn't the sole culprit.

Just a few years ago, high-speed networking was so expensive that it was really just a dream for most network managers. That's because if you wanted a fast network, you had one choice: FDDI. Originally, choosing FDDI also meant changing your cabling media to optical fiber. And that meant major bucks, which effectively priced most buyers out of the high-speed network market.

A lot has changed, however. Not only are fast transport protocols popping up like mushrooms, their components are competing in price with standard 10Mbps equipment. As well, some of them can use existing Category 3 cabling (like 100VG-AnyLAN and 100Base-T4), although some of them currently require fiber-optic cabling (such as 100Base-FX and Gigabit Ethernet, although there are proposed standards for Gigabit Ethernet over copper). Therefore, it seems only natural that the performance-starved network manager would think that now is the time to implement a high-speed network.

# READ THIS FIRST

This book is for you, the network manager poised to jump into the world of high-speed networking. The first thing we want to do is urge you not to leap just yet.

You have probably read a great deal about high-speed networks. You may have begun talking with vendors of high-speed networking products. You may have even begun the task of selecting a high-speed protocol for your network. We applaud your diligence. And we sympathize; of all the challenges that high-speed networking presents, the selection of the transport protocol is probably the most daunting.

Unfortunately, it's not the challenge you have to meet first.

## Ask Yourself Why

Before taking the plunge, be sure you really need to.

As we mentioned, it's easy to attribute slow network performance to a shortage of bandwidth. It's also easy to assume that "more is better" and forge ahead into high-speed networking because it can't hurt. But neither assumption is true, and both are dangerous. The time to learn that high-speed networking cures your network's ills is before you invest the time and money to implement it.

Before you continue with your high-speed networking plans, ask yourself why you are considering high-speed networking. Is it because you are currently experiencing slow network performance? Or is it because your networking plans for the near future involve such bandwidth-hungry applications as multimedia and videoconferencing? In either case, why do you think more bandwidth will improve the situation?

## It May Be Bandwidth

If your current problem is slow network performance, you may be on the right track. Often enough, poor network performance is indeed the result of excessive network traffic. There are a lot of factors that could be contributing to increasing network traffic. Too many workstations on one segment can generate more traffic than the available bandwidth can handle. There is also a trend in applications to use more bandwidth, due largely to the popularity of multimedia applications. Finally, the average packet size for all applications is growing. Although the current average packet size is around 512 bytes, it may soon grow to 1,500 bytes and larger. To determine whether excessive traffic is causing your network problems, you should put a protocol analyzer on each affected network segment. A protocol analyzer can be configured to monitor packets for the specific topology and protocol of the segment, letting you monitor the traffic on the segment to which it's connected. A protocol analyzer will help you determine not only the average bandwidth utilization on the segment, but also the average packet size and composition. As well, a protocol analyzer can assist in spotting trends in traffic, peak traffic periods, and devices that are generating bad packets or acting as network bottlenecks.

For your initial network evaluation, we recommend that you use a sophisticated protocol analyzer that offers packet-level decoding and analysis. If you don't have your own such protocol analyzer, you can rent one or even hire someone to bring in a protocol analyzer and do the traffic monitoring and protocol analysis for you. Most network integration firms offer protocol analysis equipment and services.

Don't feel you have to rush out to purchase a high-end protocol analyzer. After you complete your initial network evaluation and have established a "baseline" traffic pattern, you can monitor your network adequately with one of the software-only protocol analyzers, such as Etherpeek from AG Group. These software-only protocol analyzers are relatively inexpensive ($500 or less), and while they don't offer the packet-level analysis that more sophisticated protocol analyzers do, they enable you to spot trends and potential problems on your network.

In any event, don't proceed with plans for implementing a high-speed network until you have monitored your network with a protocol analyzer and are satisfied that insufficient bandwidth is the problem. This is the only way to be sure that a high-speed network will improve your network's performance.

## And Then Again, It May Not Be Bandwidth

All the benefits of higher network bandwidth notwithstanding, a high-speed network isn't a panacea. There are many network problems that will slow performance that have nothing to do with insufficient bandwidth. If the real problem in your network is, for example, disk I/O on your servers, no amount of bandwidth is going to speed performance. Here are some problems that will slow your network that can't be fixed with a high-speed protocol.

# SERVER-RELATED PERFORMANCE PROBLEMS

There are several server components that affect network performance. Before contemplating upgrading to a higher-speed network, be sure to check out the following potential server bottlenecks.

## Processor Speed

The actual speed of the processor is obviously a big factor in server performance.

A heavily used server with an inadequate processor simply can't keep up with the requests for data it receives. Make sure that your servers have adequate processing power. Some network operating systems, such as NetWare 4.X, have server utilities that perform server speed tests. The results of such a speed test can give you a good idea of your server's overall performance and indicate whether it has sufficient processing power for its job. Even if you confirm that your servers have adequate processing power right now, you still may need to replace or enhance them when (and if) you implement a high-speed network. High-speed network interfaces place more demand on the server's CPU—after all, they are requiring the server to process incoming packets that are arriving many times faster than on a 10Base-T or Token Ring/16 network. Therefore, before you install your high-speed network adapter, make sure your server has processing power to spare.

## Disk Subsystem

This is the slowest part of your network. By definition, a file server provides file services: access to the data and application files stored on the file server's disk subsystem. The disk subsystem is the hard disk itself and the disk controller that manages the transfer of data between the disk and the server's processor. If the disk subsystem cannot provide fast enough access to the files stored on it, your network users will spend a lot of time waiting for the data they have sent to or requested from the file server to be processed. The data transfer rate, or speed with which a server can transfer files between its processor and disk subsystem, is a function of the disk itself, the disk controller, and the bus interfaces between the disk and the disk controller and between the disk controller and the processor. The faster these components are, the faster the network response time. The first clue that the disk subsystem is slowing performance is when server requests to read and/or write data are waiting on disk input/output. Most network operating systems have integrated utilities that will show the percentage of time requests are waiting on disk input/output. If you find that requests are waiting excessively on disk input/output (and this will vary from server to server and network to network, so "excessive" will have to be defined in terms of your particular network), it's probably time to consider installing a faster disk subsystem. However, even the fastest disk subsystems available at the time of this writing can't keep up with 100Mbps traffic.

## Random Access Memory

Too little or poorly configured random access memory (RAM) can also slow server performance. A network server caches, or holds, its most recently accessed data in memory as long as it can. When the server fills all of its memory allocated for caching, it writes the least recently accessed back to its disk. If your server has too little RAM, it will spend an excessive amount of time going to disk to retrieve data. Reading data from the disk drive is substantially slower than reading the information from RAM. Your network operating system will have an integrated utility that will tell you the percentage of cache hits, or times when requested data was retrieved from RAM. When cache hits drop below about 85 percent, you should consider adding more memory or readjusting memory caches.

The speed of your server's RAM also affects its overall performance. You should therefore check to see that your servers' memory speed fits their usage.

# NETWORK-RELATED PERFORMANCE PROBLEMS

Some performance problems are related to the connection between the host device and the network media, but aren't the result of insufficient bandwidth. Here are some of the more common performance-sapping problems that occur at the network connection.

## Network Interface Card Selection

Your choice of network interface cards, both in the server and in the workstation, can dramatically affect network performance. Network interface cards vary widely in both performance and cost, so you will have to weigh the benefits of faster performance against the relative cost of the cards. When choosing a network interface card, be sure to evaluate the following:

▼   **Data throughput**   This is the speed at which the network interface card transfers data between the host computer's memory to the network. The data throughput depends upon both the width of the bus interface to the host processor and the method the network interface card uses to transfer data.

Currently, host bus widths are 16, 32, or 64 bits. The wider the data bus to the host processor, the faster the network interface card can transfer data. Different network interface card bus architectures offer different bus widths, with Industry Standard Architecture (ISA) network interface cards offering 16-bit buses, and Extended Industry Standard Architecture (EISA) and Peripheral Component Interface (PCI) network interface cards offering 32- and 64-bit buses. Servers, with their heavy traffic over their network interface cards, should really be computers designed with one of the 32- or 64-bit architecture buses and outfitted with corresponding network interface cards.

Network interface cards transfer data to and from host memory using one of three methods: direct memory mapping, input/output ports, or direct memory addressing (DMA). Direct memory mapping is usually the fastest data transfer method, so for highest performance, choose a network interface card that employs the direct memory mapping data transfer method.

▲ **Onboard processor**   Network interface cards that employ an efficient onboard processor can improve the performance of the card and therefore of the network as a whole. Therefore, to improve performance, use network interface cards with high-performance onboard processors.

## Chattering Cards

If you have a card chattering, or sending out streams of bad packets, no amount of bandwidth will improve network function. This is because the malfunctioning card may very well fill all available bandwidth with errant packets, meaning that increasing bandwidth to 100Mbps will only give you ten times the network garbage you now have.

## Poor Network Interface Card Driver Support

If the drivers—those lines of code that translate network redirector program calls into instructions for your network interface cards—are poorly written, your users will experience all kinds of network difficulties, including slow performance. The poor performance comes from the retransmissions necessary to send a packet successfully from the network interface card to its addressee. Other problems associated with poorly written drivers are network time-outs, lost connections, and "hung" servers.

# WORKSTATION-RELATED PERFORMANCE PROBLEMS

Another aspect of network performance that is often overlooked is the workstation performance. Workstations with slower processors, slow hard disks, and/or insufficient memory won't be able to process quickly all the data they send and receive from the server. This will give your users the impression of a slow network, although the problem is really much closer to home.

# HOW TO DETERMINE THAT HIGH-SPEED NETWORKING WILL HELP

Now that you have some idea of the scope of the many problems that high-speed networking won't solve, you're probably wondering how to go about determining if it will solve your particular network difficulties. Using the following worksheets and flowchart will help you determine whether high-speed networking will really help your network.

## Step One: Evaluate Your Server Usage

Use the following form to determine whether your server is experiencing performance problems.

### Server utilization:

The average server utilization should probably be below 60 percent. However, this will vary from operating system to operating system and network to network. Consult your network vendor to determine the appropriate server utilization for your network. If server utilization averages over 60 percent, consider upgrading the server's processor or moving some applications to another server.

### Cache utilization:

Cache hits should average around 85 percent. If not, check the amount of memory and allocated cache buffers. The rule for most network operating systems is the more memory, the better. However, there are exceptions, especially when you are working with older versions of these network operating systems.

### Disk utilization and swapping:

If server requests are waiting on disk input/output, or if the server is *disk swapping* (using disk storage to augment random access memory), consider adding memory or increasing cache buffers.

If the server disk itself is more than 80 percent full, you'll need to increase disk capacity or remove some data from the existing disks.

### Component device utilization:

With component device technologies such as *Small Computer Systems Interface (SCSI)*, the throughput is always reduced to the lowest common denominator. So, if you have a bunch of devices attached to a single SCSI host adapter, the signaling throughput for the entire chain will match that of the slowest device in the chain.

## Step Two: Evaluate Your Server Configuration

Using the following form, describe your server hardware and configuration. Make copies of the form as needed.

**Server 1:**

Processor:

Type:

Clock speed:

Random Access Memory:

Amount:

Speed:

Total cache buffers:

Disk Subsystem:

Controller type:

Disk access speed:

Disk capacity:

RAID level (if applicable):

Network Interface Card:

Manufacturer:

Model:

Host bus width:

Memory access method:

Onboard processor type:

Driver name:

## Step Three: Evaluate Workstations

It's important to evaluate the processing power of the workstations on network segments that are experiencing poor performance. Even when the server and network are operating well, an underpowered workstation can give users the impression of a slow network.

**Workstation 1:**

  Processor:

    Type:

    Clock speed:

  Random access memory:

    Amount:

    Speed:

    Total cache buffers:

  Disk subsystem:

    Controller type:

    Disk access speed:

    Disk capacity:

  Network interface card:

    Manufacturer:

    Model:

    Host bus width:

    Memory access method:

    Onboard processor type:

    Driver name:

# Step Four: Evaluate Current Application Requirements

List in the next form the names and types of applications resident on each server. Database, statistical modeling, and CAD/CAM applications put a strain on server resources. If you see a server—or disk within a server—that has a disproportionate number of these types of applications, try to move them to another server or disk to try to balance the load. Imaging and multimedia applications, on the other hand, generate a lot of network traffic, and therefore indicate a need for a high-speed network protocol.

**Server 1:**

*Disk 1*

Operating system:

   Number of users:

   Location of users:

Word processing applications:

   Number of users:

Spreadsheet applications:

   Number of users:

Database applications:

   Number of users:

CAD/CAM applications:

   Number of users:

Imaging applications:

   Number of users:

Multimedia applications:

Number of users:

Groupware applications:

Number of users:

*Disk 2*

Operating system:

Number of users:

Location of users:

Word processing applications:

Number of users:

Spreadsheet applications:

Number of users:

Database applications:

Number of users:

CAD/CAM applications:

Number of users:

Imaging applications:

Number of users:

Multimedia applications:

Number of users:

Groupware applications:

Number of users:

*Disk 3*

Operating system:

  Number of users:

  Location of users:

Word processing applications:

  Number of users:

Spreadsheet applications:

  Number of users:

Database applications:

  Number of users:

CAD/CAM applications:

  Number of users:

Imaging applications:

  Number of users:

Multimedia applications:

  Number of users:

Groupware applications:

  Number of users:

*Disk 4*

Operating system:

  Number of users:

  Location of users:

Word processing applications:

Number of users:

Spreadsheet applications:

Number of users:

Database applications:

Number of users:

CAD/CAM applications:

Number of users:

Imaging applications:

Number of users:

Multimedia applications:

Number of users:

Groupware applications:

Number of users:

Also, make a note of the number of users for each application and the location of these users. The more users, obviously, the more load on the server—but also the more network traffic. Furthermore, users that must cross bridges to access servers are generating traffic on networks other than their local segment.

## Step Five: Evaluate Future Application Requirements

Looking at your network's strategic and budget plans, list the names and types of applications you plan to add in the next 18 months. Beside each, list the number and location of the users of these applications.

## Step Six: Evaluate Network Usage

If, however, after making the suggested changes to your network, summarized in Figure 1-1, you still have a performance problem, it's time to put a protocol analyzer on your network. This will tell you the amount and type of traffic being generated.

It will also tell you that you have network-related problems, such as chattering cards, that will cause slow network performance.

## Step Seven: Read On

If traffic monitoring with a protocol analyzer reveals exceedingly heavy network utilization, often characterized by an abundance of collisions, it's time to start planning your high-speed network. The following chapters show you how and why to implement high-speed protocols on different segments of your network.

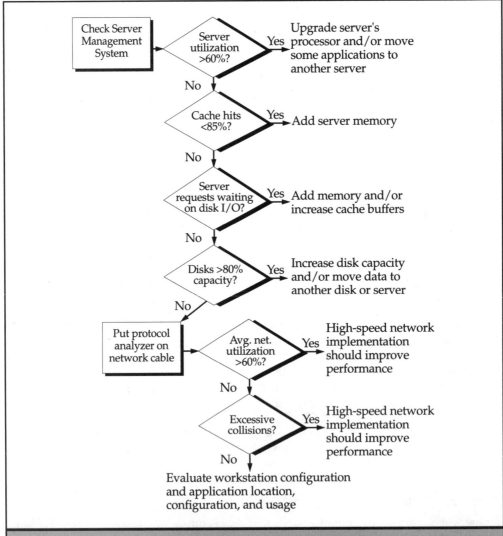

**Figure 1-1.**    Flow chart summarizing how to troubleshoot poor network performance

# CHAPTER 2

## The Backbone Is Connected to the...

P robably the first place you will start feeling the bandwidth pinch is on your network's backbone. By its very nature, a network backbone is prone to congestion and slow network response. As a result, it is usually the first place high-speed networking is indicated—and implemented—in a network. However, before you conclude that a high-speed backbone is the answer to your performance problems, be sure that you understand the function of the network backbone, as well as your options for improving the handling of high traffic volume.

## HOW IT ALL BEGAN

Back in the early days of networking, all networks were linear networks. This meant that a network consisted of a number of workstations connected by a single cable. At the time, this was fine, because networks tended to be small, and so cable problems were fairly easy to isolate. On larger networks, however, locating a loose connection or cable break could be a difficult and time-consuming process, often requiring special—and expensive—equipment to determine the type and location of the cable problem.

To solve the problem caused by a single network cable, wiring centers, or hubs, were developed. The first hubs were nothing more than signal repeaters. They took a data signal from one cable segment and repeated it over another, extending the length of the network, as shown in Figure 2-1. However, these simple repeaters made it easy to divide networks into segments, meaning physical and/or logical groups of network users and resources. Dividing networks into segments enabled network managers to keep network users as close as possible to the network resources they used the most. This allowed the network administrator to control and isolate network traffic to a certain extent.

The potential usefulness of hubs went well beyond that of the first simple network repeaters. Soon after the appearance of the first basic hubs, a second generation of hubs appeared that offered management features. These hubs could collect management information from each network connection, then convert that information into a standardized format (for example, Simple Network Management Protocol), then export that information to a number of management reporting systems. Often these hubs also

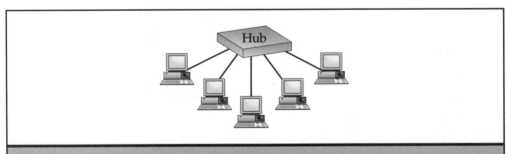

**Figure 2-1.**    A basic hub configuration. The hub regenerates, or *repeats*, the transmission signals coming from the workstations

had buses that allowed them to support multiple transport protocols on the same high-performance backplane. Then, thanks to the high-performance backplane, hubs appeared that could support multiple logical network segments within the hub, meaning that a hub could now contain more than one segment and that each of those segments could be managed separately. This enabled network managers to reconfigure network segments, making moves, adds, and changes on the fly and even from a remote console.

With these sophisticated new features came new roles for network hubs. Soon, network managers were using hubs to concentrate, or collapse, network nodes into increasingly complex hierarchies of networks, often within a single chassis. Simple, unmanaged wiring center hubs were used to connect end-user nodes to their login servers. These simple hubs were in turn connected to one another by more sophisticated hubs. These intermediate-level hubs were then connected by extremely feature-rich and highly manageable chassis-based hubs, some employing bridging or routing modules. (See Figure 2-2.)

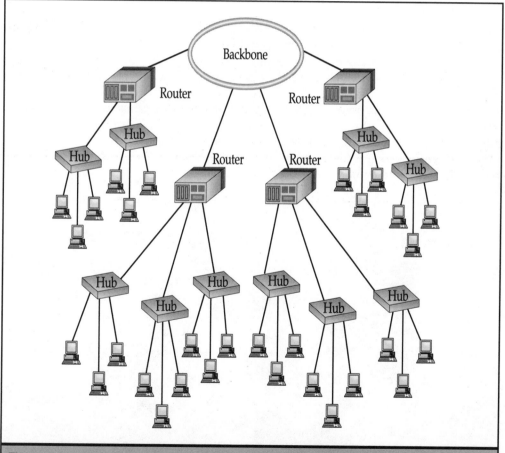

**Figure 2-2.** A hierarchical network with hubs and routers concentrating network nodes at discrete levels

With this, the concept of structured wiring was born, and network managers began to realize its many benefits, including the following:

▼ Easier moves, adds, and changes

■ Centralized management

■ Improved scalability

■ Better monitoring of network events and statistics

■ Improved reporting

■ Easier troubleshooting

■ Improved fault tolerance

■ Support for multiple transport protocols

▲ Support for multiple communications protocols

## Types of Backbones

The term backbone, although it is tossed around rather loosely, really means a network that connects multiple local area network segments. In this sense, a backbone is a "network of networks" that handles internetwork traffic—that is, traffic that originates in one LAN segment and is transmitted to another. Network segments, on the other hand, handle local network traffic. Because the backbone provides both a physical and logical data path among all the nodes connected to it, the network segments and subnetworks must be connected to the backbone by devices capable of performing the necessary bridging and routing of data packets being transmitted. These devices may be bridges (Figure 2-3), routers (Figure 2-4), and/or file servers (Figure 2-5) performing the bridging and routing functions among the network segments.

**Figure 2-3.**   A backbone connected by bridges

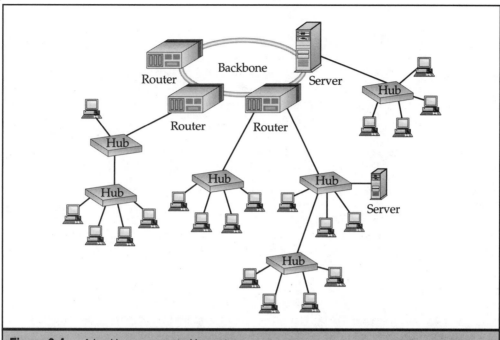

**Figure 2-4.**    A backbone connected by routers

**Figure 2-5.**    A backbone connected by file servers

# Why Build a Backbone?

A well-designed backbone can bring order, ease of management, and the potential for improved performance to your network. Backbones enable network managers to centralize their network structures by providing a single point of monitoring, management, and control. Because all network servers are attached to a common cable, they can be moved to a central location. This centralization makes the network easier to configure, secure, and manage because:

- ▼ Repairs and maintenance are easier to schedule and perform.
- ■ All backups and archiving can be handled simultaneously.
- ▲ Telecommunications connections can be pulled to one central location.

What's more, network backbone designs have given rise to two related network designs that we touched on earlier: structured wiring and collapsed backbones. These two techniques further increase ease of network management.

## Structured Wiring

Although any cable plant that involved a little forethought could be called a structured wiring system, the term is usually reserved for those standards-based wiring schemes that are hierarchically designed for easy management and expansion. Structured wiring systems generally incorporate a network design in which a central hub controls the flow of information between departments and also serves as a connection point for enterprise resources such as communications and applications servers. (See Figure 2-6.)

There are two keys to a good structured wiring system. The first is to keep network users as close as possible—both physically and logically—to the network resources they use the most. In Figure 2-6, for example, the members of the Accounting Department (in Building A) are directly attached to the server they use most frequently. This eliminates unnecessary internetwork traffic that can slow down the performance of the whole network. The second key is to design the system so that adding, moving, and changing users (which you will occasionally have to do to keep them as close as possible to their preferred network resources) are as easy as possible.

## Collapsed Backbones

A collapsed backbone is essentially a "backbone in a box"—that is, an entire physical and logical data internetwork contained within a single device. (See Figure 2-7.)

Instead of running backbone media throughout the walls, ceilings, and floors of the building, each network segment is attached to a single hub or stack of hubs that connect all the segments and subnetworks to form the enterprise internetwork. The collapsed backbone design was a logical outgrowth of the centralized backbone network design. After all, if all the servers are in a central location for management purposes, the next step

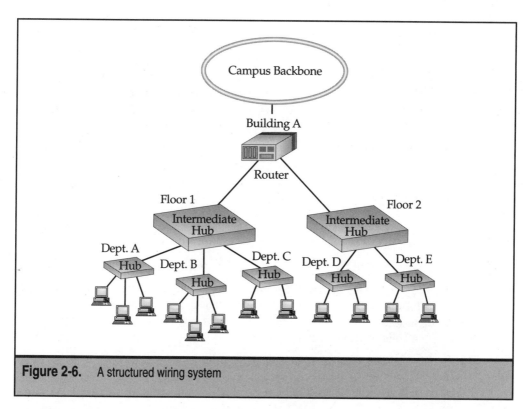

**Figure 2-6.**    A structured wiring system

**Figure 2-7.**    A collapsed backbone network

is to connect them to a single hub, replacing the backbone cable with the backplane of the hub. The advantages to this are many:

▼ Hubs are modular and easily scalable.

■ Hubs are built on a chassis with high-speed backplanes that provide a high-speed bus for expansion boards.

■ Most chassis-based hubs can simultaneously support multiple transport protocols, such as Ethernet, token ring, FDDI, and WAN.

▲ Most hubs offer optional integrated diagnostic and management tools.

Furthermore, a collapsed backbone extends the manageability of the centralized backbone by:

▼ Providing a central point for management of the entire network

▲ Providing better management of and security for network resources

A collapsed backbone design provides better management because it offers a single point of network monitoring and control, which also makes troubleshooting easier. It improves security because all servers are moved to a central management area. Most important of all, a collapsed backbone design makes it easy to implement a high-speed network.

# How Do You Build a Backbone?

You can configure backbones physically to accommodate your segmenting scheme. For example, local area network segments on each floor of an office building are connected to a backbone that runs through the conduit from one floor to the next.

Regardless of the physical configuration of your backbone, the network segments and subnetworks must be connected to the backbone by devices capable of performing the necessary bridging and routing of data packets being transmitted.

## Building a Backbone with Switches

This is one of the simplest and most straightforward ways to build a backbone, as shown in Figure 2-8. A switch is simply a specialized bridge that creates a virtual one-to-one connection between a sending node and a receiving node. When a switch receives a packet, it sets up a connection between the sending node and the receiving node just long enough to transmit the packet. The switch then takes down that connection and waits for the next packet.

To build a backbone with switches, just connect the segments and/or individual nodes to switches, and the switches in turn are connected to one another on the backbone cable.

## Building a Backbone with Routers

In a router-based backbone, a router or routers connect the segments to the backbone cable, as shown in Figure 2-9. A router functions as the connection point to the backbone

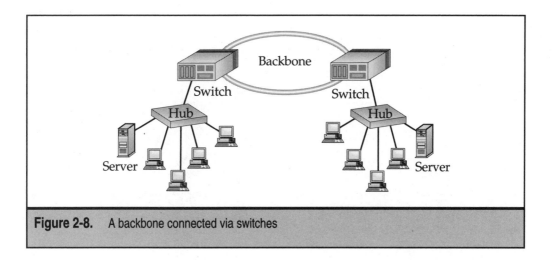

**Figure 2-8.**    A backbone connected via switches

for each segment. Using routers as the backbone can provide a level of fault tolerance that bridges can't achieve. When the backbone is constructed of a dual-ring medium, such as fiber-optic cable, the ring will loop back on itself, the routers will adjust the paths, and the data will continue uninterrupted across the backbone.

## Building a Backbone with Network File Servers

In a server-based backbone, like the one shown in Figure 2-10, each server forming the backbone contains two or more network adapters. One of the adapters connects the server to the backbone. This provides backbone access for the server and for all the network segments attached to the server. The other network adapters provide the connection between the server and its network segments.

**Figure 2-9.**    A backbone connected via routers

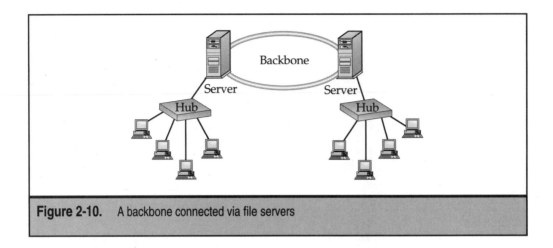

**Figure 2-10.** A backbone connected via file servers

The backbone is by nature a high-traffic area, so it will be one of the first places to experience slow performance caused by high traffic. This is especially true in server-based backbones, in which the network file server or servers connect the network segments to the backbone cable. Most network operating systems have integrated bridging and routing functions that enable them to connect the segments, although requiring the server to perform these functions steals processing cycles from other vital server activities such as file management. Therefore, managers of large networks and/or networks with heavy traffic should dedicate file servers either to file management or bridging and routing functions, or consider building a backbone using bridges or routers. In small-to-medium-sized networks that have relatively low traffic, however, the servers may be able to provide backbone connectivity without seriously affecting server performance.

## Effects of Excessive Internetwork Traffic

As we mentioned earlier, the backbone is probably the area of your network where you will first feel the effects of excessive traffic. If you are experiencing slow network performance, therefore, the backbone is probably your first suspect. A fairly reliable indicator of a clogged backbone is slow network response when handling internetwork traffic (packets that originate on one network segment and are then transmitted to another), despite the fact that all the servers and workstations are not overworked.

## Causes and Cures for a Clogged Backbone

To be sure that the problem is indeed excessive backbone traffic, however, you will need to conduct a few tests. First, check to make sure that the slow performance you experience is occurring only during internetwork transmissions. If slow performance is characteristic of all network transmissions, the problem may not be your backbone—or at least not the backbone alone. Determine the physical location of the network applications you are using when the network response slows. If these applications are on another network segment, you may indeed be suffering from excessive traffic on the network backbone.

## Location of Applications

Before you conclude that more backbone bandwidth is what you need, however, ask yourself whether it's possible to move the applications onto the same segment as the user without slowing down performance for users on other segments. Be sure all users are as close as possible—both physically and logically—to the network resources they use most frequently. This eliminates unnecessary internetwork traffic.

*TIP:* Balancing the location of your applications is much more efficient—and much less expensive—than implementing a high-speed protocol on your backbone.

## Inadequate Hardware

Next, check your workstations and servers. Ensure that your workstations have sufficient memory and processing power for the job. Also, check servers to make sure that they are not the bottleneck. If your servers are waiting on disk input/output, that's probably the cause of the network slowdown, and it can be alleviated by installing a faster disk subsystem. Likewise, insufficient memory (often indicated by memory swapping to disk), low throughput to and from the network adapter (resulting in dropped packets and retransmissions), and inadequate processors can all slow your servers and cause them to be a bottleneck on your backbone.

## "Chatty" Communication Protocols

Another, although now very rare, cause of congested backbones is the communication protocol used by your network operating system. Among the functions of the communication protocol are creating service connections, getting network station addresses, and other tasks associated with transferring data from a station on one network to a station on another network. The communication protocol operates at the network layer, as described on the International Standards Organization's Open Systems Interconnection model. Communications protocols include Internet Protocol (IP) and NetWare's Internetwork Packet Exchange protocol (IPX).

Some communication protocols generate a lot of traffic because for every request for service they send, they require a response from the station that is granting the services. Because of this constant "conversation" between the requester and grantor of services, these protocols are called "chatty" protocols. IPX, for example, is the classic example of a "chatty" protocol—request then response, request then response. Often these requests and responses are larger than one packet. Therefore, a chatty protocol significantly increases the number of packets being transmitted. Consequently, chatty protocols are not a good choice for backbone deployment. Luckily, the networking world as a whole is moving away from IPX and has adopted the Internet Protocol as the network layer protocol of choice.

Internet Protocol (IP), on the other hand, is not a chatty protocol. Rather than sending a request for service, waiting for a reply, then sending the next request for service, IP sends all requests for service in a single burst, sometimes called a "packet burst." It then receives multiple responses from the grantor of those services. This makes it a better choice for a backbone protocol than IPX.

**TIP:** If you're still using IPX, you may want to implement Novell's PBURST NLM, a NetWare Loadable Module that enables the server and workstations to function in Packet Burst mode, sending all service requests in a single burst. However, PBURST is not turned on by default. You will have to load PBURST manually or add the LOAD PBURST command to your STARTUP.NCF file.

## Small Packet Size

Also, bigger is better when it comes to packet size on the backbone. That's because one large packet obviously represents less traffic than a lot of little ones. This has a couple of indications. First, you should select a backbone protocol with the largest packet size available. Second, if you're running NetWare, you may have to make some adjustments.

Your NetWare servers could be needlessly creating more backbone traffic because they are limiting packet size to a 512KB maximum. By default, NetWare servers route a default packet size of 512KB. This is because 512KB used to be the largest packet that all routers could route. However, most routers these days will route at the maximum packet size for each protocol. Therefore, if you have a NetWare 4.X network, check to make sure your routers can handle a larger packet size. If they can, you may want to consider enabling the Large Internet Packet support.

## The Trend Toward Switched Networks

Lately the trend has been to interconnect all workgroups with switches, creating one large, flat switched network fabric. This goes against the traditional structured wiring precepts of keeping applications close to users. However, with the use of virtual LANS, or VLANS, which we will discuss in later chapters, it can make for a faster, easier-to-manage network.

To successfully implement a VLAN, you will need to have an infrastructure with sufficient bandwidth to handle all traffic from all groups on the flat, switched network. This is where high-speed links are necessary.

# The Final Analysis

Of course, the true and indisputable determination of where your backbone's bottleneck lies comes from in-depth analysis of your network traffic with a protocol analyzer (see Chapter 1). A protocol analyzer will help you determine whether packets are being dropped, resulting in retransmissions, and pinpoint where those packets are being dropped. It will also help you confirm whether your network has heavy internetwork traffic (data packets addressed to a node not on the same segment where they originated). You can also use the protocol analyzer to determine bandwidth utilization, or the average percentage of bandwidth being used, on your network's backbone. If you are experiencing slow network performance or dropped packets, and if your network's bandwidth utilization over the backbone consistently averages over 50 percent, it's fairly safe to say that the problem is too much backbone traffic, and your network is a good candidate for implementing high-speed networking protocols.

# What You Gain

Putting a high-speed protocol on the backbone will result in higher network throughput, and will eliminate any bottleneck caused by insufficient internetwork bandwidth. However, please be aware that a high-speed backbone usually gives subtle network improvements: faster internetwork transmissions and better server-to-server communication. The dramatic improvements in network response time—the kind that will make your boss call you to congratulate you and talk about your next raise—are not usually the kind realized through increasing bandwidth on the backbone. Those types of performance increases generally come from adding bandwidth within a local segment from the workstation to the local server.

# Selecting a High-Speed Backbone Protocol

If you have conducted the necessary tests and have determined that you need to implement a high-speed protocol on your backbone, it's time to establish the selection criteria for this protocol. Overall, the most important features for a backbone protocol are:

▼ Manageability

■ Fault tolerance

■ Scalability

■ Packet size

■ Packet overhead

▲ Maximum network span

Because manageability and fault tolerance are so important on the backbone, these two qualities must be paramount when you are selecting a high-speed protocol for this implementation. A protocol that currently supports only limited management systems is clearly a bad choice, as is a protocol that can't support a backup ring, spanning tree, or other disaster recovery system.

Easy and broad scalability is also another necessary feature of a backbone protocol because the protocol will need to be able to ensure low response times, even as you are adding servers. Important things to remember are the number of stations the protocol can support on a single LAN as well as the packet size. Internetwork and server-to-server packets tend to be larger than local segment packets. Therefore, a protocol that can support large packet sizes tends to be more efficient on a backbone. As well, the amount of overhead (addressing and management information) per packet should be low to eliminate unnecessary traffic on the backbone.

Furthermore, consider maximum network extent. Backbones tend to be spread out over buildings or campuses, so be sure that the protocol you select can span your network without a lot of expensive repeating devices.

Finally, the backbone is not the place to pinch pennies. Losing a backbone link could cost you your job, so don't select backbone equipment on the basis of cost alone. Remember, the protocol that you select for your backbone doesn't have to be the same protocol you use throughout your network. Therefore, implementing a more expensive protocol on the backbone doesn't condemn you to overrunning your cabling budget on every segment.

# CHAPTER 3

## Down on the Farm

The second most likely place to have a bandwidth crunch (after the backbone) is in a server farm. If you have one of these, you're probably not experiencing the network throughput your users need. However, because the term is used so loosely, you're probably not even sure whether you have one, much less how to improve its performance. So, in this chapter we'll begin by defining the structure of the server farm, illustrated in Figure 3-1, and then discuss the specific requirements it demands of its transport protocol. Next, we'll discuss the indications of insufficient bandwidth in a server farm environment and how to alleviate it.

## DO SERVERS GROW ON FARMS?

Many manufacturers of high-speed networking devices recommend their products for use in server farms. However, rarely do these same manufacturers define what they mean by "server farm." Often, they mean anything from a backbone to a UNIX workgroup. For the purposes of this book, however, let's define a server farm as a group of servers that share processing responsibility for a common information system. This type of environment is often called a distributed computing system, or more recently, a distributed information access architecture. Before you can design a network to support a

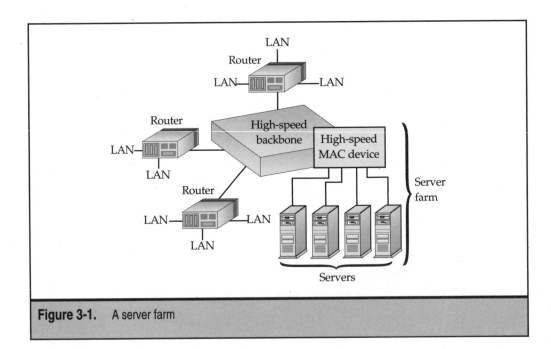

**Figure 3-1.**    A server farm

distributed computing system, you first need to understand the function of this architecture and the tools used to implement it.

A distributed computing environment, such as the one shown in Figure 3-2, generally has two goals:

▼   Allow enterprise-wide access to information

▲   Distribute processing load across specialized platforms

## Enterprise-Wide Access to Information

Enabling all users throughout the enterprise to access corporate information is truly the most important goal of a distributed computing environment. It is the driving force behind developing a distributed computing environment, and so we will address this goal first.

**Figure 3-2.**   A distributed computing environment

## How It All Began

For decades now, companies have developed and maintained databases—at times huge and very expensive—containing vital corporate information of all kinds. These databases were developed independently on a variety of computing platforms using many different development tools and programming languages. All of these databases fulfilled their intended functions (some better than others), but they existed for the most part as islands of information. The users who needed access to the information had to have specialized software loaded on their specialized workstations, which were in turn connected by specialized cables to the specialized host computing platform that held the database.

During the past decade or so of mergers, takeovers, consolidations, and downsizing, however, maintaining these large, expensive, and disparate databases has become both unwieldy and uneconomical. Executive managers wanted fast, seamless, integrated access to all corporate information. MIS managers wanted to be able to access all databases from one desktop platform rather than having to support a terminal, a UNIX workstation, and a PC for each user so that he or she could access all the various corporate databases. Users didn't want to have to learn how to work on three different workstations and six different host platforms to pull their daily reports, then have to spend hours manually consolidating them. Furthermore, as companies discovered that many of their databases could be moved from expensive mainframe platforms to more economical local area and wide area networks, they began pressuring their data processing departments to port applications and databases to these less expensive platforms.

The result of these different forces—corporate mergers, downsizing, the emergence of local area networks, and plain old economic pressures—is the emergence of distributed computing systems. A distributed computing system is a logical evolutionary step from centralized computer systems and even client/server computer systems, as shown in Figure 3-3.

## Issues and Concerns About Distributed Computing Systems

A distributed computing system is really client/server computing on a grander scale. While in a client/server system, data is located on one server; in a distributed computing system, the data is located on many servers. Furthermore, these servers can be located anywhere—in the next room or in the next state.

Obviously, a distributed computing system has a lot of advantages over the old centralized computing systems, including fault tolerance. Because data is replicated on several servers, users are protected from loss or downed systems. A distributed computing system also makes more computing power available as it is needed. However, there are some problems associated with implementing a distributed computing system. Among these are

▼  **Management**  Because distributed computing systems by definition include multiple platforms, the time required to manage them increases exponentially over that required for a centralized system. Also, distributed computing systems are often the result of merging existing systems, which involves finding and resolving integration problems.

■ **Data synchronization**   Keeping all data updated and consistent across all computing platforms is a major management challenge.

■ **Time synchronization**   The system must have some means of resolving updates when more than one user creates a transaction to change the same field in the same record at the same time.

▲ **Security and control**   Multiple platforms means multiple points of access, and general concerns about data location, content, control, and management.

## Distribute Processing Load Across Specialized Platforms

A distributed computing system is very similar to a client/server environment except that rather than a single server with many clients, there are many servers and many clients who can—and do—access any one of those servers at any time. This opens up many possibilities for efficient use of computing hardware, but also presents challenges as to how to make the best use of each platform.

In some ways, distributed computing is similar to multiprocessing. A multiprocessing computer system divides processing functions into multiple discrete tasks, then assigns

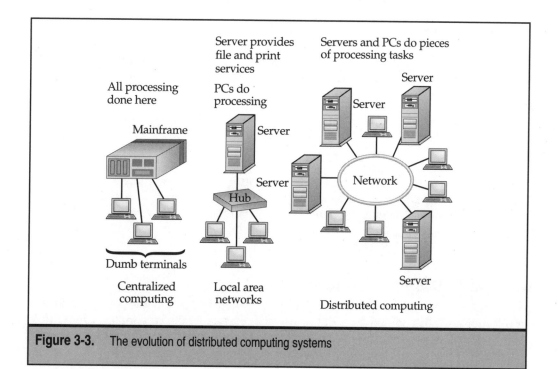

**Figure 3-3.**   The evolution of distributed computing systems

these tasks to each of its multiple processors. The multiprocessing computer balances the load so that no one processor becomes overwhelmed. Distributed application processing does the same thing, except that it balances processing across computers rather than just across processors in the same computer platform. Furthermore, there are, theoretically at least, more kinds of computing resources available in the distributed computing system, such as random access memory and disk storage space. For example, in many offices around the world, thousands of megabytes of memory lie idle every evening as workers turn off their desktop systems and leave for the day. It is possible, however, for a distributed application to use this idle memory.

Distributed systems have some clear advantages. First, in a client/server environment, inexpensive personal computers can relieve the server of many tasks. Likewise, relatively inexpensive local area network servers can handle some of the processing that once required CPU cycles from a mainframe. Furthermore, using multiple server platforms allows network managers a flexibility in hardware upgrades, moves, and changes that simply wasn't possible in centralized mainframe systems.

However, as we mentioned, distributed computing systems present their share of challenges, mostly in the area of network design. For example, distributed computing systems theoretically allow a client system to locate other computer systems on the network to process all or part of a task. The criteria for delegating processing tasks might include load balancing or processing power. Developing applications that can seek out appropriate computer platforms and take advantage of them is a challenge in and of itself. However, these distributed applications must be supported by a network that is fast enough, manageable enough, and fault-tolerant enough to make such distributed processing possible. For example, the only way to make our scenario of using workstation memory during idle periods possible is by using extremely high-speed links to make memory of one platform available for use by another.

# IMPLEMENTATIONS OF DISTRIBUTED COMPUTING SYSTEMS

In the move to consolidate corporate data and port it to the most efficient and economic platforms available, certain types of distributed computing systems have become standard for commercial environments. These different types of systems determine the design of the networks that support them, so we'll take some time to describe these tools and their requirements.

## Distributed Application Processing

As we mentioned earlier, distributed computing environments can employ distributed applications. A distributed application is one that can take advantage of multiple computing platforms by running different processes on different computers attached to the same network. Groupware applications, for example, are distributed applications because they let users work with the same data at the same time or take advantage of the network to share information easily. Document processing, scheduling, electronic mail, and workflow software are examples of groupware. Some applications automatically integrate data from systems attached to the network. For example, Windows NT lets users take information stored in other places on the network and "paste" it in their own documents. The original source of the information can still be updated by other users. When the original data is changed, the copies of that data that are pasted in other users' documents are automatically changed as well.

# Distributed Databases

By definition, a distributed computing system has data located at multiple sites. Users everywhere should be able to access all data no matter where it is located. Users should therefore only have to concern themselves with the data, not with the design of the network.

These distributed databases generally reside in server-based database management systems (DBMS) and mainframe-based information systems. In the centralized computing model, users accessed only their local database server. In the new distributed computing model, however, users can—and do—access any server in the enterprise. The network challenge here is providing transparent access from any user on the network to any database. Furthermore, distributed databases may also require some level of local control so that managers at the local site can secure the data.

# Data Warehousing

While data warehousing is not itself a distributed computing system—and is actually the antithesis of distributed computing—it is a practice that often enables distributed computing systems to exist. Data warehousing is the practice of extracting working copies of databases and storing these copies on a database warehouse server or servers—usually large multiprocessor computers. The data is extracted from various distributed databases, cleansed, and transformed in the information warehouse, making distributed access quicker and easier (as well as often providing more accurate results). This practice allows users to access actual, current corporate data, running involved and processors-intensive queries, without affecting the production systems. This not only protects the integrity of vital data and production systems, it also is often the most efficient way of allowing access to multiple databases of differing designs. It is also one of the more practical ways of storing and managing historical information, accounting detail, and other data that may be too unwieldy to manage on local systems.

Many companies have used data warehousing successfully to preserve their distributed computing systems while simultaneously allowing users "one-stop shopping" for all the data contained in the various distributed databases. As a result, data warehouses are becoming increasingly popular.

To keep the data in the warehouse sufficiently current to meet the needs of its users, data may have to be transferred from the production databases to the warehouse (after cleansing and normalization) many times a day. This frequent transfer of data places special demands on the network, because the data will need to be transferred quickly enough to keep the warehouse up to date (if you need to update the warehouse every six hours, but a data transfer takes eight hours, you've a real problem on your hands) while not bringing the network traffic for the production databases to a standstill.

One thing to keep in mind when you are designing a network to support a data warehouse is that usually the primary reason for implementing data warehousing is cost. Therefore, any additional cost incurred to develop a network for a data warehouse system will likely be closely scrutinized by corporate management. As a result, a lower cost, high-speed networking alternative is probably the best choice for this environment.

# BUILDING BLOCKS OF DISTRIBUTED COMPUTING SYSTEMS

So far we have discussed the goals of distributed computing systems as well as some of the ways these systems are implemented. All of these systems are designed and built using a common set of database tools and techniques. Understanding these basic "building blocks" of distributed computing systems will help you better understand their networking requirements, so we'll describe them in some detail.

## Relational Databases

The relational database has become the data structure of choice for most corporate distributed computing systems. One reason is that its structure is, by definition, transparent to its users. Here's how it's designed: All relational databases consist of only two-dimensional tables with rows. The rows are not in any particular order. Rows are, however, supposed to have a unique primary key that defines a sort order or other criteria. A single column is common to every row in the table, as shown in Figure 3-4.

The model doesn't specify exactly how tables are represented physically, so they could take pretty much any form—indexed files, for example. However, all the users see is a table with rows and columns.

## Structured Query Language

Almost every relational database product available supports a Structured Query Language (SQL) interface. SQL, invented by IBM and now standardized by the American National Standards Institute (ANSI), started life as a database query language for the VM/370 and MVS/370 operating systems. Today, SQL is used to access data on all

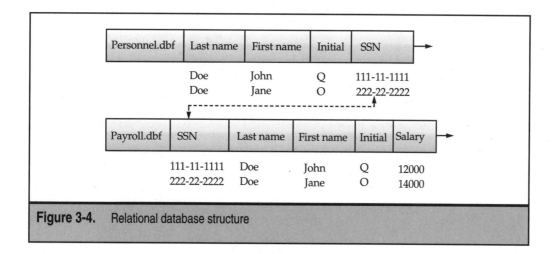

**Figure 3-4.**   Relational database structure

different types of database systems, including mainframes, midrange systems, UNIX systems, and network servers.

SQL is both a data definition language and a data manipulation tool that can be used to develop complex queries. SQL takes advantage of the inherent strengths of relational databases: efficient optimizers that make all the decisions about data access at the time the database is compiled or at execution. Therefore, SQL specifies the targeted values of the queries or updates, but specifies nothing about how the data is to be accessed. For example, in SQL you can't save a pointer or select indices.

SQL plays a key role in a client/server environment. It provides a standard interface between the user's front-end application and the DBMS engine. This interface can be implemented through application programming interfaces embedded in the programming language (embedded application program interfaces—APIs) or called externally (call-level APIs). In either case, SQL enables the communication between the front-end application—which usually resides on the user's desktop computer—and the back-end database—which usually runs on a server located elsewhere on the network.

# Middleware

Middleware is software that lets users access data on a server using a wide variety of front-end applications. Using middleware is now a well-established practice in client/server networks, because it lets users select any front-end application they want to access any "back-end" server on the network, hiding the underlying network from applications. This allows users and programmers to use and develop applications without having to know anything about the networks on which they will run or the communication protocols that will be used on those networks. This lets the programmers concentrate on the applications and the users concentrate on doing their work. It also provides a mechanism for integrating legacy database applications with new ones. Clearly, middleware is especially helpful for programmers developing applications that will run on networks that use different network communication protocols.

## Caught in the Middle

Like its name suggests, middleware acts as an intermediary between front-end applications and back-end engines, as shown in Figure 3-5.

Its role is something like that of a diplomat mediating an agreement among countries that don't share common cultures or languages. The diplomat provides language translation services as well as a standard etiquette by which all parties agree to conduct themselves. Therefore, citizens of Country A may know nothing about the culture of Country W, but they know if they conduct themselves by the standard etiquette, or protocol, they will be able to carry on trade with Country W successfully. Likewise, middleware translates between the APIs of front-end and back-end applications and provides a standard interface to which developers of both types of applications can write for successful interaction.

Middleware is crucial to client/server computing for a couple of reasons. First, it hides the differences among various vendors' SQL. Although SQL is supposed to provide a standard interface between front-end applications and back-end data, each vendor has slight differences in how they have implemented SQL. Thus, middleware plays an important role in making back-end data available to all vendors' SQL.

Second, it keeps application development generic. For example, without middleware, a programmer developing an application for a multiprotocol environment would have to develop a variation of the application to work with each of the protocols present in the network. Middleware, however, was developed to negotiate the multiprotocol environment, so all the programmer has to do is write the application to the middleware interface and middleware takes care of the rest.

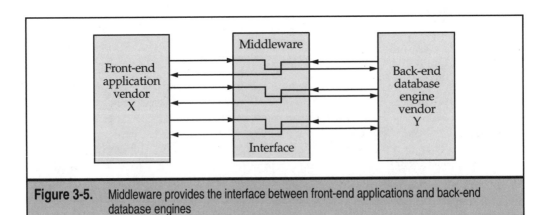

**Figure 3-5.**    Middleware provides the interface between front-end applications and back-end database engines

## Types of Middleware

Middleware comes in three flavors. Each has a different impact on network traffic, so we'll briefly discuss each of them. The three types of middleware are

▼ Conversations

■ Messaging systems

▲ Remote procedure calls

**CONVERSATIONS** A conversation is a continuous stream of requests and replies between two or more systems. Because of its continuous nature and many-to-many orientation, conversations are generally used in situations where full synchronization of databases is critical.

**MESSAGING SYSTEMS** Messaging systems are store-and-forward systems that can be likened to a voice mail system. They allow applications to leave messages—in the form of commands and data—for other applications to pick up and process at a later time.

Because messaging systems aren't real-time and require no synchronization among systems, messaging systems are connectionless. Because messaging systems don't operate in real time, they are generally deployed in widely dispersed networks and/or networks with low transfer rates. Obviously, therefore, middleware based on messaging systems is not crying out for a high-speed network to support it.

**REMOTE PROCEDURES CALLS** Remote procedure calls (RPCs) are requests from one machine to another over a network, as shown in Figure 3-6. In an RPC, the requester waits

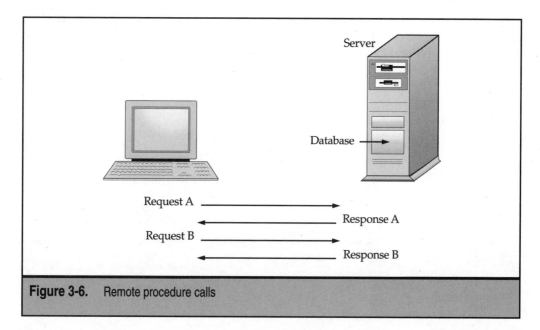

**Figure 3-6.** Remote procedure calls

for a response before issuing the next request. Consequently, RPCs are usually real-time calls that take place over connection-oriented interfaces. The Open Software Foundation has written specifications for an environment called the Distributed Computing Environment (DCE) that includes a set of middleware RPCs that can break processing tasks down into smaller routines, any of which can then be run on any server on a network.

### Developing Standards in Middleware

As middleware becomes more prevalent and more crucial in the development of distributed computing environments, different organizations and companies are attempting to develop standards that will allow interoperability among all front-end and back-end systems. Currently, the major standards seem to be Microsoft's Open Database Connectivity (ODBC) standard and the Independent Database Application Program Interface (IDAPI), which was jointly developed by IBM, Novell, and Borland. At the time of this writing, Microsoft's ODBC appears predominant.

## Data Propagation

Data propagation is really just copying data in whole or in part. As well as copying, data propagation may also involve some level of data processing, such as summarizing or aggregating. The concept of data propagation plays a key role in designing a distributed computing system because it is the means by which the data is distributed to various platforms around the network.

A carefully planned system of data propagation, such as the one shown in Figure 3-7, allows database administrators to divide processing tasks among the server platforms that are best able to perform them. It lets administrators break large processing tasks into several smaller tasks and distribute them throughout the network. It also allows them to maintain security by providing users with only those parts of the data absolutely

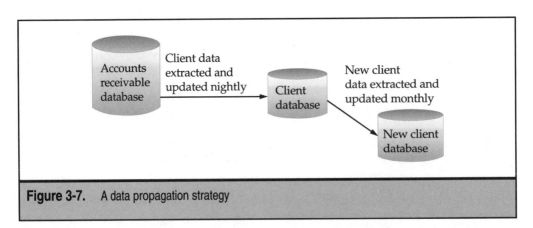

**Figure 3-7.** A data propagation strategy

necessary to perform their jobs. This explains why it is so popular for financial analysis and decision support systems.

Data propagation has many costs associated with it. As a result, you must carefully plan your data propagation strategy. Data propagation obviously increases network traffic, data storage requirements, data communications facilities, and management time. Management is especially crucial because maintaining the consistency of the directories, synchronizing data, and providing adequate storage on the various server platforms require careful planning and frequent review. As well, the security of data both over the wire as it is being propagated and on the hard drives of the server platform may be critical.

# NETWORK REQUIREMENTS OF A SERVER FARM

Now that we've had a fairly thorough discussion of the what, why, and how of a server farm, it's time to translate that into network needs. From the preceding discussion, we can see that a network that connects a distributed computing environment like the one illustrated in Figure 3-8 must support

▼ A wide variety of communications protocols

■ Real-time connection-oriented requests to servers

■ Quick updates to a directory naming service

■ High-speed replication of data to various servers

■ High-speed transfers of extracted data to data warehouse computers

■ Database connectivity

■ Security

■ Rapid synchronization of data

■ Transparency to users

■ Quick response to users, even during extract transfer replications and backups

■ Fault tolerance

■ Easy installation and configuration, because you will probably be moving it around frequently to balance the load on servers

■ Driver support for many different server platforms

▲ Support for fiber-optic cabling and other high-speed, high-security media

**TIP:**  Security may be far more important on a server farm than on other portions of the network. This is because distributed computing systems are most frequently used to handle accounting systems and decision support systems that include sensitive financial data.

**Figure 3-8.**   A distributed computing environment

# INDICATIONS OF BANDWIDTH DROUGHT ON THE FARM

The empirical evidence that your server farm is suffering from insufficient bandwidth includes:

▼ Delayed replication of databases

■ Corrupted databases caused by poor synchronization

■ Slow response time to users during data extract transfers

▲ Slow updates to directory naming service

# OTHER CAUSES AND CURES FOR SLOW PERFORMANCE ON THE SERVER FARM

Even if the network supporting your server farm is suffering from one or more of the problems listed above, it is still premature to conclude that implementing a high-speed network is the solution. There are other situations that can cause slow performance on a server farm. And there certainly may be other—often less expensive—solutions.

## Location of Data and Applications

Before you conclude that you need more bandwidth on the server farm, however, ask yourself whether it's possible to balance the load more equitably among the servers. If you can move databases and/or applications from busier servers to more idle servers, you may notice performance problems alleviating or disappearing altogether. Also, whenever possible, be sure all users are as close as possible—both physically and logically—to the databases they use most frequently. Although the point of a distributed computing system is that users anywhere can effectively access data anywhere, you can sometimes spot trends in data usage and keep users as close to their data as possible. This helps keep network traffic to a minimum.

*TIP:*  Balancing server load and keeping users close to their data is much more efficient—and much less expensive—than implementing a high-speed protocol on your server farm. The problem is that today's traffic patterns (80 percent of traffic now leaves the local area) make it almost impossible to keep users close to their applications and data.

## Inadequate Hardware

You should also check your workstation hardware configuration. Client/server application front-ends tend to demand a lot of processing power from workstations, so be sure that they are up to the task. Ensure that your workstations have sufficient memory and processing power for the job.

Also, check servers to make sure that they are not the bottleneck. Database engines can put a strain on disk input/output. If your servers are waiting on disk input/output, that's probably the cause of the network slowdown, and it can be alleviated by installing a faster disk subsystem. Likewise, insufficient memory (often indicated by memory swapping to disk), low throughput to and from the network adapter (resulting in dropped packets and retransmissions), and inadequate processors can all slow your servers and cause them to be a bottleneck on your server farm.

## Buying the Farm

Of course, the true and indisputable determination of where your server farm's bottleneck lies comes from in-depth analysis of your network traffic with a protocol analyzer (see Chapter 1). A protocol analyzer will help you determine whether packets are being dropped, resulting in retransmissions, and pinpoint where those packets are being dropped. It will also help you confirm whether your network has heavy internetwork traffic (data packets addressed to a node not on the same segment on which the packets originated). You can also use the protocol analyzer to determine bandwidth utilization, or the average percentage of bandwidth being used, on your server farm's network.

If you are experiencing slow network performance and dropped packets, and if your network's bandwidth utilization over the server farm's segment(s) consistently averages over 50 percent, it's fairly safe to say that the problem is too much network traffic, and your server farm's network is a good candidate for implementing high-speed networking protocols.

# CHAPTER 4

## Closer to Home

ervers aren't the only causes of network traffic jams. In this era of collaborative computing and client/server architectures, workstations often generate more traffic than their network protocols can handle efficiently. This heavy traffic is usually generated by power workgroups—users who collaborate via their computers, sending massive amounts of electronic mail to one another, constantly surfing the Internet, and often employing bandwidth-gobbling applications such as multimedia, client/server databases, groupware, and workflow software.

To understand if and when these applications might dictate a high-speed protocol for your network, we'll first take a look at each of them and how they affect network performance. Then we'll discuss the symptoms of excessive bandwidth in the workgroup, and the special requirements a workgroup has for a high-speed protocol.

## COMPONENT TECHNOLOGIES

Web development environments have enabled us to create applications that allow users to share all types of information regardless of their physical location. For example, Java—a special type of programming language based on *component technology* developed by Sun Microsystems—features downloadable Web *components*, called applets, that can run on any kind of computing platform. This frees developers to concentrate on the content of their applications rather than on their interoperability with computing platforms. It also allows users to download components at will and use them as they need them. Microsoft also has developed a component technology, called Active X. Active X enables Web developers to create distributed object applications as well as dynamic Web pages.

Component technologies have given developers unparalleled freedom in developing applications. They've also given users access to applications in a way they have never before known. Unfortunately, they have also caused some bandwidth issues as more and more users download more and more components.

## ELECTRONIC MAIL AND MESSAGING

Electronic mail is everywhere. Nearly everyone who has turned on a computer has used electronic mail. It is undoubtedly one of the most widely used network applications in existence. More important to your network traffic, however, is electronic messaging (on which electronic mail systems are based), which is a system for exchanging data commands among applications. An electronic message may carry an electronic mail or it may contain a request for service from a user to a remote database, which in turn replies with a message back to the user.

Despite all the benefits of electronic mail—instant communication, elimination of telephone tag, and others—it can pose a traffic problem. Often, careful management can alleviate mail-induced bandwidth problems, or even avoid them altogether. However, sometimes the only answer is more bandwidth. To understand how to manage electronic mail and messaging, let's first take a look at how it works.

## An Electronic Mail System

The basic components of an electronic mail system are a mail-enabled user application, a back-end mail application, and a mail directory. The user application would reside on the user's workstation and allow the user to create, address, and send electronic mail. The back-end mail application resides on a server and would handle the delivery of the messages, including any document conversion and gateway operations required among different types of electronic mail systems. The electronic mail directory is a database of electronic mail addresses that would also reside on a server or servers. A typical electronic mail system would look something like the one in Figure 4-1.

## Electronic Messaging Systems

An electronic messaging system is something like an electronic mail system for applications rather than people. As we mentioned earlier, an application may send an electronic message containing a request to another application. The receiving application can then send its reply in an electronic message to the application making the request.

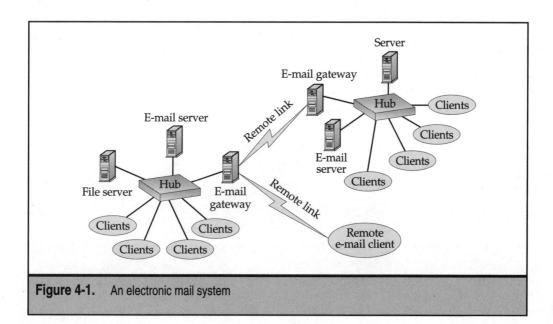

**Figure 4-1.**   An electronic mail system

Electronic messaging is a store-and-forward operation. That means the exchange of electronic messages doesn't take place in real time—the requesting application does not wait for a reply before continuing with its other processing. While this wouldn't be acceptable in many systems, it's perfect for collaborative workgroups. That's because it allows members of workgroups to exchange information and work together without having to establish and maintain real-time sessions with one another. They can send information and messages that other users can read and act upon later, enabling widely dispersed users to function as a workgroup. Furthermore, you can attach text and graphics files to messages, making it easy to exchange documents, photos, and other types of images with other users.

## Electronic Messaging System Standards and Tools

As you can imagine, as the number of widespread workgroups increases, the amount of electronic mail and messaging increases even faster. This has the potential for causing performance problems, depending upon the traffic characteristics of the electronic messaging being used. This in turn depends upon which electronic messaging standard the messaging-enabled applications use. Some are more efficient than others, so we'll discuss the most popular ones here.

### Mail Systems and Standards

A number of e-mail standards have been proposed to span all computing environments, including mainframes and local area networks. Probably the two most widely used are the CCITT's X.400 standard, and Novell's Message Handling Service (MHS). The two function at different layers in the application interface, as illustrated in Figure 4-2, and unfortunately are not always compatible.

**Figure 4-2.**   How X.400 and MHS interoperate

**X.400** The Consultative Committee for International Telegraph and Telephone (CCITT) has defined the X.400 store-and-forward message exchange system. The goal of X.400 is to provide message exchange interoperability among a wide variety of platforms. The basic components of X.400 are

▼ **User agent (UA),** which resides on the client computer as part of the front-end mail application.

■ **Message transfer agent (MTA),** which accepts messages from the UA and routes them to other MTAs. The MTA may perform data conversion and translation if required.

■ **The message store (MS),** which is a storage directory for messages that are currently undeliverable. For example, if the addressee isn't logged in to the network when the MTA first tries to deliver a message, the message will be stored in the message store, where the addressee can collect it later.

■ **Access unit (AU),** which is an interface to the mail system for dissimilar systems, such as fax machines.

▲ **Directory system,** which is a database of names and electronic mail addresses.

**NOTE:** In X.400, the directory system is called X.500 and includes a special format for electronic mail names and addresses.

**LIGHTWEIGHT DIRECTORY ACCESS PROTOCOL (LDAP)** Lightweight Directory Access Protocol (LDAP) is a directory service protocol designed on a client/server architecture that runs over Transport Control Protocol/Internet Protocol (TCP/IP). LDAP organizes information about a network object, called an *attribute,* into records called *entries.* Attributes all have a type, which identifies what kind of object it is—such as an e-mail address or a compressed video file—and at least one value. In the example of an e-mail address, the value would be the actual e-mail address of the object. Each entry is identified by its *distinguished name* (DN).

All of this information is arranged in a hierarchical tree. The tree is built to represent geographical as well as organizational structure. For example, the object at the top of the LDAP tree is the country in which the object resides. Below that would be the state or enterprise in which the object resides. Below that might be the department or functional area. Below that would be the individual entry for the objects.

Because it is designed to run on a client/server model, the actual LDAP database can be located on one or more servers. When an LDAP client wants to find information on an object in the LDAP directory, it connects to an LDAP server and queries it. The server either replies by sending the client the requested information or it sends the client a pointer to another server on which the requested data resides.

**NOVELL MESSAGE HANDLING SERVICE (MHS)**    Novell developed NetWare MHS to provide messaging for both LANs and wide area networks (WANs). MHS is designed to function as the messaging engine for both electronic mail systems and application message systems. Therefore, developers can use MHS to create applications that talk to other applications and exchange information. For example, queries can be made to databases on other systems using MHS as long as both client front-end and server back-end applications support the MHS interface.

Figure 4-3 shows an MHS installation. MHS is built on the client/server model, so in an MHS environment host systems provide messaging services for a group of clients. MHS hubs route messages and establish connections. Because MHS was developed to support both local and wide area networks, it supports remote connections.

## Mail-Enabled Applications

As we mentioned earlier, many client/server applications use store-and-forward messaging systems to communicate with each other. Mail-enabled applications are applications that use messaging systems to let the application users communicate with each other. Electronic mail is an organic, integrated function of a mail-enabled application, allowing users to create, address, and mail data and documents from within the application. Vendors are now shipping mail-enabled word processors, databases, and applications. Figure 4-4 shows how these standards interoperate.

## Electronic Mail Application Programming Interfaces (APIs)

So, how do programmers design support for messaging systems into their applications? By using application program interfaces (APIs) developed to provide application support for these systems. These APIs define such things as address formats and file

**Figure 4-3.**    An MHS system built on the client/server model

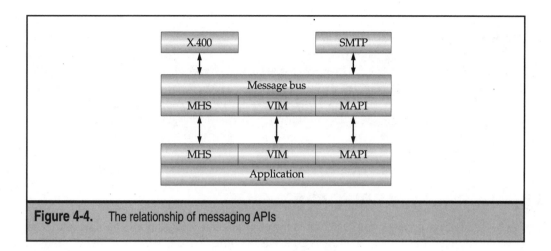

**Figure 4-4.**   The relationship of messaging APIs

attachment services. Several standard APIs have emerged to provide interoperability among applications and various mail systems. Some of these standard APIs are described below.

**VENDOR-INDEPENDENT MESSAGING (VIM)**   Vendor-Independent Messaging (VIM), developed by Lotus Development Corporation, is an API that allows developers to create mail-enabled applications that work on many different platforms.

**MESSAGING APPLICATION PROGRAMMING INTERFACE (MAPI)**   Developed by Microsoft to enhance Windows interoperability, MAPI provides a way for Windows applications to access messaging systems like Microsoft Mail and Novell's MHS.

**STANDARD MESSAGE FORMAT (SMF)**   This is the messaging API provided by Novell for MHS.

## Electronic Mail and Messaging on the Internet

It's now a cliché to say that the Internet has revolutionized how people locate information and each other. Nearly everyone has turned to the Internet for research and communication, both for business and personal use. While this has made information in heretofore unheard of variety and quantity available to record numbers of people, the Internet is something of a curse to network designers. That's because "surfing the 'Net" involves downloading huge, graphics-laden files as well as sending and receiving electronic mail in astonishing amounts. Workgroups that use the Internet frequently are among the first to experience slow network performance.

Electronic messaging on the Internet employs systems and standards that are different from, but interoperate with, those of local and wide area private networks. Refer again to Figure 4-2. For example, the messaging standard for electronic mail on the Internet is Simple Mail Transfer Protocol (SMTP), which can support any user interface as a front end. Therefore, users can exchange SMTP-based electronic mail with anyone on the Internet without going through a gateway. Furthermore, using Multipurpose Internet Mail Extension (MIME), a standard built on SMTP constructs, users can exchange multimedia e-mail messages that include both text and multimedia components.

# CLIENT/SERVER APPLICATIONS

For the past several years, one of the most popular phrases in the computing industry has been client/server computing. However, it has become obvious that the concept of what constitutes client/server computing varies dramatically from vendor to vendor. For the purposes of this book, client/server computing is a distributed computing model in which users work at intelligent computers running front-end applications that share processing functions with back-end applications that run on network servers. The servers running the back-end applications provide far more than storage, file, and print services. Taking advantage of the server's often far superior processing power, the back-end applications perform applications processing tasks such as complex calculations and queries. Most commonly, client/server systems are composed of a database management system (DBMS) in which clients query back-end servers using structured query language (SQL), which we discussed in some detail in Chapter 3.

## Client/Server Architecture

The client/server architecture defines a relationship between the client and the server. The client can't be a dumb terminal. It must have its own processing ability, but it doesn't have to bear all the burden of processing as it generally does in the file server model. There are several possible client/server configurations. One of the most common is shown in Figure 4-5, in which clients access a distributed database located on several servers.

## How to Build a Client/Server Application to Minimize Traffic

Currently there are no strict standards on how to build client/server architectures or applications. There are, however, four broad models for client/server systems, each with its own strengths and weaknesses. Therefore, you can base your client/server system on the model that suits your network's particular needs, whether those be minimal server load, minimal client load, or minimal network traffic.

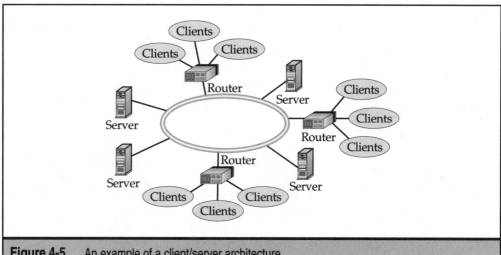

**Figure 4-5.**   An example of a client/server architecture

## Standard Model

The client portion in this model does little more than transmit requests to the back-end server portion. The server then responds to the requests. This model probably puts the greatest traffic burden on the network, especially if the server responses involve large amounts of data.

## Stored Procedures

Think of stored procedures as macros stored on the server. The client sends a request to the server and receives a response, just like in the standard model. However, in this model the client doesn't send quite as many requests to the server because stored on the server are these macros—or procedures—triggered by requests from the clients, which automatically perform a complete task. This model moves closer to the object-oriented model in which procedures are stored with data.

## Object-Oriented Model

In this model, data and procedures are encapsulated in objects. In the object-oriented model, procedures and data are stored together as a single object, minimizing network traffic. Objects communicate with one another using message-passing procedures, managed by a mechanism called an object request broker (ORB). The ORB receives a request from a client, then locates the most appropriate service on the network to respond to a request. By combining procedures and data into objects, and giving the system the intelligence to find the best network resources to process the object, this model generally results in optimum performance with minimum traffic generation.

### Data Warehouse

In this model, data is stored in a back-end server "warehouse" that is not usually directly accessed by the users. Instead, a system sitting between the user and the warehouse extracts the appropriate data from the warehouse and prepares it for delivery to the user. Furthermore, this system may already have the requested information, so it may be able to reply to client requests without accessing the warehouse server. This system minimizes the processing burden on the warehouse server, but can result in more network traffic in those instances when the secondary or intermediate server is unable to reply to a client request.

## Effects of Client/Server Computing on Network Traffic

In some instances, client/server computing reduces the amount of traffic on the network. The reason is that in the file server model, when a user wants to work on a particular file, he or she requests it from the server. The server then sends a copy of the entire file as well as the program the user will use to work on it across the network to the workstation, which does all the processing. When the user finishes working on the file, he or she sends the entire copy of the completed data across the network to the server. You can see how network traffic increases at the beginning and end of working on a file.

However, the file server model was made for a "feast or famine" model of network traffic. When users began working on files, the network traffic was heavy as entire copies of the data (executable) and overlay files were transmitted to the workstation. When they completed work, network traffic was heavy as an entire copy of the data was transmitted back to the server. However, in between these operations there was almost no traffic between workstation and server.

The client/server model has pretty much eliminated the flood of traffic at the beginning and end of tasks. Network traffic is reduced because the server only gives the client the information requested, not large blocks of information that the workstation must process. However, it has made for a consistently higher level of traffic at any given time.

# MULTIMEDIA

Multimedia is the bane of any network traffic management scheme. Multimedia involves sending not only text, but also voice, video, and graphics files across the network, often in real time. Multimedia files are huge, requiring not only large amounts of disk space for storage, but (more critically for us) massive bandwidth for transmission. More and more applications, especially groupware applications, are including multimedia support. Therefore, we can only warn you that it is probably a matter of when, not if, multimedia support becomes an issue on your network.

Some multimedia applications are less bandwidth-greedy than others. Image and graphics files, while large and complex, generally don't require synchronized delivery of multiple frames like video and sound files usually do. By the same token, store-and-forward messages that don't require immediate delivery don't demand the high-bandwidth transmission rates necessary for real-time video, which must have dedicated bandwidth during the transmission and a fast transmission rate.

**NOTE:**    Flicker-free, full-motion video requires a delivery speed of 30 frames per second (fps). Viewers find the quality of video with a delivery speed below 10 frames per second to be unacceptably "jumpy."

# WORKFLOW SOFTWARE

Workflow software combines electronic messaging with document management and imaging. The concept is to move a document through various stages of processing by sending it to people within a group who have the equipment and skills to manipulate the document or the authority to sign and validate it.

Typical environments where workflow software is beneficial would be a tax preparation firm. A document containing an income tax return would travel through the firm as shown in Figure 4-6. Raw data for the tax return would be entered by a typist

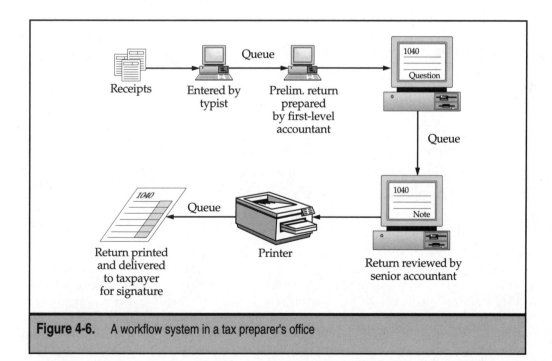

**Figure 4-6.**    A workflow system in a tax preparer's office

working from original client documents. Once the data entry is completed, the tax return document would go into a queue for review by a first-level accountant, who would actually perform the necessary calculations and apply the necessary tax regulations to complete the return. When the first-level accountant's work is completed, the tax return document would then go into a queue for review by a senior accountant, who would check the return for accuracy and completeness. Once the review is finished, the tax return document would be printed and presented to the taxpayer for signature and approval. At that point, the tax return would go into a queue awaiting electronic filing. When the return was filed and confirmation received, the document would then be archived.

**NOTE:** In this example, as in many workflow environments, software must provide a high level of security, perhaps through some implementation of passwords and login authentication.

What distinguishes a workflow system from other document processing systems is that in a workflow system, documents:

▼ Contain routing information

■ Allow simultaneous access

■ Have a filing system, queue, and workflow manager

■ Allow "user sign off" at various stages

▲ Lock all or part of approved documents to prevent further modification

# GROUPWARE

Groupware is exactly what its name implies: software used by a group of people to enable them to work together more efficiently and effectively. It lets users conduct discussions and debates, schedule meetings, and work collaboratively. By definition, it should allow several people to:

▼ Access the files and documents simultaneously

■ Make and track modifications to files and documents

▲ Monitor projects

## Groupware in Action

An example of groupware is Windows for Workgroups' object linking and embedding (OLE) features. It lets users collaborate on one document simultaneously, letting them create and modify text, graphics, and spreadsheet information. The resulting document, called a compound document and illustrated in Figure 4-7, actually contains links to a file on the workstation of the person who created a given element. If that file is changed, the element linked to it in the compound document also changes. Therefore, the next time any user anywhere opens the compound document, the document is automatically updated.

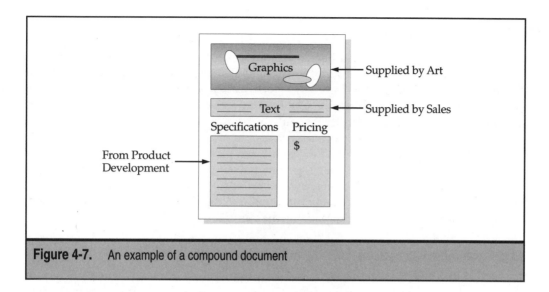

**Figure 4-7.**    An example of a compound document

There are lots of companies offering groupware now. Among them are the following:

▼   Microsoft Windows for Workgroups is a workgroup-based network operating system and a suite of applications and interfaces that aid in collaborative computing.

■   Novell's GroupWise is a workgroup suite that provides e-mail, project management, workflow, and calendaring and scheduling applications.

▲   Lotus Development's Notes is a groupware environment for developing and using document processing, messaging, and database applications.

## Groupware Tools

With so many vendors offering so many different types of groupware—all of which offer similar, overlapping functionality—you may be wondering whether each of these implementations is proprietary and thus restrictive. The answer is both yes and no. Yes, each company's implementation of groupware is proprietary, but fortunately each employs—to varying degrees—standard interfaces that enable the collaborative environment. Among these technologies are the following.

## Standard Generalized Markup Language (SGML)

Like the American Standard Code for Information Interchange (ASCII), Standard Generalized Markup Language (SGML) is a standard means of storing data in documents. However, unlike ASCII, SGML defines procedures for sharing within the same document data that was created in other environments. SGML files can have attributes that define each element of a document (such as page style, footers, and paragraphs) that can be transferred to any other application that supports SGML.

# GROUP THERAPY

Now that you know how much bandwidth a workgroup can consume, how can you determine whether your network traffic problems are being caused by the workgroup or by something else? Luckily, there are a few signs of an overactive workgroup. First, if you have workgroups using multimedia applications, especially full-motion video systems like the one shown in Figure 4-8, they should be prime suspects when the network starts to slow. Furthermore, if slow performance is limited to just one segment on your network (not a backbone or server farm), chances are the problem lies in the activities of the workgroup or workgroups on that segment rather than with the server. As well, if network time-outs, packet collisions, and packet retransmissions seem to occur only in one segment, and all the network adapters, hubs, and cables test out fine, it's fairly safe to say that the workgroup on that segment is the culprit.

## Location of Applications

Before you conclude that more bandwidth in the workgroup is what you need, however, ask yourself whether it's possible to move all the applications the workgroup needs onto the same segment as the user without slowing down performance for users on other segments. Be sure all users are as close as possible—both physically and logically—to the network resources they use most frequently. This at least eliminates unnecessary internetwork traffic.

**Figure 4-8.**    The type of video system will definitely affect performance

# Inadequate Hardware

Next, check your workstations and servers. Ensure that they have sufficient memory and processing power for the job. Also, check servers to make sure that they are not the bottleneck. If your servers are waiting on disk input/output, that's probably the cause of the network slowdown and it can be alleviated by installing a faster disk subsystem. Likewise, insufficient memory (often indicated by memory swapping to disk), low throughput to and from the network adapter (resulting in dropped packets and retransmissions), and inadequate processors can all slow your servers and cause them to be bottlenecks on your power workgroup segment.

# "Chatty" Communication Protocols

Just as with backbones, another cause of congested workgroup segments is the communication protocol used by your network operating system. Among the functions of the communication protocol are creating service connections, getting network station addresses, and other tasks associated with transferring data from a station on one network to a station on another network. The communication protocol operates at the network layer as described on the International Standards Organization's Open Systems Interconnection model. Communication protocols include Internet protocol (IP) and NetWare's Internetwork Packet Exchange protocol (IPX).

Some communication protocols generate a lot of traffic because for every request for service they send, they require a response from the station that is granting the services. Because of this constant "conversation" between the requester and grantor of services, these protocols are called "chatty" protocols. IPX, for example, is the classic example of a "chatty" protocol—request then response, request then response. Often these requests and responses are larger than one packet. Therefore, a chatty protocol significantly increases the number of packets being transmitted. Consequently, chatty protocols are not a good choice for deployment in power workgroups. Luckily, the networking world as a whole seems to be moving away from IPX and adopting Internet Protocol as its network-layer protocol of choice.

Internet protocol (IP), on the other hand, is not a chatty protocol. Rather than sending a request for service, waiting for a reply, then sending the next request for service, IP sends all requests for service in a single burst, sometimes called a "packet burst." It then receives multiple responses from the grantor of those services. This makes it a better choice for a power workgroup protocol than IPX.

*TIP:* If you are still using NetWare's IPX as your network layer protocol, you may be able to ease the congestion that IPX can cause by using PBURST NLM. This is a NetWare Loadable Module that enables the server and workstations to function in Packet Burst mode, sending all service requests in a single burst. However, PBURST is not turned on by default. You will have to load PBURST manually or add the LOAD PBURST command to your STARTUP.NCF file.

## Small Packet Size

Also, bigger is better when it comes to packet size in segments that are using multimedia applications. That's because multimedia applications involve large files with rapid delivery rates, and one large packet obviously represents less traffic than a lot of little ones. This has a couple of indications. First, you should select a protocol with the largest packet size available. Second, if you're running NetWare, you may have to make some adjustments.

Your NetWare servers could be needlessly creating more traffic because they are limiting packet size to a 512KB maximum. By default, NetWare servers route a default packet size of 512KB. This is because 512KB used to be the largest packet that all routers could route. However, most routers these days will route at the maximum packet size for each protocol. Therefore, if you have a NetWare network, check to make sure your routers can handle a larger packet size. If they can, contact Novell for the workaround that will enable the server to default to a larger packet size.

Finally, look at the history of the workgroup. If you've had to make smaller and smaller segments to isolate high-bandwidth users from the rest of the network, any recurring or persistent performance problems are probably workgroup-related.

## Group Encounters

Of course, the true and indisputable determination of where your workgroup's bottleneck lies comes from in-depth analysis of your network traffic with a protocol analyzer (see Chapter 1). A protocol analyzer will help you determine whether packets are being dropped, resulting in retransmissions, and pinpoint where those packets are being dropped. It will also help you confirm whether your network has heavy internetwork traffic (data packets addressed to a node not on the same segment where they originated). You can also use the protocol analyzer to determine bandwidth utilization, or the average percentage of bandwidth being used, on your workgroup's segment. If you are experiencing slow network performance and dropped packets, and if your network's bandwidth utilization over the server farm's segment(s) consistently averages over 50 percent, it's fairly safe to say that the problem is too much network traffic, and your workgroup's segment is a good candidate for implementing high-speed networking protocols.

# GROUP THINGS

When selecting a high-speed networking protocol for the workgroup, there are a few issues unique to this environment that you should consider:

▼ **Applications transparency**   Applications transparency means existing applications can run over the new network protocol. This is especially important when considering Asynchronous Transfer Mode.

- **Computer compatibility**   When converting to a new network protocol, each computer in the workgroup must be equipped with a new network interface card. The NIC must be compatible with the bus type, operating system, and model of the connected workstation. It is important that the NIC card has been tested with the specific product you are using. Also, choose a vendor that has experience with NICs across a variety of platforms.

- **Physical network compatibility**   Ideally, the new network protocol should support the type of cable that is already installed in the workgroup. Another consideration is the wiring hub location. Be sure you have enough space, power, and air conditioning to meet the requirements of any new equipment.

▲ **Special multimedia considerations**   To maintain deterministic frame delivery, video traffic should not be directed through routers. Therefore, you'll need to keep video users within the same area or network segment. Furthermore, prioritization of real-time video traffic can ensure that it has enough bandwidth in the available signal to ensure quality delivery. Switched microsegmented Ethernet, Asynchronous Transfer Mode (ATM), and new 100Mbps Fast Ethernet technologies can provide the bandwidth.

# CHAPTER 5

## The Wide Area

In many organizations, there is a distinct division of responsibilities between "network management" and "telecommunications management." Network managers handle all aspects of the local area network up to the building walls or the campus gate.

All data communications outside the local area network are administered by the telecommunication managers. Whether or not this is the case in your organization, you probably still need to read this chapter as well as the other wide area networking chapters in this book.

If you are a network manager, you probably already know that most wide area equipment vendors assume you know enough about data communications over the wide area to select and manage their wares. If you're a telecommunications manager, you know that the fastest growing part of your job is wide area data communications, and that requires an understanding of local area networking. In either case, you'll need an understanding of wide area networking and how it interoperates with local area networking.

The most compelling reason to read the wide area networking chapters in this book, however, is that your users don't know the difference between local and wide area data communications—and they don't want to. Network operating systems and networked applications are becoming very "wide area aware," and are so good at hiding the location of data and programs that users mistake wide area performance problems for local performance problems. For example, I know of a situation in which a user complained about how doggedly slow the network was because it had taken her almost a minute to retrieve a document. Upon investigation, I discovered that the document was on a server in another city, and she was accessing it over a 19.2Kbps dial-up line. The network operating system and the document management application she was using had done a great job of making the location and retrieval transparent to the user. It was so transparent, in fact, that I had a hard time explaining to the user that the problem wasn't an underpowered server or workstation, or a slow LAN, but rather a wide area link that was many times slower than the local links—and couldn't be cost-justifiably upgraded.

This brings up another reason for studying the wide area. Whether you are in telecommunications or network management, because of the previously mentioned wide area transparency of applications and NOSes, you will have to troubleshoot wide area problems as well as recommend and justify the cost of wide area solutions.

With the advent of the Internet and intranets, which are local networks run with Internet and Web-based technologies, the 80/20 rule of network traffic has turned inside out. Traditionally, 80 percent of network traffic was local, and only 20 percent was remote. Currently, however, only 20 percent of network traffic stays local, while 80 percent leaves the network. This means that wide area links are going to become more and more of a concern to you.

Java and other popular Web development environments are stretching wide area resources to their limits. Downloading applets across a distributed computing environment can put a strain on available bandwidth. So read on!

# THE WIDE AREA DEFINED

A wide area network (WAN) uses dedicated or switched connections to link computers in geographically remote locations that are too widely dispersed to be directly linked to the local area network media. These wide area connections can be made either through the public network or through a private network built by the organization it serves.

A typical WAN and the equipment required for WAN connections are shown in Figure 5-1. A router sends traffic addressed to a remote location from the local network over the wide area connection to the remote destination. The router is connected either to an analog line or a digital line. Routers are connected to analog lines via modems or to digital lines via channel service units/data service units (CSU/DSUs). The type of carrier service determines the exact type of equipment the wide area will need to function.

## Dedicated Versus Switched Lines

Wide area networks can include either dedicated or switched lines. A dedicated line is a permanent connection between two points that is usually leased on a monthly basis, as shown in Figure 5-2.

A switched line service doesn't require permanent connections between two fixed points. Instead, it lets users establish temporary connections among multiple points that last only for the duration of the data transmission, as shown in Figure 5-3.

There are two types of switched services available, circuit-switching services that are similar to the services used to make garden variety voice telephone calls, and packet-switching services, which are better suited to data transmission, as explained next.

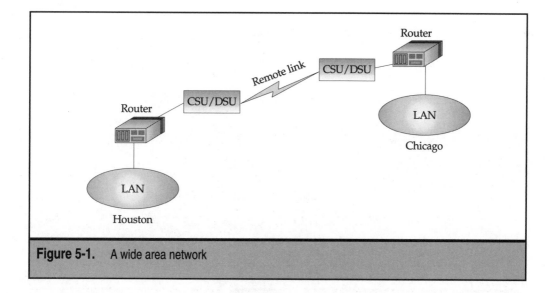

**Figure 5-1.**   A wide area network

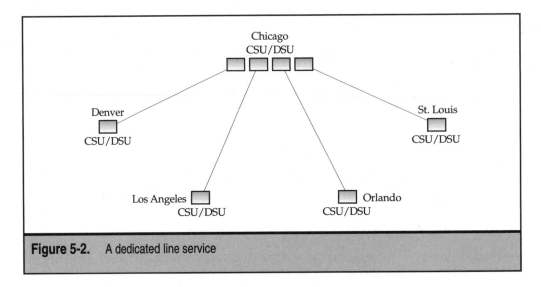

**Figure 5-2.**    A dedicated line service

## Circuit-Switching Services

In a circuit-switched connection, a dedicated channel, called a circuit, is set up between two points for the duration of the call. It provides a fixed amount of bandwidth during the call, and users pay for only that amount of bandwidth for the amount of time on the call. Occasionally there is a delay at the beginning of these calls while the connection is

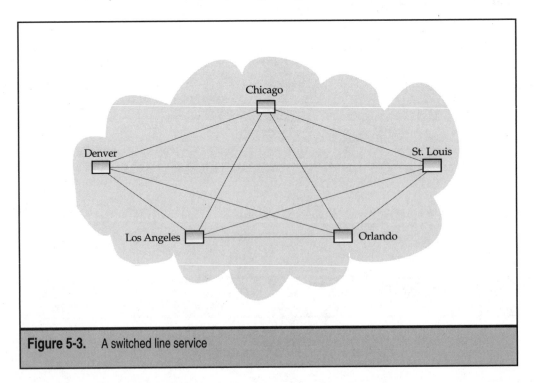

**Figure 5-3.**    A switched line service

being made, although new switching techniques and equipment have made this connection delay negligible in most cases.

Circuit-switching connections have a couple of serious drawbacks. First, because the bandwidth is fixed in these connections, they don't handle bursts of traffic well, requiring frequent retransmissions. Given that WAN connections are relatively slow anyway, retransmissions can make the performance crawl. The second drawback is that these virtual circuits have only one route, with no alternate paths determined. Therefore, when a line goes down, either the transmission stops or one of the users intervenes manually to reroute the traffic. Figure 5-4 illustrates a circuit-switched network.

## Packet-Switching Services

Packet-switching services do away with the concept of the fixed virtual circuit. Data is transmitted one packet at a time through a network mesh or cloud, with each packet having the ability to take a different route through the network cloud. This is illustrated in Figure 5-5. Because there is no predefined virtual circuit, packet switching can increase or decrease bandwidth as required, and therefore handles bursts in packets elegantly. Taking advantage of the multiple paths of the network cloud, packet-switching services can route packets around failed or congested lines.

## Which Switch?

Whether to choose circuit-switching or packet-switching services depends upon two things:

▼   The type of traffic your network generates

▲   Your budget

If the traffic generated on your network is delay sensitive, such as that generated by video applications, you'll need the fixed, guaranteed bandwidth of a circuit-switched service. Unfortunately, these services are very expensive. On the other hand, if your traffic can stand delays, especially if it is "bursty" in nature, packet-switching services are reliable and also more economical than circuit-switched services.

**Figure 5-4.**   A circuit-switched network

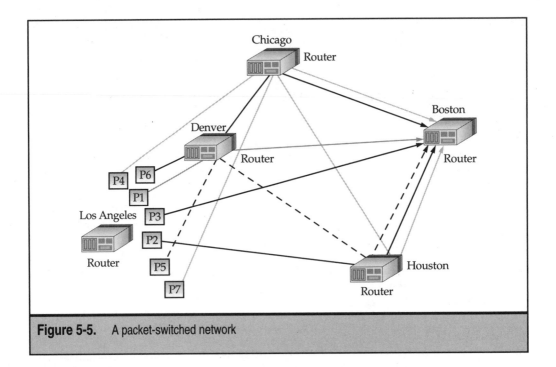

**Figure 5-5.** A packet-switched network

# Public Networks

Public networks are the wide area telecommunications facilities owned by common carriers and resold to users by subscription. These common carriers include the following:

▼ Local exchange carriers

■ Interexchange carriers

▲ Value added carriers

Each type of common carrier may offer wide area data services, and they often compete against one another in this market. Therefore, it's a good idea to check service availability and pricing with all of them.

## Local Exchange Carriers (LECs)

Local exchange carriers are companies such as the Regional Bell Operating Companies (RBOCs), GTE, and other companies that handle local telephone and telecommunications connections. Until recently, these companies were restricted by federal law to handling local communications, providing point-of-presence (POP) facilities for long-distance carriers, and offering wide area communications services only within their local service areas, known as local access and transport areas (LATAs). However, recent legislation has permitted them to compete with long-distance carriers and eventually to discontinue providing POP facilities to their competitors in the long-distance markets.

## Interexchange Carriers (IXCs)

An interexchange carrier (IXC) is a long-distance telecommunications carrier, such as AT&T, MCI, and US Sprint. Customers can choose the IXC of their choice. While many IXCs use the local point-of-presence facilities that local exchange carriers were required to provide, some IXCs built their own POPs, allowing customers to bypass the LEC and connect directly into the IXCs' long-distance services.

Just as the Telecommunications Act of 1996 has allowed LECs to go into the long-distance business, it has also allowed IXCs to compete in the local exchange carrier service market. Therefore, look for the lines between the LECs and the IXCs to disappear in the near future.

## Value Added Carriers (VACs)

VACs, such as GE Information Service, often provide WAN services as a sideline to their core business. Typically, a VAC has a national private data network (PDN) it established for its own use, and resells the excess capacity of that PDN to its customers. Using a PDN saves you the trouble of acquiring the various carrier services and setting up your own switching equipment, because the switching is done in the carrier's network. The VAC also handles the management and maintenance of the WAN services, and may even be able to do some protocol conversion for you.

# Private Networks

A private network is just that: a private communications network built, maintained, and controlled by the organization it serves. At a minimum, a private network requires its own switching and communications equipment. It may also use its own carrier services, or it may lease them from public networks or other private networks that have built their own communication lines.

A private network is extremely expensive. The organization that builds one must be prepared to maintain and manage its own switching and communications equipment, as well as either build its own microwave or other long-haul carrier service or negotiate to lease such service at a reasonable price. However, in companies where tight security and control over data traffic are paramount, private lines are the only guarantee of a high level of service. Furthermore, in situations where data traffic between two remote points exceeds six hours a day, employing a private network may actually be more cost effective than using the public network.

Figure 5-6 shows a private network connecting two separate sites.

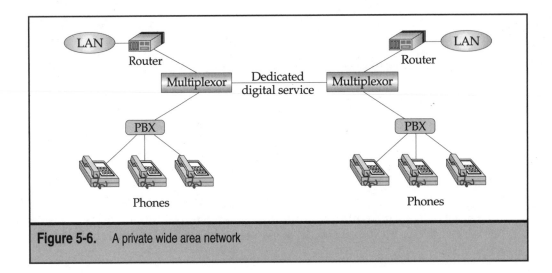

**Figure 5-6.**   A private wide area network

## A Word About Routers and Routing

Routers play a crucial part in determining the efficiency of a WAN connection. Routers connect the LAN to the WAN, learning the destination of devices on the internetwork and determining the best path for data traffic to take to reach its destination. For users of delay-sensitive applications, the router can make the wide area connection either completely transparent or a frustrating swamp. For switched-services customers, who pay only for the bandwidth they use, an efficient router can save huge amounts of money in carrier service fees.

When selecting a router for your WAN, be sure to test how efficiently it uses the carrier service. Does it terminate the connection when no traffic is being transmitted? Does it allow you to select the criteria for route determination—cost, shortest route, etc.? Does it correctly select the transmission route based on these criteria?

*TIP:*   When purchasing wide area routers, try to get a substantial trial period or return period. This will enable you to test the router thoroughly before making a final commitment.

## Analog Lines

Analog lines are garden-variety voice lines that were originally developed to carry voice traffic. Analog lines are a part of plain old telephone service (POTS), and as such they are everywhere. Although digital data traffic isn't compatible with analog carrier signals, you can transmit digital traffic on analog lines by using a modem, which modulates digital signals onto analog carrier services. The maximum achievable transmission rate of digital traffic over analog lines is about 52,000 bits per second, although the international standard for this rate of transmission hasn't been completed. Currently, the fastest modems available transmit about 32,600 bits per second, which is the transmission rate of the CCITT ITU V.34bis standard. Even when modems are available that transmit at the higher rate, it will still be significantly slower than the transmission rates achievable with digital lines.

# Digital Lines

Digital lines are designed to carry data traffic, which is digital in nature. Therefore, your computer equipment won't need a modem to load data onto the digital carrier signal. Instead, it will use a channel service unit/digital service unit (CSU/DSU), which simply provides an interface to the digital line. Digital lines can transmit data traffic at speeds up to 45Mbps and are available as either dedicated or switched services.

# Carrier Services

Different networks require different transmission rates, data prioritization, and levels of service. They also have different budgets available for wide area connections. Luckily, there are a variety of wide area carrier services available. We'll briefly describe the most popular.

## Switched Analog Lines

As we mentioned earlier, traditional analog voice lines are made up of the POTS we all know. They are widely available and inexpensive, and can theoretically support a data bandwidth of up to about 52,000 bits per second, although the current practical limit as established in the V.34bis standard is 32,600 bits per second with compression. Analog lines come in two basic flavors: dial-up lines and dedicated lines.

**DIAL-UP LINES**    In dial-up access, a connection is made only when there is data to transmit. It is especially good for traffic that is not delay sensitive, such as file transfers and electronic mail.

**DEDICATED LINES**    These analog lines provide the same data rates as dial-up lines, except that customers have a contract with the carrier that stipulates, in return for a flat fee, that the lines will always be available for the customer's immediate use.

## Circuit-Switched Services

Circuit-switched services are switched carrier services that establish a virtual connection before transmitting data. Two of the most commonly used are Switched 56 Service and Integrated Services Digital Network (ISDN).

**SWITCHED 56 SERVICE**    This is a digital data service that transmits at 56Kbps. Because it is digital, it doesn't require a modem. Instead, it uses a CSU/DSU to provide an interface between the router and the carrier service. Switched 56 is most often used as a backup to higher-speed data services as well as for fax transmissions and file transfers.

**INTEGRATED SERVICE DIGITAL NETWORK (ISDN)**    ISDN is the first all-digital dial-up service. Note that it is a high-speed digital circuit-switching service that provides integrated voice and data services on which many other high-speed offerings are based, including switched T1 services.

The basic ISDN service unit, called the basic rate interface (BRI), has three channels (although some carriers don't offer all three in their packaging of the BRI): two provide 64Kbps data channels (called the "bearer channels" or "B channels") and the other is a 16Kbps signaling channel (called the "D channel"). The ISDN primary rate interface (PRI) provides 23 B channels and 1 D channel. In either interface, the D channel provides call setup and monitoring, keeping the B channels free to transmit data.

## Packet-Switching Services

Packet-switching services, described in greater detail earlier in this chapter, do not function on the model of the virtual circuit. Connections don't need to be established before data transmission begins. Instead, each packet is transmitted separately, and each may take a separate path through the mesh of network paths that make up the packet-switching network. Although it is not as well suited for delay-sensitive traffic as circuit-switching services, packet-switching services do handle bursty traffic better. The most popular packet-switching services are X.25 and frame relay.

**X.25**    X.25 networks have been around since 1976, when X.25 was mostly used to provide remote terminal connections to mainframes. They perform extensive error checking that ensures reliable delivery. However, X.25 networks are not suitable for most LAN-to-LAN traffic because of the time and bandwidth consumed by this extensive error checking. Still, X.25 operates at speeds up to 2Mbps, which is much higher than the previously described carrier services.

**FRAME RELAY**    Frame relay, which began life as a service of ISDN, provides services similar to X.25, but is faster and more efficient. Frame relay doesn't employ the extensive error checking of X.25.

## Cell-Switched Services

In cell-switched services, the smallest unit of data switched is a fixed-size "cell" rather than a variable-size packet. This cell-based technology allows switching to be accomplished in hardware without complex and time-consuming frame-by-frame route calculation. This makes switching both faster and less expensive.

**ASYNCHRONOUS TRANSFER MODE (ATM)**    ATM can currently transfer data at rates of 25Mbps to 622Mbps and has the potential to transfer data at rates measured in gigabits per second. Many carriers already offer ATM services, with many more scheduled to do so in the near future.

**SWITCHED MULTIMEGABIT DATA SERVICE (SMDS)**    Like ATM, Switched Multimegabit Data Service is another cell-based service provided by the Regional Bell Operating

Companies (RBOCs) in selected areas. SMDS uses cell switching and provides services such as usage-based billing and network management.

## Digital Services

Digital services are often used to carry voice, video, and data. Digital circuits can transmit data at speeds up to 45Mbps. Usually, digital lines are made possible by "conditioning" analog lines to handle higher data rates. The lines are usually leased from a local exchange carrier and installed between two points (point-to-point) to provide dedicated, service.

**T1**    The standard—and most widely used—digital line service is the T1 channel. A T1 channel provides transmission rates of 1.544Mbps and can carry both voice and data. The 1.544Mbps bandwidth of a T1 is usually divided into twenty-four 64Kbps channels. This is because a digitized conversation requires 64Kbps of bandwidth, so when T1s are divided into 64Kbps channels, voice and data can be carried over the same T1 service.

**FRACTIONAL T1**    Fractional T1 is for those who need 64Kbps wide area channels but don't need a full T1. A customer can start with a number of fractional T1 lines and grow into a full T1 line when and as necessary. When a customer orders fractional T1 service, the carrier sets up a full T1 interface but only makes the contracted bandwidth available until more is needed. The lines are fractional, meaning that they can be divided into channels for voice or data.

**T3**    A T3 line is equivalent to 45Mbps, or 28 T1 lines, or 672 64Kbps channels.

# SYMPTOMS OF A BANDWIDTH SHORTAGE OVER THE WIDE AREA

As we mentioned earlier, right now the wide area will always seem slower than the rest of your network. That's because currently most wide area carrier services simply aren't designed to carry the megabits per second bandwidths that local area protocols can sustain. This will change as ATM becomes available over the wide area. However, until then, users who access programs and data over wide area connections will not receive anything near the performance they are accustomed to receiving over the local area.

If users complain of slow performance when accessing remote data and applications, you can almost be certain the problem is a slow remote link. However, to be thorough, check the following to make sure that the problem can't be solved locally:

▼    Hardware (may be inadequate)

■    Location of applications and data

■    Traffic patterns

■    Packet size

▲    Communications protocols

## Is Your Hardware Adequate?

As mentioned in Chapter 2, it's important for you to check your workstations and servers and ensure that they have sufficient memory and processing power for the job. Also, check servers to make sure that they are not the bottleneck.

## Can Applications Be Moved to the LAN?

Before you conclude that more bandwidth in the workgroup is what you need, ask yourself whether it's possible to move all the data and applications, or at least the applications, onto the local area network. This goes back to ensuring that all users are as close as possible—both physically and logically—to the network resources they use most frequently. This at least eliminates unnecessary internetwork traffic, which is especially important when the internetwork link is over a wide area connection (with its generally much slower transmission speeds).

## Are Traffic Patterns Localized?

Try to limit the data that travels over wide area connections to that which absolutely has to. That means making sure that, whenever possible, database and application maintenance, server backups, and software upgrades are done locally rather than over the wide area link.

## Can Your Servers Handle Larger Packet Sizes?

Your NetWare servers could be needlessly creating more wide area traffic because they are limiting packet size to a 512KB maximum. By default, NetWare servers route a default packet size of 512KB. This is because 512KB used to be the largest packet that all routers could route. However, most routers these days will route at the maximum packet size for each protocol. Therefore, if you have a NetWare network, check to make sure your routers can handle a larger packet size. If they can, you may want to implement the Large Internet Packet parameter on your NetWare Server.

## Are Your Communication Protocols Too "Chatty"

Just as with backbones, another now-rare cause of congested workgroup segments is the communication protocol used by your network operating system. Among the functions of the communication protocol are creating service connections, getting network station addresses, and other tasks associated with transferring data from a station on one network to a station on another network. The communication protocol operates at the network layer as described on the International Standards Organization's Open Systems Interconnection model. Communication protocols include Internet protocol (IP) and NetWare's Internetwork Packet Exchange protocol (IPX).

Some communication protocols generate a lot of traffic because for every request for service they send, they require a response from the station that is granting the services.

Because of this constant "conversation" between the requester and grantor of services, these protocols are called "chatty" protocols. IPX, for example, is the classic example of a "chatty" protocol—request then response, request then response. Often these requests and responses are larger than one packet. Therefore, a chatty protocol significantly increases the number of packets being transmitted. Furthermore, if a route fails, the delay required to rebuild routing tables using this chatty protocol can delay the establishment of a new route. Consequently, chatty protocols can slow a wide area link tremendously. Fortunately, most of the networking world has moved away from using these protocols and has shifted to using Internet Protocol (IP).

Novell has solved many of these problems by replacing IPX with a new routing protocol, called NetWare Link Services Protocol (NLSP). NLSP doesn't use the request-reply routines that IPX does. Instead, it uses a link-state routing based on the Open Shortest Path First and intermediate system-to-intermediate system routing algorithms. This makes routes easier to manage and faster to recalculate should a path fail. It also lets network managers program a preferred route selection based on cost, traffic congestion or priority, line speed, or other criteria.

Transmission Control Protocol/Internet Protocol (TCP/IP), on the other hand, is not a chatty protocol. Rather than sending a request for service, waiting for a reply, then sending the next request for service, TCP/IP sends all requests for service in a single burst, sometimes called a "packet burst." It then receives multiple responses from the grantor of those services. This makes it a better choice for a wide area link than IPX.

To ease the congestion that IPX/SPX can cause, with version 4 of NetWare Novell introduced PBURST.NLM, a NetWare Loadable Module that enables the server and workstations to function in Packet Burst mode, sending all service requests in a single burst. However, PBURST is not turned on by default. You will have to load PBURST manually or add the LOAD PBURST command to your STARTUP.NCF file.

# TESTS TO CONFIRM INSUFFICIENT WAN BANDWIDTH

Just as with the local area, the true and indisputable determination of where your wide area bottleneck lies comes from in-depth analysis of your network traffic. This analysis will reveal whether lack of bandwidth is the culprit or whether there is some other problem on your wide area link that is causing the poor performance.

However, unlike on the local area, for the wide area connection analysis you will have to rely on your carrier service provider to conduct these tests and report the results. From my experience, relying on these test results requires a leap of faith—don't be surprised if the report comes back with "nothing wrong." Even when you receive such a report, wait a couple of days to see if network performance improves anyway. On many occasions I've had a wide area link magically improve after I notified the carrier service we were having problems, even when the carrier service's investigation turned up "No Trouble Found."

*TIP:* When you first report a performance problem to your wide area carrier, just ask for a traffic analysis. Don't tell them you're considering upgrading to a faster wide area protocol.

# REQUIREMENTS FOR WIDE AREA PROTOCOLS

If you have conducted the necessary tests and have determined that you need to implement a high-speed protocol on your wide area connections, it's time to set the selection criteria for this protocol. Overall, the most important features for a wide area protocol are almost the same as for the backbone protocol:

▼ Performance

■ Manageability

■ Fault tolerance

■ Packet size and overhead

▲ Cost

## Performance

Performance is paramount in a wide area connection because, with the exception of ATM, wide area protocols are much slower than local area network protocols. Therefore, to limit performance degradation as much as possible, select the fastest protocol you can manage.

## Manageability

Manageability and fault tolerance are critical on the wide area, and yet they are largely out of your hands unless you have a private network. The majority of network and data communications managers will have to work with the public network providers to manage, troubleshoot, and repair their wide area links. Therefore, it's essential that you select both a protocol and a vendor you feel are capable of supporting that protocol.

## Packet Size and Overhead

Packet size and overhead are more critical on wide area connections than on any other segments. This is because wide area network protocols are often slow anyway. Adding unnecessary overhead and error checking—as well as smaller, less efficient packets—will simply slow them even more. Because many carrier services charge their customers only for the bandwidth they use, larger, more efficient data packets will save bandwidth and money.

Internetwork and server-to-server packets tend to be larger than local segment packets. Therefore, a protocol that can support large packet sizes tends to be more efficient on a backbone. As well, the amount of overhead (addressing and management information) per packet should be low to eliminate unnecessary—and potentially expensive—traffic over the wide area link.

# Cost

Finally, the wide area is not the place to pinch pennies, and yet wide area protocols—with their frequent dependence on outside carrier services—can be wildly expensive to implement. The wide area is one place where it's very important to make sure that you have all the features your network requires, but no "extras" that you can live without.

# CHAPTER 6

## The Cost of Converting to High Speed

Now that you know where to expect slowdowns, and why they occur, it's nearly time to start talking about how to speed things up. However, before we do that, we need to prepare you for sticker shock. High-speed networking is not cheap, it's not easy, and therefore it's not always worth it. Therefore, before you launch into an implementation project, I recommend that you do the following:

1. Determine exactly which segments will benefit from a high-speed protocol, as detailed in the first four chapters of this book

2. Carefully estimate the costs of converting to a high-speed protocol

To help you "put a pencil" to these potential expenses, I have prepared worksheets that outline the major cost components of a high-speed network and describe how to calculate the cash outlays associated with each. These worksheets appear at the end of the chapter.

# TO SPEED OR NOT TO SPEED

Before you can estimate costs, you'll need to determine which segments of your network you want to upgrade. This can be your most difficult planning task, because you'll want to implement high-speed networking widely enough to provide you with adequate bandwidth for the foreseeable future, but not implement any more than you'll really need during that time because of the high costs associated with it. Here are a few guidelines to help you develop a good scope for your network conversion project:

▼ **Upgrade your network to see you through the next 18–24 months.** Upgrades intended to last less than that amount of time will be nearly outdated before they are complete. The future beyond 24 months is too unpredictable. Under no circumstances should you claim that no further upgrades will be required for more than two years—the networking industry is changing too fast to make such dangerous assertions!

■ **Whenever possible, upgrade your cable plant universally.** For example, if you're going to have to upgrade high-speed segments from Category 3 to Category 5 cable, go ahead and upgrade your whole network to Category 5. The incremental cost of upgrading cable is fairly low, and having a versatile cable plant will save you time and money in the future.

▲ **Upgrade the busiest 20 percent of your network.** The 80-20 rule usually applies on the LAN as well, so upgrading the top 20 percent of bandwidth-starved segments should cover most of your problem areas.

**NOTE:** A little speed and a lot of management go a long way. There are many things you can do to prevent a bandwidth crunch on the segments that you don't upgrade to a high-speed protocol. Among these bandwidth management tools are virtual networking, microsegmentation, and full-duplex protocols.

# HARDWARE WORKSHEET

The cost of equipment is probably the first and most obvious expense related to installing a high-speed network. What may not be so obvious, however, are the many costs directly and indirectly related to installing new hardware. The Hardware worksheet outlines the equipment and related costs you will have to consider, along with the quantity and the cost of each.

## Servers

When upgrading servers, be sure to contact your NOS vendor to find out exactly which network adapters and drivers are fully certified for the version of the NOS you now have. Remember, some high-speed networking technologies are relatively new, so the version of the network operating system you currently have installed may not support high-speed protocols. If it doesn't, a NOS upgrade—with all the attendant heartache—will be in order. Furthermore, a new version of the operating system—or even a high-speed NIC driver—may require other hardware upgrades, such as increased memory or disk space. Be sure to ask your vendors about system hardware requirements, and figure any upgrades into your cost estimate.

## Hubs

The number of hubs you require depends on two things:

▼ How many ports you will be converting to a high-speed protocol

▲ The port density of the hubs you want to purchase

If you are purchasing stackable hubs, the smallest unit you can buy is a hub. Note that some stackable hubs require separate terminators, so be sure to include the cost of these terminators in your estimate.

If you have purchased or are planning to purchase a chassis-based unit, the smallest unit will be a chassis module. In either case, be sure to include the cost of the special cables and connectors required to attach the high-speed ports to your existing network.

Finally, remember to include the cost of any changes that you'll need to make in your wiring closet to accommodate the new hubs, such as additional racks and patch panels.

## Routers

Your routers may require new physical interfaces, either internal or external, as well as software and firmware upgrades to work with a high-speed protocol. They may even have to be replaced altogether. In either case, some manual configuration will be necessary, so be sure to include all the associated costs.

## Switches

You may need to purchase or upgrade existing switches. Upgrading your switches may involve high-speed interfaces or firmware upgrades. Be sure to quiz your vendor to make sure you know everything involved in preparing your switches for high-speed networking.

## Workstations

Implementing high-speed networking at the workstation involves many of the same considerations as upgrading servers. Contact your workstation vendor to make sure the network adapters you have chosen are compatible. Select network adapters with PCI buses if at all possible. Also, make sure the workstations are running a version of the operating system that supports the network adapter driver, and that they have sufficient memory and hard disk storage to accommodate the operating system and drivers. And remember, to get the desired performance, you may need to replace the workstation altogether.

## And a Smooth Road

Don't forget that you may need to upgrade your cable plant. The Hardware worksheet will make sure you consider what kind of work will have to be done and the number of cable drops that will need this kind of work. Also, remember that new media will require new patch cables—which may seem insignificant at first, but add up to no small expense in most shops!

# SERVICE COST WORKSHEET

You may need help with all of this. Use the Service Cost worksheet when considering the cost of any outside service providers you may retain to help you with your high-speed networking implementation. This will include contract programmers to help you enhance applications and network integrators to help you upgrade your servers and network operating system as well as your switches and routers. Don't forget PC maintenance companies that can help you upgrade your desktop workstations. Finally, you may need to hire cabling contractors to help upgrade racks, risers, and patch panels in your wiring closets.

# STAFFING AND STAFF DEVELOPMENT WORKSHEET

Hiring and/or training a staff to install and maintain a high-speed network is a significant expense. Because, as we have mentioned earlier, high-speed networking technologies are relatively new, chances are your current staff hasn't been adequately trained in them. Therefore, before you dive into a high-speed network implementation, you'll need to make sure that your staff has acquired the necessary skills in both troubleshooting and management. This means they need to learn not only how to physically connect devices to the high-speed network but also to optimize drivers and operate management applications for the protocol.

Preparing your staff to handle these responsibilities includes sending them to courses and seminars, purchasing books and other reference materials, and possibly hiring temporary staff to keep your network running while your regular staff acquires expertise in high-speed networking.

Sometimes developing existing staff isn't enough. You may even have to hire additional staff that are already experienced in high-speed networking. If that's the case, be sure to include recruiting and hiring costs into your implementation budget. The Staffing and Staff Development worksheet can help you estimate your budget.

# TIME ESTIMATE WORKSHEET

One of the hardest figures to estimate is that of time. Using the Time Estimate worksheet, come up with an estimated time to upgrade each server, hub, router, workstation, and switch; then, multiply that by the number of units of each piece of equipment you will convert.

Don't forget, the cost isn't limited to just time spent on the actual installation and configuration of your high-speed network. A major expense of converting your network protocol will be the costs of downtime, reduced productivity of everyone in your organization while systems are being optimized and the inevitable conversion problems are being solved, and reduced productivity of your staff while they become comfortable with the new equipment, software, and systems. Also, don't forget the opportunity cost associated with a network conversion: what won't get done well, or get done at all, while your staff is concentrating on implementing the high-speed protocol?

# APPLICATIONS WORKSHEET

In some instances, you will need to upgrade applications as well as hardware. For example, you may need new network management applications to monitor and manage the new protocol. In the case of Asynchronous Transfer Mode, applications on both the clients and the servers may need to be upgraded to support the transport protocol. As well, if you will be upgrading the network and/or desktop operating systems, application upgrades may be necessary or desirable to get the required performance and support of the operating system.

# LIVE FAST, DIE YOUNG

Another issue to consider before undertaking a conversion to high-speed networking is the emotional cost. Whether and when it is worthwhile to install a high-speed network depend a lot on the condition of your company and your department. Implementing a high-speed network is an expensive, laborious, time-consuming, and nerve-wracking project. Therefore, if your company is in the midst of, say, a reorganization, a financial crisis, or an SEC audit, the stress of such a conversion will more than likely far outweigh its benefits. The same is true of your department. If you're having morale problems before you begin a high-speed networking conversion, you may not even have a department left when it's complete.

# IF YOU STILL FIND IT'S WORTH IT

Okay, you've figured in the cost of equipment, staff, applications, services, and morale, and it still seems cost-effective to implement a high-speed networking protocol. Now it's time to select the specific protocol or protocols that will best meet the needs of your network. In the next section, we will discuss in detail the high-speed networking protocols that are currently available for both the local and wide area.

# Hardware Worksheet

### Servers:

| Equipment | No. of Units | Cost per Unit | Total |
|---|---|---|---|
| Network adapters | | | |
| NOS upgrades | | | |
| Memory upgrades | | | |
| Disk upgrades | | | |
| Driver upgrades | | | |
| Other hardware upgrades | | | |

**Total**

### Hubs—Number of ports to upgrade:

| Equipment | No. of Units | Cost per Unit | Total |
|---|---|---|---|
| New hubs | | | |
| Modules | | | |
| Chassis | | | |

**Total**

### Routers:

| Equipment | No. of Units | Cost per Unit | Total |
|---|---|---|---|
| New routers | | | |
| Router interfaces | | | |
| Firmware upgrades | | | |
| Software upgrades | | | |

**Total**

# Hardware Worksheet *(continued)*

### Switches—Number of switched ports needed:

| Equipment | No. of Units | Cost per Unit | Total |
|---|---|---|---|
| New switches | | | |
| Switch upgrade modules | | | |
| Firmware upgrades | | | |
| | | | |
| **Total** | | | |

### Workstations:

| Equipment | No. of Units | Cost per Unit | Total |
|---|---|---|---|
| New | | | |
| Operating system upgrades | | | |
| Network adapters | | | |
| Memory | | | |
| Disk space | | | |
| | | | |
| **Total** | | | |

### Cable, media, and wiring closet:

| Equipment | No. of Units | Cost per Unit | Total |
|---|---|---|---|
| New drops | | | |
| Upgraded drops | | | |
| Additional pair terminate | | | |
| Patch cables | | | |
| Connectors | | | |
| Terminators | | | |
| Racks | | | |
| Patch panels | | | |
| | | | |
| **Total** | | | |

# Service Cost Worksheet

| Service | No. of Hours | Cost per Hour | Total |
|---|---|---|---|
| Contract programmers | | | |
| Client applications | | | |
| Server applications | | | |
| Management applications | | | |
| Network integrators | | | |
| Server upgrades | | | |
| Network operating system upgrades | | | |
| Cabling contractors | | | |
| Wiring closet upgrades | | | |
| Rack installation | | | |
| Riser wiring/installation | | | |
| Patch panel installation | | | |
| **Total** | | | |

# Staff Development Worksheet

## Staff development costs:

| Seminars | No. of Enrollees | Cost per Enrollee | Total |
|---|---|---|---|
| Management systems | | | |
| Cabling | | | |
| Switches | | | |
| Routers | | | |
| Hubs | | | |
| General protocol | | | |
| | | | |
| **Total** | | | |

| Courses | No. of Enrollees | Cost per Enrollee | Total |
|---|---|---|---|
| Management systems | | | |
| Cabling | | | |
| Switches | | | |
| Routers | | | |
| Hubs | | | |
| General protocol | | | |
| | | | |
| **Total** | | | |

| Books and Reference Materials | No. of Units | Cost per Unit | Total |
|---|---|---|---|
| Management systems | | | |
| Cabling | | | |
| Switches | | | |
| Routers | | | |
| Hubs | | | |
| General protocol | | | |
| | | | |
| **Total** | | | |

# Staffing Worksheet

| Temporary Staff Costs | No. of Hours | Cost per Hour | Total |
|---|---|---|---|
| Network management | | | |
| Programming/ analyst | | | |
| Hardware maintenance | | | |
| Network administration | | | |
| **Total** | | | |

| New Staff Recruiting Costs | No. of Positions | Cost per Position | Total |
|---|---|---|---|
| Advertisements | | | |
| Search firm fees | | | |
| Orientation costs | | | |
| **Total** | | | |

# Time Estimate Worksheet

| Installation Time | No. of Hours | Cost per Hour | Total |
|---|---|---|---|
| Servers | | | |
| Hubs | | | |
| Routers | | | |
| Switches | | | |
| Workstations | | | |

| Upgrades and Optimization | No. of Hours | Cost per Hour | Total |
|---|---|---|---|
| Servers | | | |
| Hubs | | | |
| Routers | | | |
| Switches | | | |
| Workstations | | | |

| Application Upgrades | No. of Hours | Cost per Hour | Total |
|---|---|---|---|
| Workstations | | | |
| Servers | | | |
| Network management | | | |
| **Total** | | | |

## Time Estimate Worksheet *(continued)*

| Segment | No. of People on Segment | Average Cost per Hour for Person on Segment | Estimated Downtime in Hours | Total Cost of Segment Downtime |
|---------|--------------------------|---------------------------------------------|-----------------------------|--------------------------------|
|         |                          |                                             |                             |                                |

**What Won't Get Done**

**Total Downtime Lost**

# Application Worksheet

| Client Applications | No. of Licenses | Cost per License | Total |
|---|---|---|---|
| Upgrade | | | |
| New | | | |

| Server Applications | No. of Licenses | Cost per License | Total |
|---|---|---|---|
| Upgrade | | | |
| New | | | |

| Management Applications | No. of Licenses | Cost per License | Total |
|---|---|---|---|
| Upgrade | | | |
| New | | | |
| **Total** | | | |

# WAN Services Worksheet

|  | Quantity | Cost per Unit | Total Cost |
|---|---|---|---|
| Wide area service links |  |  |  |
| Customer premises equipment |  |  |  |
| Local access links |  |  |  |

# PART II

# How to Speed Up:
# Local Area Solutions

# CHAPTER 7

## Fiber Distributed Data Interface (FDDI)

Fiber Distributed Data Interface, or FDDI, was perhaps the first 100Mbps transport protocol available for local area networks. When it first appeared in the late 1980s, FDDI was expensive both to install and to manage. This was largely because the protocol ran only on fiber-optic cabling, which was scarce and difficult to install. Therefore, it was reserved almost exclusively for backbone use. Although most FDDI nodes are still mostly found on backbone segments, with the introduction of the protocol's copper wire implementation—twisted-pair-physical media dependent (TP-PMD)—along with a drop in the cost of installing optical fiber, this protocol is finding its way to the desktops more often than ever before. Although, with the recent advent of other high-speed transport protocols that require less investment of time and money to implement, FDDI may have missed its chance for widespread deployment, it still may be the right choice for your network's backbone or power workgroup.

# WHAT MAKES IT THE SAME—AND WHAT MAKES IT DIFFERENT

While there is nothing magic about FDDI as opposed to the other local area network transport protocols discussed in this book, FDDI is a significant departure from protocols we find defined in the IEEE 802 committee specifications. FDDI is a standard developed by the X3T9 committee of the American National Standards Institute (ANSI), and was originally conceived to transport data over fiber-optic cabling at 100Mbps. Since then, a copper cable implementation called TP-PMD has emerged, but has never enjoyed widespread popularity. Therefore, we will focus on the fiber-optic cabling implementation.

In its most basic form, an FDDI network is a group of computers, each with an FDDI network adapter installed, passing data packets around a ring. When operating in default mode, a computer receives a data packet from its neighbor on one side, then retransmits the packet to its neighbor on the other side.

In this scenario, each computer in the network is acting as a repeater, regenerating the data packet when it retransmits it. However, most FDDI adapters have a bypass mode, in which the device lets data packets pass by without retransmitting them. Bypass mode is used to keep the FDDI ring intact even when a computer is inactive. However, because a computer operating in bypass mode is not acting as a repeater (regenerating the data packets it receives), if too many computers placed next to each other in the ring are operating in bypass mode, the data signal may become very weak and limit the span of the network.

While a computer retransmits every data packet it receives, it sends a data packet of its own origination only when it receives the token. A token is a special data packet that serves the sole purpose of letting computers know that it has permission to originate a data packet on the ring. When a computer receives a data packet that it originated—after that packet has completely traversed the ring—the computer doesn't retransmit the packet. If it did, packets would continue circling the ring ad infinitum, eventually overwhelming the network with unnecessary traffic. Instead, when the originating computer receives its data packet, it removes the data packet from the ring.

The network just described is a very basic FDDI ring. As we will see, the functions of an FDDI network quickly become more complex.

## Framing the Data

FDDI uses a frame type different from that described in either the IEEE 802.3 (Ethernet) or IEEE 802.5 (Token Ring) standards. Although a comprehensive discussion of the types and contents of FDDI frames is beyond the scope of this book, it is important to understand that FDDI has its own frame structure. Figure 7-1 illustrates the composition of a frame.

FDDI carries much the same information in its header field, as do other protocols. The header contains information on originating station, frame classification, and unique frame identification.

The Class field identifies the frame as belonging to one of the eight (soon to be twelve) frame classes now defined in the FDDI protocol. Currently these are:

▼ Neighbor information frames (NIF)

■ Extended service frames (ESF)

■ Parameter management frames (PMF)

■ Status report frames (SRF)

■ Status information frames (SIF)

■ Echo frames (ECF)

■ Resource allocation frames (RAF)

▲ Request denied frames (RDF)

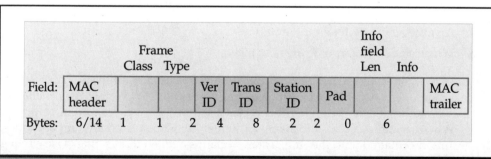

**Figure 7-1.** Structure of a Fiber Distributed Data Interface frame

The Type field identifies to which of the six frame types the frame belongs: token, void, media access control (MAC), station management (SMT), implementor, and Logical Link Control (LLC). The Ver ID field shows the version of SMT protocol. The Transaction ID field is a unique identifier for each frame. The Station ID field gives the FDDI (not the MAC) address of the originating station. This is because some FDDI stations have multiple MAC addresses, and therefore need identifiers for the protocol. This Station ID field also comes in handy if you are using hot-swappable FDDI devices because it will maintain a constant ID for the station even when the MAC addresses change.

# Determining the Path

As mentioned earlier, FDDI is a protocol that employs a token-passing scheme to determine station access. Stations send and receive data packets when they receive the token—data transmission is not managed by a central controlling station as it is with 100VG-AnyLAN. This token-passing scheme guarantees each station on the network a certain amount of bandwidth. If you take the number of nodes on the network and multiply it by the amount of time it takes each node to transmit a data packet, then you have the maximum amount of time it can take for any station to receive the token. This is what makes FDDI a deterministic network: each node will receive a minimum throughput that you can calculate.

While throughput on an FDDI network is fixed at any given time, it varies according to the number of nodes transmitting on the ring. Therefore, to join an FDDI segment, a station must follow a fairly strict set of procedures, which are part of FDDI's integrated management capabilities called *station management protocols*, or SMT (these are discussed later in the "Manageability" section of this chapter). These ring initiation protocols first initialize and test the link from the new station to the ring. Next, the station initiates its connection to the ring using a distributed algorithm called the *claim token process*. The claim token process determines whether a token already exists and, if so, reconfigures the token's path to include the new station. However, if no token is detected, the claim token protocol requires that all stations attempting to join the FDDI segment transmit special packets, called *claim frames*. The stations use the claim frames to determine both

▼ An exact value for token rotation time

▲ Which station will initiate the new token

Once the token has been created and transmitted, it is used to arbitrate shared access for the stations using a timed token protocol. The first station to join the ring establishes and tests its link with the ring, then generates a token that is passed from station to station. When a station receives the token, it can then transmit a fixed amount of frames. To transmit information onto the ring, a station claims a token that is otherwise circling the ring.

FDDI has prioritization mechanisms implemented via bandwidth allocation. The first mechanism, called *synchronous bandwidth allocation* (SBA), enables managers to assign a fixed amount of bandwidth to a certain station or stations, thus giving them greater access to the token. In SBA, bandwidth is allocated to stations as a percentage of *target token rotation time* (TTRT), which is the preset time it takes the token to make one rotation of the ring. Obviously, the total bandwidth allocated via SBA should not exceed 100 percent of the available bandwidth. See Figure 7-2.

The second mechanism, referred to as the asynchronous class of service, takes the bandwidth that is not allocated via SBA and divides it equally among the stations on the ring. The asynchronous service works like this: each station keeps a token rotation timer that tells the station when next to expect the token. When the token next appears, the station compares the *target rotation time* (TRT), or expected time of arrival, to the TTRT, which is the preset time for the token to make one rotation. The TTRT is usually set at 8 milliseconds. If the TRT is less than the TTRT, the station can grab the token and send asynchronous data frames. If the TRT is greater than the TTRT, the token is late, so stations that have only asynchronous class of service must defer to stations with synchronous bandwidth allocation.

During times of heavy traffic, the TRT can get so long that stations sending data packets with low priorities can be completely restricted from access to the ring for a time. Eventually, however, all the stations with high-priority packets will send their data,

**Figure 7-2.**   Synchronous bandwidth allocation ensures that bandwidth is available to the stations that need it most

lowering the TRT and thereby letting stations with low-priority transmissions have a chance to claim the token.

# Cabling Considerations

FDDI networks are composed of a set of counterrotating dual rings and attached devices and segments. The set of counterrotating dual rings is called the *trunk* ring. While devices can be directly attached to the trunk ring, as described in our initial description of a basic FDDI network, they can also be attached to the trunk ring via *concentrators*. Concentrators are devices similar to multistation access units (MAUs) in the token ring world that provide trunk connections to multiple stations. Devices that are directly attached to the trunk must be *dual-attachment stations* (DAS)—in other words, devices that are attached to both of the counterrotating rings. Devices that are attached to the trunk ring via a concentrator are *single-attachment stations* (SAS)—stations that attach to one ring only.

## Making the Connection

In FDDI, network connections are made through a series of strictly defined protocols that require that all FDDI ports have one of four identities: A, B, S, and M. Table 7-1 defines the various port types.

All stations on an FDDI network must have both an A and a B port. A *tree* connection occurs when an A, B, or S port connects to an M port. In this configuration, the node isn't attached directly to the trunk ring, but rather to a port on a concentrator attached to the trunk ring. See Figure 7-3.

| Port Type | Function | Location |
|---|---|---|
| A | Exit point from station to secondary (backup) ring | All dual-attachment stations |
| B | Exit point from station to primary ring | All dual-attachment stations |
| S | Connects stations to one ring only | All single-attachment stations |
| M | Distribution ports that extend both primary and secondary rings | Concentrators |

**Table 7-1.** The Four Types of Network Connections Supported by FDDI

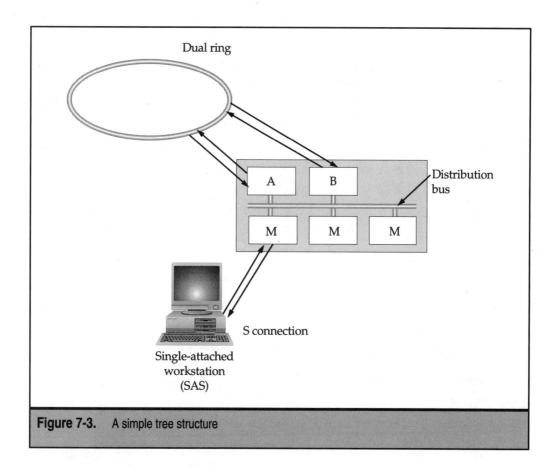

**Figure 7-3.**   A simple tree structure

## Supported Media

FDDI can run on both multimode fiber (PMD) and single-mode fiber (SMF-PMD), as well as Category 5 unshielded twisted-pair cable and 150-ohm shielded twisted-pair cable (TP-PMD).

## The Topology

The general topology used in FDDI networks is a dual ring with trees (see Figure 7-4). However, there are variations, including the following:

▼   **Dual rings without trees**   This just means that all the stations are directly connected to the dual ring via DAS connections. See Figure 7-5.

■ **Wrapped ring with or without trees**    A *wrapped ring* is really a dual ring in which a cable fault or break has occurred. When the protocol senses a cable fault, it reroutes traffic from its direct path to the destination station to the roundabout secondary data path, essentially "wrapping" the data back around the ring until it reaches its destination. See Figure 7-6 for an example of a wrapped ring without trees. This type of topology is obviously inefficient, and should be used only as a disaster recovery measure in the event of a cable fault. Wrapped-ring configurations should be rectified as quickly as possible.

▲ **Single tree**    This is simply an FDDI network consisting of one tree. See Figure 7-7.

Whichever of these topologies you use, the cardinal rule remains the same: FDDI supports a maximum of two data paths—a primary data path and a secondary data path.

**Figure 7-4.**    The basic FDDI topology: a dual ring with trees

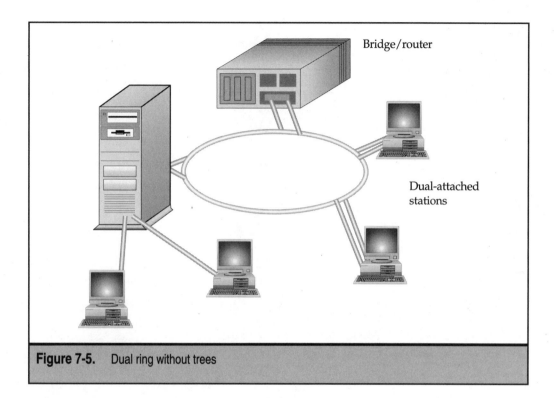

Bridge/router

Dual-attached
stations

**Figure 7-5.**    Dual ring without trees

## Cost of Ownership

FDDI is an expensive protocol to implement. Hubs cost an average of about $1,500 per port, and network adapters for a server or desktop average a little over $1,000 each. What's more, if you use fiber-optic cable, you're going to encounter a major expense in training your staff to install and/or work with this medium. And then you're going to have to spend money to keep them, because there is a fairly strong demand for employees who are familiar with fiber-optic technology. Still, fiber-optic cabling has the capacity to support protocols that far exceed FDDI's current bandwidth so, depending upon your network strategy, it could be a good investment.

As we mentioned earlier, FDDI runs on either optical fiber or Category 5 UTP. However, the pinout for FDDI is different than that for Ethernet, so you'll need FDDI patch cables (it's a good idea to color code these patch cables). Therefore, be prepared for some trouble calls resulting from Ethernet patch cables inadvertently being plugged into TP-PMD ports.

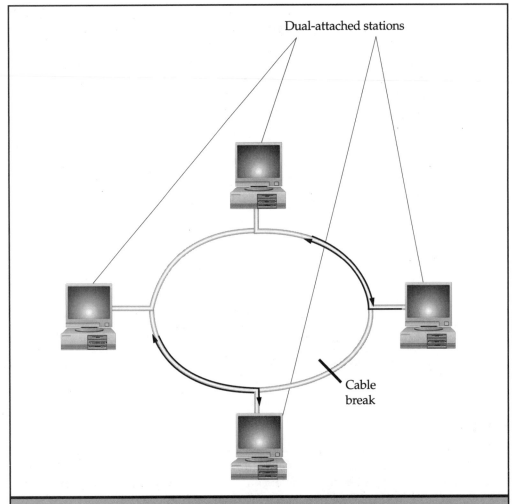

**Figure 7-6.** Wrapped ring without trees. This topology is nearly always the result of a cable break

## Scalability

FDDI is probably the most scalable of all the high-speed local area network protocols, with the exception of ATM. Its deterministic protocol, along with its synchronous and asynchronous bandwidth allocation mechanisms, make it easy to add stations while ensuring that response times meet the needs of the applications. What's more, FDDI supports up to 500 stations on a single LAN, and its maximum network extent is 200 kilometers when running over fiber-optic cabling.

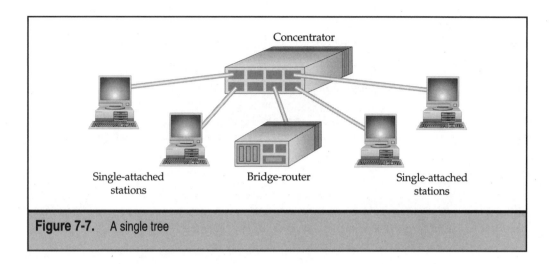

**Figure 7-7.**    A single tree

FDDI's large packet size makes it a very efficient transport protocol for large packet sizes. However, for the current average packet size of between 256 bytes to 512 bytes, FDDI has extremely high overhead per packet.

If you are integrating FDDI into an existing 10Base-T network, there are many hubs available that support switching between the two protocols. Also, several vendors have recently announced the development of FDDI switches, which may enhance the performance of FDDI networks as they grow.

## Setup and Configuration

As we mentioned earlier, installing FDDI is relatively difficult. However, because FDDI has been around for several years now, it should be fairly easy to find technical assistance. The initialization scheme required for stations wanting to enter the ring may cause some headaches during the initial configuration. However, once the FDDI network is up and running, it proves to be a solid and stable machine that needs very little maintenance.

## Manageability

FDDI is both extremely fault tolerant and manageable. Because FDDI supports dual-homed, dual-attached backbones, each server on the ring can be connected to as many as two hubs on the same ring, so there is always an alternate path. Also, its support for counterrotating rings provides great fault isolation while simultaneously keeping the network running.

Unlike Ethernet, FDDI has a built-in network monitoring and management protocol called *station management* (SMT). Unlike the rest of the protocols in this comparison book, FDDI was designed with SMT as an integral part of it. SMT includes both network monitoring facilities at the link, node, and network levels, as well as remote network management capability via management information bases (MIBs). It provides capabilities for fault isolation and recovery, statistics gathering, data error monitoring, and noise monitoring. In addition, it provides connection and configuration management. Even the previously described ring initiation procedures are a part of the station management protocol. However, providing these management and monitoring facilities also adds to the overhead of the protocol, and therefore can limit the efficiency and cost effectiveness of the protocol, especially in desktop implementations.

## Performance

FDDI has been a proven performer for some time. The elegance of the bandwidth allocation mechanisms really shows up in multimedia and video applications. As you run video applications, for example, you can add workstations to the FDDI ring without experiencing the slightest stall or shudder.

Furthermore, FDDI has a maximum data packet size of 4,500 bytes, which makes more efficient use of available bandwidth than 100Base-T with its 1,500-byte maximum. This larger packet size is especially helpful in applications with a large average packet size. In short, FDDI's performance gets very high marks.

## Evolving to Survive

A related standard, FDDI-II, has emerged to transport data that cannot sustain delays. An example of this would be real-time, full-motion video. To accomplish the "zero-delay" standard, FDDI-II borrows from the circuit-switching technology of long-distance telephone carriers. FDDI-II multiplexes bandwidth into dedicated circuits that ensure packet delivery. These circuits can then provide isochronous, or *circuit-based*, services that offer a regular, fixed-length transmission slot that essentially provides a dedicated channel between stations. FDDI-II can support as many as 16 such circuits. Bandwidth on these circuits is allocated to stations on the basis of need, so maximum bandwidth varies from 6.144Mbps to 99.072Mbps. In turn, each of these channels may be subdivided into 64Kbps circuits. FDDI-II supports a maximum of 96 64Kbps channels.

FDDI-II has some drawbacks, however. First, all nodes on the network must be FDDI-II. If all nodes aren't, then the FDDI-II devices begin operating as FDDI devices. This lack of compatibility is not only inconvenient, it's extremely expensive because you will have the cost of replacing FDDI devices with FDDI-II devices as well as the cost of redesigning your network to make sure that all FDDI devices are on their own ring.

## SUMMARY

While FDDI has proven itself as a solid, fault-tolerant, high-performance vehicle for backbone deployment, there are several obstacles to implementing it at the desktop. Its high price, high overhead, and complete departure from the familiar 10Base-T cabling rules may prevent its widespread use at the desktop. You will probably have to spend a significant amount of time and money in finding, training, and then retaining expertise in fiber-optic cabling. Also, due to differences in pinout between Ethernet and FDDI, if you have both protocols at your site, there may be some confusion—and resulting troubleshooting—resulting from misplaced patch cables.

## Recommended for:

▼ Multimedia and video because synchronous bandwidth allocation mechanism can ensure adequate bandwidth

■ Server farms and backbones because of manageability and fault tolerance

▲ Backbone segments

## Not Recommended for:

▼ Standard desktop deployment because of relatively high cost and high overhead associated with SMT

## Strengths:

▼ Extensive management support built into the protocol

■ Largest network diameter of all 100Mbps network options

▲ Established protocol with fairly broad vendor support

## Weaknesses:

▼ Relatively expensive

■ Relatively difficult to install

▲ High overhead associated with SMT

# CHAPTER 8

## 100VG-AnyLAN

In June 1995, the IEEE certified the 100VG-AnyLAN specification for the 802.12 standard. Long before that date, however, its proponents—led by Hewlett Packard Company, Inc.—heralded it as the ultimate trade-in opportunity for 10Base-T networks. Ethernet users were told that the conversion from 10Base-T to 100VG-AnyLAN would be so inexpensive and easy that there would be no reason *not* to go with 100VG-AnyLAN. However, while 100VG-AnyLAN was a logical and cost-effective migration path for some applications, there were enough caveats to prevent it from inheriting 10Base-T's preeminence. At the time of the writing, market forces have largely passed 100VG-AnyLAN by.

# SO CLOSE, BUT SO FAR FROM 10BASE-T

Although 100VG-AnyLAN has many similarities to the familiar 802.3 protocol, it employs data access and signaling methods that differ drastically from both Ethernet and Fast Ethernet. Rather than the familiar collision-based CSMA/CD protocol that the 802.3 and 802.3u standards use, the 802.12 data access method is known as *Demand Priority Access* (DPA), in which the workstation initiates data transfers and the hub acknowledges data and directs the transfer. This differs from CSMA/CD in two critical ways:

▼ Data transfer is controlled by the hub rather than the network adapter.

▲ Collisions are eliminated because each node is guaranteed a turn at sending data.

Theoretically, this deterministic protocol increases available bandwidth by eliminating collisions and retransmissions. However, being a complete departure from 802.3, it therefore will likely require some rethinking on the part of your technical staff and some redesign for your network.

## Getting Framed

Although 100VG supports the frame formats of the existing 802.3 and 802.5 protocols (but not both simultaneously), the 802.12 transport protocol is nothing like either. The emerging IEEE 802.12 standard for transmitting 100Mbps over voice-grade unshielded twisted-pair wire represents a significant departure from the existing Ethernet standard in the area of data access.

### Setting Priorities

One of the key differences between the 802.3 and 802.12 standards is also one of the prime advantages of the latter protocol: its ability to recognize two levels of priority in transmission requests. The 802.12 100VG-AnyLAN protocol recognizes normal-priority and high-priority transmission requests, with high-priority requests taking precedence.

The priority level can be set either by the workstation or by the application, although as of this writing there were no generally available applications that took advantage of this ability to set priority. If a normal-priority request remains pending for more than 300ms, it is moved to the high-priority service queue.

DPA does more than simply allow you to set transmission priority. It also improves performance by removing the network overhead associated with the CSMA/CD access method. In CSMA/CD, all workstations contend for access to the channel. Collisions, which are fairly frequent, require detection and retransmission of the packet. Furthermore, the DPA scheme has a performance edge on CSMA/CD. This is because as collisions become more frequent as traffic increases on CSMA/CD networks, the resulting packet retransmissions slow performance. The DPA network, which has no contention for transmission and hence no packet collisions, is able to handle more traffic.

100VG-AnyLAN has something of a security advantage over the 802.3 standard as well. The 100VG-AnyLAN hub transmits packets only across ports attached to the destination address of the packet. This reduces the opportunity for unauthorized monitoring of transmissions.

# The Architecture

The 100VG-AnyLAN topology must be in a physical star, with no loops or branches. The centerpiece of this topology, as specified by the DPA scheme, is a central hub, called the root hub, that controls the traffic. Each lower level hub maintains its own per port address table that contains the addresses of the stations connected to each of its ports. If this sounds like the familiar polling architecture of yore—that's because that's exactly what it is.

## How the Demand Priority Access Scheme Works

When a station sends a transmission request, the request is first received by the hub to which the station is directly attached. If the directly connected hub is the only hub in the network, it is the root hub and thus the central controller for network transmission. It will therefore service the transmission request in the station's turn in the polling and priority sequence. However, if the directly connected hub is not the root hub, it will send the station's transmission request on to the next higher level hub, which in turn will transfer the request on if it is not the root hub. Eventually, the transmission request reaches the root hub, which will then allow the local hub to service the transmission request in its turn. See Figure 8-1 for a bird's-eye view of the progress of a data packet across this topology.

## Here We Go Round the Network

A 100VG-AnyLAN network functions something like a "round-robin," because each hub is polled in sequence, and each hub in turn polls each of its ports in sequence. Here's the process: Between packet transmissions, stations and hubs send a signal to each other indicating that the channel is available to make a transmission request. This signal is called an *idle signal*. When a station has a packet to transmit, it sends a *transmission request*

**Figure 8-1.**    The path of a packet across a 100VG-AnyLAN network

*signal* to the hub. The transmission request signal includes the priority of the transmission request. The transmitting station then waits for a response, originating from the root hub, which grants it permission to transmit one packet onto the network.

In 100VG-AnyLAN, the root hub controls all the data transmission. If the hub that receives the transmission request is the only hub in the network, it is the root hub, so it waits for any transmission in progress to complete, then services the port that is next in the polling sequence, giving that port permission to transmit one packet. However, if the hub is connected to a hub higher in the network, it waits for any network transmission in progress to complete, then signals a transmission request to the higher level hub. In the same manner, the higher level hub will pass the transmission request to the next higher level of hub—if any—until the transmission request eventually reaches the root hub.

The root hub determines which lower level hub can then begin servicing transmission requests. When the right to service network requests passes to a hub, it services requests in port order (i.e., port 1, then 2, up to port N), and then passes control back to the higher level hub. If a high-priority request is made anywhere on the network, however, the control passes immediately to the hub that has that request, and returns to the original hub after all high-priority requests have been serviced throughout the network. High-priority transmission requests occurring anywhere on the network always take precedence, and the root hub always allows the local hub that received the request to service the request, then return control to the hub whose turn it is. See Figure 8-2.

## Joining the Club

Because of the deterministic nature of 100VG-AnyLAN, a station can't simply join the network and start transmitting. It must register itself with the root hub, which will assign

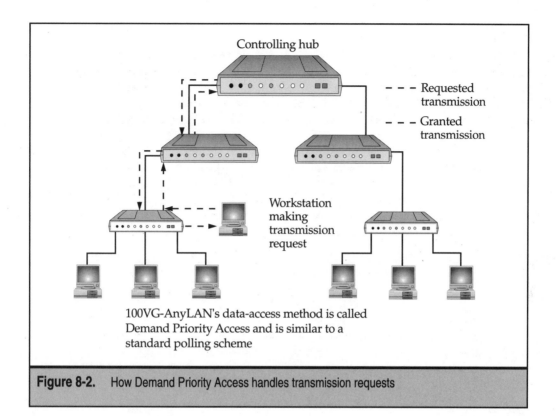

Controlling hub

- - - Requested transmission

- - - Granted transmission

Workstation making transmission request

100VG-AnyLAN's data-access method is called Demand Priority Access and is similar to a standard polling scheme

**Figure 8-2.**    How Demand Priority Access handles transmission requests

the new station a place in the polling sequence. It works like this: when a station or hub wishes to join the network, it transmits and receives frames to and from the attached port. This is called a *training sequence* of frames. The training sequence helps the hub determine whether the new device is a station or another hub, which frame type it is using (either 802.3 or 802.5 frames), and whether the port will be allowed to operate as a promiscuous listener. If the connecting device is a station, the training sequence also determines the MAC address of the connecting station. While training is occurring, the network suspends its polling operations; fortunately, completing the training sequence takes about 5 microseconds. Based on the results of the training sequence, the hub either allows the new device to join the network or denies it access and transmits the reason why it will not be admitted.

## Cable Design Considerations

The cabling rules for 100VG-AnyLAN are very similar to 10Base-T. In fact, of all the high-speed transport protocols, 100VG-AnyLAN has cabling rules closest to that for 10Base-T. However, there are some important differences.

## Wiring Issues

In the 802.3 standard, one pair of wires is dedicated to transmitting data and another to receiving. Currently, in the 802.12 100VG-AnyLAN standard all four pairs of wires both transmit or receive data (a two-pair implementation is planned), enabling each pair to operate at a signal rate of 25MHz. Because the deterministic protocol eliminates collisions, data throughput is theoretically at 100 percent, resulting in a 100Mbps network operating rate.

By sending out 25MHz signals, the protocol keeps radio frequencies within required standards. It also allows the use of voice-grade cable (Category 3). Using 4-pair wiring, the 25MHz signal enables 100VG-AnyLAN to send and receive data simultaneously. 100VG-AnyLAN supports Categories 3, 4, or 5 UTP cable, Type-1 STP cable, and fiber-optic cable. Depending on the cable type, network span varies from 100 meters to 2,000 meters. See Figure 8-3.

**NOTE:** 100VG-AnyLAN doesn't support flat cable in a twisted-pair topology.

Because 100VG-AnyLAN supports such a wide variety of cable types, you may be able to preserve your investment in your current network cable infrastructure. However, keep in mind that because 100VG-AnyLAN currently requires all four pairs of Category 3 UTP, you must be sure that all four pairs are terminated—and that may cost you some extra bucks.

**TIP:** Be sure that your twisted-pair cabling has twists all the way up to the pins of the cross-connect blocks. A section of untwisted pairs can cause crosstalk.

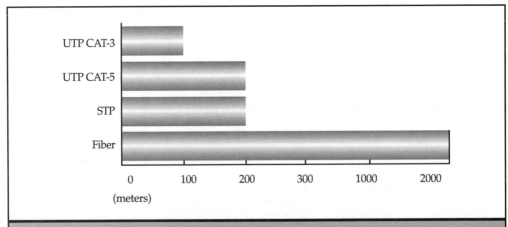

**Figure 8-3.** In 100VG-AnyLAN, type of cabling determines the maximum network span

## Hub Issues

The maximum number of hub levels in a 100VG-AnyLAN network is five. However, your network will perform best if you keep it to three levels of hub cascading. Because three is the maximum number of hub levels allowed by 802.3, your network is probably already designed this way. However, each level of hubs shortens the maximum distance allowed between a root hub and an end node by 1km. Table 8-1 will help you determine the maximum distance between the root hub and an end node.

As a final cabling plant note, keep in mind that you shouldn't have more than seven bridges or switches between any two nodes in a network. This is a result of the IEEE 802.1d spanning tree protocol, not a limitation of 100VG-AnyLAN.

# Preparing for 100VG-AnyLAN

One of the most unsettling things about plunging into 100VG-AnyLAN is its current limited vendor support. Lack of competition in this market not only potentially limits the technical expertise available, but also may keep prices higher than for other better established protocols. So, let the buyer beware.

| Type of Media | Number of Hubs Between Root Hub and End Node | Number of Levels in Network | Recommended Maximum Distances Between Root Hub and End Node |
|---|---|---|---|
| Category 3 | 1 | 2 | 100mm |
| Category 3 | 2 | 3 | 75mm |
| Category 3 | 3 | 4 | 50mm |
| Category 3 | 4 | 5 | 25mm |
| Category 5 | 1 | 2 | 200mm |
| Category 5 | 2 | 3 | 150mm |
| Category 5 | 3 | 4 | 100mm |
| Category 5 | 4 | 5 | 50mm |
| Fiber optic | 1 | 2 | 4km |
| Fiber optic | 2 | 3 | 3km |
| Fiber optic | 3 | 4 | 2km |

**Table 8-1.**    Maximum Distances Allowed Between End Node and Root Hub

You should scrutinize your cable plant before implementing 100VG-AnyLAN, carefully removing any 25-pair cables connected to devices operating in promiscuous mode (in which the device monitors all frames it receives), including the following:

▼ A cascaded (hub-to-hub) link, because the default configuration of an uplink port is promiscuous. The entire cable path from hub to device must be unbundled cable. Otherwise, the result will likely be severe crosstalk, retransmissions, and unreliable performance.

■ Links between routers and hubs.

■ Links between bridges and hubs.

▲ Links between a network analyzer and a hub. Network analyzers have to be configured as promiscuous so they can capture all network data.

You'll also have to check to make sure the distance between hubs does not exceed the specifications for 100VG-AnyLAN. Refer again to Table 8-1 for more information.

**TIP:**   Spend a significant amount of time reviewing your cable plant to comply with 100VG-AnyLAN media and distance requirements. Also, if you are internetworking 100VG-AnyLAN with a 10Base-T network, be prepared to resegment your network to accommodate 100VG-AnyLAN bridging limitations.

## Scalability

While the deterministic Demand Priority Access scheme makes 100VG-AnyLAN easily scalable with little drop in performance, growing a 100VG-AnyLAN network has its obstacles. Most of the scalability problems we noted are ones that you are most likely to encounter when migrating in phases from 10Base-T to 100VG-AnyLAN. For example, like all high-speed protocols, 100VG-AnyLAN requires a translational bridge between itself and 10Base-T. Furthermore, while there are no limitations on the number of nodes on a single shared 100VG-AnyLAN, it's a good idea to limit the number of nodes to 250 to maintain performance.

The rules governing network span in a 100VG-AnyLAN network depend not only on the type of cable used (see Figure 8-3), but also on the number of hub levels employed. Maximum network span for 100VG-AnyLAN networks varies from 100m to 2,000m, depending on the media used. The maximum network length with Category 5 cabling is around 200m. Refer again to Figure 8-3 for information on maximum network span. Also, you can cascade up to five hubs (it supports four repeater hops per network segment, just like Ethernet). However, we recommend that you review your network design carefully and compare it to the 100VG-AnyLAN cable rules so you can be alerted to any potential problems. That's because each level of hubs shortens the maximum distance allowed between a root hub and an end node. For example, when using fiber-optic cabling, each level of hubs shortens the maximum distance from root hub to end node by 1km. Table 8-1 will help you determine the maximum distance between the root hub and an end node for fiber-optic cabling. Figure 8-4 illustrates the maximum distance between a root

**Figure 8-4.**    The distance allowed between a root hub and an end node varies depending on the number of cascaded hubs in between and type of media

hub and an end node. In this example of a 3-hub cascade using fiber-optic cabling, the maximum distance allowed is 3km.

*TIP:* Minimize the levels of cascading. Every level of cascading adds to arbitration overhead, which slows performance.

## Manageability

Because 100VG-AnyLAN supports standard Ethernet packet types, interoperability problems are nonexistent. However, the protocol currently has no management tools that natively support bandwidth allocation and management. Right now, the only security offered is the private-mode operation described earlier, which, when enabled, allows ports to receive only those packets addressed to the device attached to it. All ports not associated with the destination address receive an idle signal while the packet addressed to that destination is being transmitted. Although this level of security is sufficient for most installations, it may not be sufficient for extremely high security sites.

## Performance

Performance is the strong suit of 100VG-AnyLAN. Because 100VG-AnyLAN can handle packet sizes of either 4,500 bytes or 1,500 bytes, it can support the current smaller average packet sizes and still maintain fast and efficient performance.

The real strength of 100VG-AnyLAN is highlighted when running multimedia applications. Even full-motion video runs under heavy network load with nary a flicker, thanks to the DPA scheme that assigned high priority to all the video frames. Furthermore, Hewlett Packard has stated that they have plans to add full-duplex capability 100VG-AnyLAN (which can be implemented only in two-pair environments such as two-pair shielded twisted-pair or two-pair fiber, support for which is currently unavailable), which will increase performance even more. All in all, however, the performance is extremely impressive right now.

## Continuous Improvement

100VG-AnyLAN has improved since its introduction in 1994. When it was originally introduced, it didn't support redundant paths or the spanning tree protocol. Now, however, it supports redundant paths between any two hubs made via the spanning tree protocol, provided only one such path is active at any one time.

# SUMMARY

The Demand Priority Access scheme makes 100VG-AnyLAN a robust protocol that's especially well suited for multimedia and video applications. However, the protocol's lack of fault tolerance and dearth of management facilities make it less than ideal for backbone deployment. Finally, because it almost but not quite complies with 10Base-T cabling rules, network managers should approach a broad-scale implementation with caution.

## Recommended for:

▼ Multimedia and video applications because of its capability to prioritize and ensure packet delivery

■ Installed base that doesn't include 25-pair cable, because 100VG-AnyLAN doesn't operate over 25-pair cable connected to devices running in promiscuous mode

▲ Power workgroups, because its deterministic data access scheme will ensure consistent performance under high traffic

## Not Recommended for:

▼   Backbones, because the centralized polling design can potentially cause a single point of slowdown or even failure

▲   Installed bases that have network spans that don't comply with 100VG-AnyLAN specifications

## Strengths:

▼   Low price of components

▲   Can prioritize packets

## Weaknesses:

▼   Limited security

■   Limited—but growing—vendor support

▲   Considerable preparation required before implementing into a legacy 10Base-T network

# CHAPTER 9

## 100Base-T

From the beginning, the Fast Ethernet Alliance has heralded 100Base-T as the true and rightful heir of 10Base-T. With the IEEE's adoption of 100Base-T as the 802.3u standard in June 1995, the coronation is now complete. On its face, the succession seems logical, because in many ways 100Base-T appears to be just supercharged 10Base-T. For example, 100Base-T has retained the CSMA/CD media access method and most of the traditional cabling rules of 10Base-T.

Some argue, however, that 100Base-T is faster than most desktops require, yet slower than backbones demand. Moreover, the similarity but not strict conformity to 10Base-T cabling rules can cause confusion. This debate notwithstanding, it's probably the easiest high-speed protocol to merge into your existing 10Base-T environment—if you carefully choose the 100Base-T specification that's right for your network, familiarize yourself with and plan for the differences between 10Base-T and 100Base-T, and implement the protocol accordingly.

# A SMORGASBORD OF SPECS

The 802.3u specification adopted by the IEEE is defined in two parts. The first part defines the data link layer, which is the layer in the OSI reference model that describes how the protocol handles sending and receiving data between nodes that are connected directly to one another. The second part of the IEEE 802.3u specification, and the part that is most significant to the network manager, is the physical layer specification. This is the part of the specification that defines the type of media over which you can run the 100Base-T protocol. The 100Base-T physical specification comes in four different flavors. Each is designed to accommodate 100Base-T on a different type of physical cable plant and is exacting in its requirements. Therefore, be sure to select the physical layer specification that suits your existing cable plant or be prepared to upgrade your cabling to meet the standard required by the specification.

> ▼ **Media-independent interface (MII)**    This specification provides MAC-layer connectivity to 100Base-T. This is similar to that of the attachment unit interface (AUI) connection in 10Base-T. The MII interface defines the way the 100Base-T protocol accesses the physical transmission media. In other words, the MII describes a generic 100Base-T interface that can connect to a transceiver that will connect in turn to 100Base-TX, 100Base-T4, or 100Base-FX. See Figure 9-1.

**NOTE:**   The MII specifications allow only a 1-meter distance between the network adapter and the transceiver.

> ■ **100Base-TX**    This specification is used for running 100Mbps Ethernet over 2-pair unshielded twisted-pair (UTP) cable and 2-pair Type-1 shielded twisted-pair (STP) cable. This is probably the most familiar of the 100Base-T specifications. It provides for 125MHz signaling over each pair of cables, which can supply only 80 percent throughput due to its encoding scheme (called

**Figure 9-1.** The MII describing MAC-layer connectivity to 100Base-T

4B5B). The 100Base-TX specification is described for both RJ-45 and DB-9 connectors. As you can see in the diagram in Figure 9-2, pinout for the 100Base-TX RJ-45 cabling is identical to that for 10Base-T, transmitting over wires 1 and 2 and receiving over wires 3 and 6.

**Figure 9-2.** 100Base-TX is 100Mbps 802.3u running on 2-pair twisted-pair cable

*CAUTION:*   Although you may be able to run 100Base-TX over Category 3 STP for short distances, don't try it. The errors caused by this implementation will outweigh the benefits of the increased bandwidth.

■ **100Base-T4**   This specification is used for running 100Mbps Ethernet over 4-pair Category 3, 4, or 5 UTP cabling. Until September 1995, there were no commercially available devices that supported this standard, and by the time such devices arrived on the market, 100Base-T4 had largely missed its opportunity. Category 5 cable became the predominant cable type in most enterprise networks, so 100Base-T4 was really unnecessary. 100Base-T4 provides for 25MHz signaling over 3-pair, with 133 percent throughput as a result of its encoding scheme (called 8B6T). The 100Base-T4 specification allows only RJ-45 connectors. As you can see in Figure 9-3, the RJ-45 cabling is similar to 10Base-T, adding two bidirectional pairs that 10Base-T does not have. Choosing the 100Base-T4 specification may be an expensive proposition, however. Although the majority of network sites run either Category 3 or Category 5 UTP, most are running on 2-cable pairs. What's more, the

**Figure 9-3.**   100 Base-T4 is 100Mbps 802.3u over 4-pair twisted-pair cable

additional 2-cable pairs required to meet the 100Base-T4 specification are often unavailable, having been appropriated for telephones, printers, or other uses.

▲   **100Base-FX**   This is the 100Mbps Ethernet physical layer specification for 2-strand 62.5/125 micron fiber-optic cabling. It supports standard MIC, ST, or SC connectors. Signaling for 100Base-FX uses the 4B5B encoding scheme, which provides 80 percent of total output. Therefore, signaling is at 125MHz over a single strand. Currently, there isn't a great deal of interest in the industry or the network management community in running 100Base-T over fiber-optic cabling. This is probably because sites that currently have fiber-optic cabling are already running at 100Mbps using the FDDI protocol. Sites that don't currently have fiber can very likely implement 100Base-T more cost effectively using copper.

It's important to pick the 100Base-T specification that is designed for the physical cable plant you have or are planning to build. That's because the various Fast Ethernet specifications are not interchangeable, and also because crafting the appropriate cable plant represents a significant portion of the cost of implementing 100Base-T. The decision table in Table 9-1 can help you select the appropriate physical layer interface for your 100Base-T network.

| If You Have | And You Are Using | Choose This Specification |
|---|---|---|
| Type-1 or Category 5 STP | 2-cable pairs | 100Base-TX |
| Category 5 | 2-cable pairs | 100Base-TX |
| Category 5 | 4-cable pairs | 100Base-T4 |
| Category 4 | 2-cable pairs | You must upgrade your cabling |
| Category 4 | 4-cable pairs | 100Base-T4 |
| Category 3 | 2-cable pairs | You must upgrade your cabling |
| Category 3 | 4-cable pairs | 100Base-T4 |
| Fiber-optic cabling | | 100Base-FX |

**Table 9-1.**   How to Choose the Correct 802.3u Specification for Your Cable Plant

# UNDERSTANDING THE DIFFERENCES BETWEEN 100BASE-T AND 10BASE-T

As we mentioned earlier, 100Base-T bears a lot of similarity to 10Base-T. Obviously, implementing 100Base-T will require that you replace your network adapters and hubs. Fortunately, the actual cost of the 100Base-T components is very low. Strong industry support indicates that competition may drive these costs even lower, currently ranging from $200 to $500 per managed port including network adapter. At the time of this writing, these prices were still dropping rapidly. However, there's much more to implementing the protocol than simply replacing equipment. Although it's also fairly easy to integrate 100Base-T into an existing 10Base-T network, there are some very important differences between how the two protocols work. The success of your high-speed network depends upon your knowing and preparing for these differences. These differences are discussed in the following sections.

## Interoperability and Obstacles

To plan a successful implementation, you should be aware of certain technical characteristics of the 100Base-T protocol. Knowing these will help you determine whether 100Base-T is the appropriate protocol for the segment you have in mind, as well as alert you to any potential difficulties you may experience after implementing 100Base-T.

### Narrowing the Window of Opportunity

One of the biggest obstacles in implementing a 100Mbps CSMA/CD protocol is the extremely short slot time available. *Slot time* is the window of time required for a network station to detect a collision. Figure 9-4 illustrates the effect of slot time on packet transmission. In 10Base-T, the slot time is 512 bits. A transmitting station "listens" to the network, waiting for an opening in the traffic so that it can send a packet. When an opening occurs, the station must transmit its packet before another packet comes hurtling down the network. This period of time that it has to transmit the packet and listen for a collision before another one comes is called the slot time. In 802.3, slot time is set at 5.12 microseconds (the time it takes to transmit 512 bits traveling at 10Mbps). This is the amount of time the station has to transmit a packet successfully, or "claim the channel" as it is called in 802.3 jargon. In fact, 5.12ms is all the time the transmitting station has to transmit the packet *and receive a collision signal if the transmitted packet collides with another packet.* That's because if the transmitted packet collides with another packet, the transmitting station must receive notification of the collision before the end of the slot time so that it can retransmit before another packet takes over the channel.

With the advent of 100Base-T, data throughput has been increased tenfold over 10Base-T, but the slot time of 512 bits has not been increased. A similar situation would be if you ordinarily merged onto a highway traveling 30 miles per hour in your car. As long as all the rest of the traffic on the highway is traveling at 30mph, you need only wait for a

**Figure 9-4.**   100Base-T's short slot time effectively limits network span

gap of about three car lengths to safely merge into the traffic. Imagine then, if your car and all the rest of the traffic began traveling at 300mph, but you still attempted to merge onto the highway when there was only a three-car-length space available. Collisions would seem inevitable, wouldn't they? And so they are with 100Base-T. Therefore, to ensure that collision notifications are received by the transmitting station before the end of the slot time, the network span must be shrunk proportionately. For 100Base-T, this limits the maximum network span to approximately 210m.

## Changes in Latitude

The 100Base-T standard doesn't allow the latitude in configuring segments that 10Base-T does. It allows only two repeater hops per segment, unlike 10Base-T's three hops per segment. To observe the 210m maximum span, these repeater hops can be a maximum of only 10m apart. Obviously, this will affect how you design your cable plant. See Figure 9-5.

# Scalability Considerations

Before you select 100Base-T, it's important to understand the limitations of the protocol. Most of the drawbacks of 100Base-T are due to its limited scalability. Because of its close kinship to 10Base-T, it suffers from some of the same problems (such as increased collisions and resulting slow performance) when subjected to heavy traffic. However, full-duplex Ethernet is a technology that has been implemented in 100Base-T protocols to help ease the same problem.

## Full-Duplex Fast Ethernet: Why and How

The CSMA/CD access protocol itself may inhibit scalability. As you add more users and more bandwidth-intensive applications, the increased collisions may well prevent

10m link
between repeaters

30th floor

100Base-T repeater

100m UTP
to desktops

100m UTP
to servers

Bridge, router, or switch

Servers

**Figure 9-5.**    The entire span of a 100Base-T network cannot exceed 210m

acceptable performance. However, 100Base-T switches, especially those that offer full duplex, may mitigate the collision problems of the CSMA/CD protocol. To explain how full duplex increases bandwidth, let's begin with an explanation of 100Base-T signaling.

There are two pairs of wires in star-wired 10Base-T and 100Base-T environments—one for transmitting and one for receiving. However, transmission and reception cannot take place at the same time. Full-duplex Ethernet, on the other hand, allows transmission over one pair of wires and reception over the other pair simultaneously, providing nearly full utilization of both pairs and thus sustainable high data rates. By installing MAC devices that support full-duplex Ethernet, you can double the effective bandwidth. Full-duplex Ethernet can coexist with normal half-duplex Ethernet and make use of the existing 10Base-T wiring.

As attractive as it sounds, full-duplex Ethernet has a couple of serious drawbacks. The first is that it requires an investment in NICs, hubs, switches, firmware, and driver upgrades that support full-duplex operation. The second drawback is that it makes sense only in a few situations. Specifically, this protocol is effective only in point-to-point connections, and then only when there is traffic available to flow in both directions at the same time. Still, in backbone implementations where there is a great deal of traffic among servers, full-duplex Ethernet is a technology that may be worth considering to make maximum use of the bandwidth available.

## The Good News About Scalability

The good news about 100Base-T scalability, as we mentioned earlier, is that it is fairly easy to integrate with existing 10Base-T networks. Despite the fact that it supports fewer hops than 10Base-T and thus may require some recabling, the 100Base-T protocol has a relatively small packet size for high-speed networks, and it handles smaller packet sizes well. Given the current 512-byte average packet size on networks, this gives 100Base-T an edge as a "transition-to-high-speed" protocol. Furthermore, many vendors offer hubs, switches, and network adapter cards that function both at 10Mbps and 100Mbps. These devices automatically sense whether they are attached to a 10Base-T or 100Base-T network and adjust their speed accordingly. This makes it relatively easy and cost-effective to convert from 10Base-T to 100Base-T in phases.

# Manageability Issues

Because 100Base-T is so similar to 10Base-T, many of the familiar 10Base-T management tools are available for use with 100Base-T networks, such as protocol analyzers and hub management systems. This means that 100Base-T is not only very manageable, but very manageable at a reasonable price since very little new development effort was required.

# Setup and Configuration Considerations

Because of its many similarities to familiar 10Base-T, installation and configuration of 100Base-T devices is extremely easy. Because there is no initialization routine required of stations wanting to enter the ring, it's very easy to add new stations. To make things even easier, it even uses the same pinouts as 10Base-T, as mentioned earlier.

## Cabling Considerations

Probably the biggest consideration in implementing 100Base-T is the cable plant. Differences in cabling rules between 100Base-T and 10Base-T are few but critical. For example, the maximum network span of 100Base-T is 210m. Therefore, you may have to recable portions of your network if you have made use of 10Base-T's 2,500m span. What's more, 100Base-T supports only two network hops, rather than three as with 10Base-T, and therefore you may have to reconfigure the segments that you are converting to 100Base-T to conform to this requirement.

 *CAUTION:* 100Base-T doesn't adhere fully with 802.3 cabling specifications! A careful pre-implementation review of your existing cable plant is critical.

## Special Concerns for 100Base-T4

There are also some issues unique to those who select 100Base-T4. Because 100Base-T4 requires four cable pairs to operate over Category 3 cable, if all four pairs aren't terminated at your site, you'll have to upgrade the cable plant. If yours is a legacy cable plant, be sure to review it very carefully to be certain all four pairs are terminated. If not, you'll have to correct this situation before you can proceed with your 100Base-T4 implementation. This can be both costly and tedious, so factor that into your decision to use 100Base-T4.

# SUMMARY

100Base-T is probably best described as a high-performance economy model. It is probably the easiest of the high-speed network desktop protocols to implement. At $200 to $5,000 per managed port and falling dramatically, it nearly competes with 10Base-T in cost. It also saves you money as well as time by building on proven technology and expertise. It's easy to integrate into an existing 10Base-T network. However, because it is modeled so closely after 10Base-T, it has some of the slower protocol's inherent obstacles limiting its scalability.

## Recommended for:

▼ Applications that require intermittent communication between client and server, such as database applications, because the CSMA/CD protocol offers its best performance under traffic that is intermittent as opposed to continuous.

■ Word processing and other standard desktop applications. As a general high-speed replacement, 100Base-T is hard to beat for its ease of implementation and leverage of existing expertise.

■ Geographically centralized power workgroups, because of short span (210m) and a limit of two repeater hops.

▲ Certain very specific backbone implementations only if the full-duplex feature is enabled. 100Base-T will certainly provide better performance than 10Base-T, but because the CSMA/CD architecture slows under heavy traffic, it may not offer as much improvement as one of the deterministic high-speed protocols.

## Not Recommended for:

▼ Applications that require constant, precisely timed communication between client and server, such as multimedia and video applications. This is because the CSMA/CD architecture can't deliver packets predictably.

▲ Backbones, because the CSMA/CD architecture tends to slow significantly under heavy traffic.

## Strengths:

▼ Inexpensive

■ Easy to integrate into existing 10Base-T installations

■ Uses the same pinouts as 10Base-T

▲ Uses much the same cabling rules as 10Base-T

## Weaknesses:

▼ Limited scalability because:

   ■ Allows only two repeater hops per segment

   ■ Maximum network span is only 210m

   ■ CSMA/CD access method may impede response time as more users and bandwidth-intensive applications are added.

*TIP:* As much as 100Base-T looks and acts like 10Base-T, it's not. The cabling rules are just different enough to cause you trouble, so be prepared to spend time locating and reconfiguring those portions of your cable plant that don't comply with 100Base-T specifications. However, more than any of the other protocols compared here, 100Base-T lets you lever your investment in staff training and expertise.

# CHAPTER 10

## Gigabit Ethernet

s we mentioned in Chapter 9, 100Base-T has become the high-speed networking technology of choice for most enterprises. For most networking applications, 100Mbps is more than sufficient bandwidth. However, there are some points on many networks that call for even greater bandwidth. For example, links connecting switches with multiple 100Base-T and/or 10Base-T ports, as shown in Figure 10-1, must be able to carry traffic from multiple 100Base-T ports.

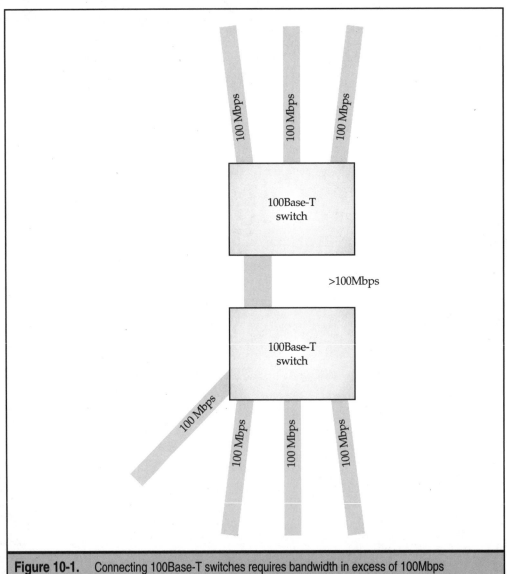

**Figure 10-1.**    Connecting 100Base-T switches requires bandwidth in excess of 100Mbps

A year or so ago, the only choice network designers had in instances like this was to turn to a radically different type of high-speed link, such as Asynchronous Transfer Mode (ATM). This led to a variety of conversion difficulties—along with the accompanying expense of solving them—in what should have been a fairly simple design issue. For example, when aggregating 100Base-T switches using ATM, frames had to be converted to cells, virtual circuits set up and torn down, and other such conversion tasks performed. And all of this had to be done simply to aggregate several 100Base-T switches. Surely there had to be a better way. And now there is.

## ENTER GIGABIT ETHERNET

Gigabit Ethernet was developed to offer high-speed Ethernet transmission for campus networks. It maintains the same frame format, frame size, and access method of Ethernet, as shown in Figure 10-2, and allows high-speed switch aggregation at considerably lower cost and greater ease than ATM or many other technologies of similar speed.

## THE 802.3 STANDARD

The IEEE 802.3z standard for Gigabit Ethernet was ratified in June 1998. While Gigabit Ethernet tries to be simply a supercharged version of the familiar 10Mbps and 100Mbps Ethernet, its high speeds have required considerable deviation from the original 802.3 specifications. Despite attempts to keep Gigabit Ethernet MAC signaling as close as possible to the familiar 10Base-T specification, there are some differences that will affect how it is implemented.

**Figure 10-2.** Gigabit Ethernet uses the same frame format as 100Base-T

Most of the work involved in finalizing the 802.3z standard centered around the specifications for the Physical layer. As the standard now exists, there are two specifications for fiber-optic cabling:

▼ 1000Base-SX

▲ 1000Base-LX

# 1000Base-SX

This is the Physical layer specification for running Gigabit Ethernet over lower-cost multimode fiber in short-span backbones.

# 1000Base-LX

This is the Physical layer specification for running Gigabit Ethernet over single-mode fiber campus backbones and long-span multimode fiber backbones.

There are also two specifications for running Gigabit Ethernet over copper cabling. At the time of this writing, neither of these had been finalized:

▼ 1000Base-CX

▲ 1000Base-T

# 1000Base-CX

This standard is for short-span copper runs used to support device clustering. Its total span is 25 meters and uses special data encoding, called 8B/10B, for high-performance data transmission. This scheme encodes each consecutive 8 bits of data (i.e., each byte) into a 10-bit transmission character. Transmitting these uniformly sized 10-bit characters enables the protocol to synchronize data transmission, thereby providing a recovery and retransmission mechanism when errors are detected. Furthermore, 8B/10B encoding uses a special character, called a comma character, to ensure byte and word alignment. The block diagram in Figure 10-3 shows the 8B/10B encoding scheme.

# 1000Base-T

This standard has not yet been finalized, but it describes Gigabit Ethernet operations over Category 5 cabling up to a distance of 100 meters or a total network span of 200 meters.

# How Gigabit Ethernet Differs from 100Base-T

As a result of the different encoding used for 100Base-T, the configuration rules for Gigabit Ethernet differ from those for standard 10Base-T and 100Base-T. The biggest difference is probably in the maximum length of cable run. In the standard, single-mode fiber runs cannot exceed 3km and multimode fiber runs should be under 550 meters. Right now, the

**Figure 10-3.**   8B/10B encoding used in 1000Base-CX

majority of campus backbones use multimode fiber, and so can span up to the 2km limit of 10Base-T. Therefore, because many backbones are now multimode fiber spanning up to 2km, before implementing gigabit Ethernet, either the backbones will need to be shortened to under 550m or they will need to be repulled with single-mode fiber.

## More Differences and Dangers

The type of multimode fiber Gigabit Ethernet will support, as well as the kind of conditioning it will require to ensure its operation, is a substantial consideration. This is due to a signaling anomaly known as *differential mode delay* (DMD). DMD is a jitter that occurs when the beams of light traveling over multimode fiber don't travel straight through the fiber cable unimpeded. Instead, in instances of DMD, the light beams bounce off the sides of the cable, throwing off the timing of the data transmission and consequently causing errors when the data is received. The farther the data travels, the more pronounced the jitter and distortion. Therefore, without a workable solution, DMD might have limited the length of fiber that could be used for Gigabit Ethernet. The Gigabit Ethernet Task Force of the IEEE didn't want to shorten the maximum length allowed in the 802.3z specification, so they came up with a solution.

The solution the Gigabit Ethernet Task Force developed is called *a conditioned launch*. In a conditioned launch, the laser at the device originating the data stream first transmits a light pattern that deliberately and *evenly* distorts the light. This prevents any one individual mode from dominating amongst the jitter, so the data pattern is overwhelmed. This is the only way to ensure error-free transmission for up to 550 meters over multimode fiber. Therefore, network managers who are considering implementing Gigabit Ethernet over multimode fiber should be sure the equipment they select adheres strictly to the 802.3z standard.

# SCALABILITY CONSIDERATIONS

Before you choose Gigabit Ethernet, you should understand that for all its speed and ease of implementation, the protocol has limitations. Most of these limitations are due to its limited scalability. Just like 100Base-T, it has all the problems of a CSMA/CD-based access method when subject to heavy traffic. And because of its extremely high speed, it currently supports fairly limited network spans.

## Gigabit Ethernet and Full-Duplex Support

Gigabit Ethernet supports full-duplex operation for both switch-to-switch and switch-to-node connections. As you will remember from Chapter 9, full-duplex operation allows simultaneous transmission and receipt of data on the cable.

**NOTE:**   Remember that full-duplex operation requires that all transmission devices support full duplex.

# CABLING CONSIDERATIONS

As we mentioned, right now Gigabit Ethernet runs only over fiber. However, the 802.3ab specification, which is under development, provides for transmitting Gigabit Ethernet over Category 5 cabling. This specification only calls for a maximum network span of 25 meters. However, as usual, the market is outrunning the standards bodies. By the end of 1998, expect to see Gigabit Ethernet Physical layer modules that will support 1000Mbps over Category 5 cabling for distances of up to 100 meters.

# MANAGEMENT

To pull off Gigabit Ethernet, you have to have the right management tools. Because Gigabit Ethernet supports the same frame format and size as 100Base-T, management tools for this technology aren't hard to find. In fact, they are most likely the very same tools that you are already using to manage your 10Base-T and 100Base-T networks.

**NOTE:** Be sure you can find and afford appropriate monitoring equipment that supports Gigabit Ethernet. As well, you may have to upgrade existing SNMP management information bases (MIBs) with Gigabit Ethernet extensions.

Of course, there are a few features no Gigabit Ethernet switch should be without. First and foremost is Layer 3 functionality. The 1000Mbps of traffic slamming through the pipes could choke a standard router, so Gigabit Ethernet switches not only need to be able to keep up at Layer 2, but also handle Layer 3 functions at wire speed. This will free routers from having to route core network protocols, preventing potentially serious traffic jams.

# COST

Gigabit Ethernet gear is decidedly expensive. At the time of this writing, Gigabit Ethernet switches range in price from nearly $15,000 to nearly $40,000. And there's no point in spending that kind of money unless people are going to notice the performance, right? Therein lies another problem.

# PERFORMANCE

When put to work, Gigabit Ethernet switches simply may not speed up networks appreciably. This isn't due to an inherent fault in Gigabit Ethernet, but rather in the design of network hosts and the operating environments running on them. With the notable exception of some flavors of UNIX, most network operating environments simply aren't prepared to process incoming traffic at rates of 1000Mbps. Compounding matters, the flood of traffic overwhelms the I/O of even the fastest SCSI drive controllers. In other words, the server is the bottleneck, making all the bandwidth superfluous.

Even should server platforms speed up, one question will remain: How long will Gigabit Ethernet be a viable high-speed protocol? This is a serious question due to the fact that network traffic is becoming an increasingly even mix of voice and data, but Gigabit Ethernet was designed for data only. Will it evolve to accommodate the demands of voice?

# SUPPORT FOR VOICE AND VIDEO

Voice and video traffic are notorious bandwidth gobblers, as well as being extremely sensitive to delays. Will these types of traffic run well over Gigabit Ethernet? For although Gigabit Ethernet provides a wide pipe, it currently has no inherent mechanism for ensuring quality of bandwidth. However, you can use other technologies and quality of service protocols in conjunction with Gigabit Ethernet, although these present their own set of concerns:

▼   Resource Reservation Protocol (RSVP)

■   Virtual LANs (vLANs)

▲   Video compression

# Resource Reservation Protocol (RSVP)

The Resource Reservation Protocol (RSVP) guarantees that a certain amount of bandwidth is set aside for a designated application. Applications use RSVP to request from the network a specific amount of bandwidth for a specific type of traffic. The job of RSVP is to set up bandwidth reservations over an established route. However, this protocol is still "emerging"—i.e., there is no standard implementation—which means that interoperability among different vendors' devices is not assured.

## How It Works

When implementing RSVP, the receiving device determines how much bandwidth it will reserve for a given type of traffic. It can change this level as necessary. However, you can centralize this control of bandwidth reservations—at least somewhat—by requiring each receiving station to specify its bandwidth reservations to one central device. This central device then sets up the reservations for the entire network. However, there is a lot of overhead required in setting up and maintaining this centralized approach. For example, every time a node wanted to reserve bandwidth for a new sending node, the central node would have to send a notification to all senders. This would tie up a lot of bandwidth, defeating the whole purpose of RSVP.

RSVP sets up bandwidth reservations using *packet classifiers* and *packet schedulers*. These are routines installed on the receiving devices that make service decisions about each packet received. The receiving device determines whether the requested bandwidth reservation is possible, based on bandwidth resources available and policy restrictions, if any. If the resources are available, the device, the packet classifier, and the packet scheduler transmit the packet. The packet scheduler makes forwarding decisions based on the bandwidth reservations. The packet classifier routes the packet based on these forwarding decisions.

## Let It Flow—But Filter It First

How do receiving devices know how much bandwidth to reserve for a given application? They determine it by examining an applications *flow specification*, or flowspec. The flowspec is a pivotal part of the RSVP architecture. It specifies the bandwidth requirements of the application in question, as well as identifying the application's data stream as coming from that application. The packet scheduler uses the bandwidth requirement specified in an application's flowspec to establish the bandwidth allocation for that application.

Not all packets will be able to take advantage of the bandwidth requested by the flowspec. That's because each receiving device also has *filter specs.* These are filters that designate which packets will receive priority treatment based on application or protocol header information. Packets that don't match the filter specs will not receive a guarantee of service. Instead, they will be transmitted on a best-effort basis only, even if they are addressed to the application's session.

The relationship of packet classifiers, packet schedules, flowspecs, and flow filters is illustrated in Figure 10-4.

# Virtual LANs (vLANs)

Setting up filters or constraints between different groups of users is awkward and time-consuming with conventional bridges and routers. Network managers think in terms of workgroups, not the physical location of users. Therefore, they shouldn't have to set up a series of filtering statements based on physical ports. The connectionless nature of Gigabit Ethernet posed some problems for setting vLANs. After all, the nature of the protocol's access method was based on broadcast. However, two emerging standards, 802.1Q and 802.1p, are enabling virtual LAN capability for packet-based networks.

## So What IS a vLAN?

A virtual LAN is a list of device media access control (MAC) or network addresses that are independent of a physical port, much like an access list used by some router vendors.

**Figure 10-4.**    How RSVP mechanisms work together to ensure quality of service

However, virtual LANs have network-wide significance. A device can access any other device on the same virtual LAN. Virtual LANs can define filters among themselves, just like routers can. Rather than configuring and reconfiguring routers every time end stations move, network managers can implement virtual LANs.

Devices on different media can be members of the same virtual LAN. Furthermore, users can move end stations onto any segment within the virtual subnet without requiring address reconfiguration.

Virtual LANs enable network managers to group devices logically regardless of physical location and provide dedicated bandwidth and services to each, as shown in Figure 10-5.

In addition to address filtering and bandwidth allocation, virtual LANs also provide the following:

▼   Simplified moves, adds, and changes

▲   Security features

## Simplified Moves, Adds, and Changes

One of the major problems network managers have in large, routed networks is the big administrative effort required to perform moves, adds, and changes. This is particularly true of Internet Protocol (IP) networks, where each physical LAN is associated with a logical subnet, as shown in Figure 10-6. If a user needs to move from one floor of a building to another, the workstation typically has to be reconfigured with a valid IP

**Figure 10-5.**    Users can plug into any port in the network, and the virtual LAN handles the rest

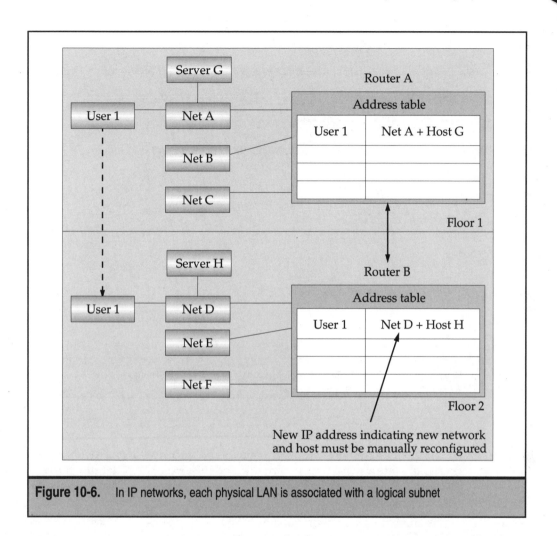

**Figure 10-6.**    In IP networks, each physical LAN is associated with a logical subnet

address on the new subnet. To handle such moves, managers of legacy networks have to reconfigure routers manually. Virtual LANs, however, eliminate all of the manual address resolution and reconfiguration.

Virtual LANs enable network managers to group devices logically regardless of physical location and provide dedicated bandwidth and services to each, as shown in Figure 10-7.

While networks obviously require routing capability, network managers would like to avoid having to manually reconfigure network address assignments every time users move from one network segment to another. Virtual networks let them do just that by identifying the physical address of a new device and associating it with a Network layer

Segment D (Station Z and U)

Segment C (Station V)

Segment B

Segment A (Station Y and W)

**Figure 10-7.** Virtual LANs enable network managers to group devices logically

address based on prior assignment without human intervention to the system or the end station. Users can plug into any port in the network, and the virtual LAN handles the rest.

### Security and Virtual LANs

Virtual LANs can increase security on Gigabit Ethernet networks. Network managers can use virtual LANs to define filtering restrictions between groups of devices, providing tight security. Furthermore, Gigabit Ethernet switches that support vLANs offer port-level security by allowing administrators to restrict virtual subnets to specific physical ports.

## Video Compression

The advent of high-quality standard video compression techniques makes it more feasible to use CSMA/CD access methods like Gigabit Ethernet for transmitting video data. The Moving Picture Experts Group (MPEG) working group of the ISO/IEC manages the development of international standards for compression and decompression of moving picture images and audio. MPEG has produced or is working on several standards for video compression:

▼   MPEG-1

■   MPEG-2

■   MPEG-4

▲   MPEG-7

## MPEG-1

This is the standard for storage and retrieval of moving picture images and audio on storage media such as hard drives and optical disks. This standard specifies the following:

▼   Medium bandwidth (up to 1.5Mbps)

■   1.25Mbps video 352 × 240 × 30Hz

■   250Kbps audio (two channels)

■   Noninterlaced video

▲   Optimized for CD-ROM

## MPEG-2

Finalized in 1994, this is the standard for digital television. Its initial goal was to develop a standard for digital encoding of television images at data rates under 10Mbps. In 1992, the goal changed to encompass coding of high density TV (HDTV). This standard specifies the following:

▼   Higher bandwidth (up to 40Mbps)

■   Up to five audio channels (i.e., surround sound)

■   Wider range of frame sizes (including HDTV)

▲   Can deal with interlaced video

**NOTE:**   MPEG-3 was originally the phase charged with developing the standard for HDTV. When MPEG-2 was broadened to include this standard, MPEG-3 became unnecessary.

## MPEG-4

Begun in 1994, this standard is currently under development, although by the time you read this it will no doubt have been finalized. It is a standard for multimedia applications. The MPEG-4 group's charter is to standardize both the tools and the algorithms for coding multimedia applications. At the time of this writing, the draft standard specifies the following:

▼   Very low bandwidth (64Kbps)

■   176 × 144 × 10Hz

▲   Optimized for videophones

## MPEG-7

Also under development, this is a standard for content representation for information searching. At the time of this writing, few of the specifications of this standard were available.

Overall, we can't recommend Gigabit Ethernet for voice and video traffic. Even the Gigabit Ethernet Alliance says that Gigabit Ethernet handles multimedia, "But application needs substantial changes." ("Gigabit Ethernet: Accelerating the Standard for Speed," Gigabit Ethernet Alliance, 1997).

# SUMMARY

We can't really foretell how robust or long-lived Gigabit Ethernet will be. After all, it provides more bandwidth than any other technology available to us today. All we can say is that Gigabit Ethernet switches are fast, fairly manageable, very expensive, and—through no fault of their own—should make little impact on overall network performance.

## Recommended for:

▼ Switch aggregation over short distances

▲ Data traffic

## Not Recommended for:

▼ Voice traffic

■ Video traffic

▲ Long network spans

## Strengths:

▼ Easy to integrate into existing 100Base-T installations

▲ Uses most of the same management tools as 100Base-T and 10Base-T

## Weaknesses:

▼ Expensive

■ More limited network span than 10Base-T

▲ No inherent bandwidth management capabilities

# CHAPTER 11

## Fibre Channel

Fibre Channel didn't begin life as a network transport protocol. In fact, the specification was not originally intended to work as a network protocol at all. It was first designed and developed to interconnect high-speed peripherals—for example, a cluster of high-performance computers—to a shared mass storage device. The result of this intent is a generic architecture that is a combination of both network and channel connection technology that concentrates on high-speed transmission and guaranteed delivery of data. This makes it suitable not only for connecting peripherals to hosts, but also for network connectivity over the short haul.

# GOING THROUGH CHANNELS

A channel connection provides either a direct or switched point-to-point connection between devices, such as a computer's processor and a peripheral device. The function of a channel isn't sophisticated in concept: it's supposed to transmit data as fast as possible from point A to point B. The destination address is not only predetermined, it is hard-wired—the data really can't go anywhere but its destination. Any error correction it performs is simple and is done in hardware. Routing and address resolution aren't done because they aren't required. Therefore, there's no address and error-correction information that needs to be carried in the data packet, so the packet overhead is very low. Because of their point-to-point nature and consequently limited processing demands, channel connections are largely implemented in hardware.

Network connections, on the other hand, are multipoint connections that rely on addressing schemes to make sure that the data gets to the appropriate destination. Each data packet traveling along a network connection must contain an address, which each device on the network reads to determine whether the packet is intended for it. Furthermore, network connections routinely have relatively sophisticated error-detection and correction capabilities. Therefore, the packet must contain the address and error-correction information in its header, resulting in higher packet overhead than in a channel connection. However, network connections can support functions, such as routing, that a channel simply isn't designed to support.

Fibre Channel has features of both a channel and a network. It is a high-speed channel that connects devices to a network fabric. The network fabric describes the matrix of connections, from a single cable connecting two devices to a mesh created by a switch connecting many devices. The fabric can be pretty much any combination of devices, including hubs, loops, mainframes, and switches. A fabric can be created specifically to suit the application being supported. In any event, no matter how complex the network fabric is, as far as an individual Fibre Channel port is concerned, it manages a simple point-to-point connection between the workstation and the network fabric.

Fibre Channel's greatest asset is speed. Ethernet, at 10Mbps, transmits data far slower than computers can produce it. Therefore, the primary goal of Fibre Channel is to provide computing devices with a throughput mechanism that is closer to the speed of their processors. And speed it has—it delivers bandwidth from 133Mbps to 1.062Gbps over a wide variety of cable types, including multimode fiber, coaxial cable, and shielded twisted-pair wire, and can support a network span of up to 10km. In fact, Fibre Channel is so efficient and fast that it can deliver speeds of 100MBps (notice that is megabytes per second) in both directions simultaneously, which means it is effectively a 200MBps full-duplex channel.

Fibre Channel is extremely versatile because it is protocol independent. It is a generic transport mechanism, meaning that it can support command sets from several different other channel protocols, such as Small Computer System Interface (SCSI), Internet Protocol (IP), and High Performance Parallel Interface (HIPPI).

Its speed and guaranteed packet delivery make Fibre Channel a good protocol for connecting network devices in a relatively local environment, such as a workgroup or even a campus environment, as shown in Figure 11-1. But because of its high performance, wide network span, and support of various topologies such as point-to-point, arbitrated loop (which we will discuss in detail later in this chapter), and

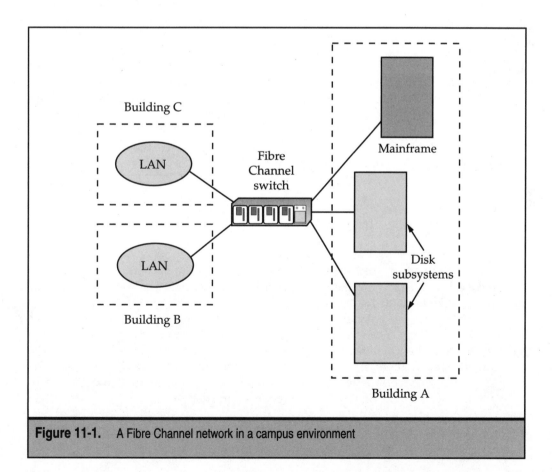

**Figure 11-1.** A Fibre Channel network in a campus environment

switched fabric, Fibre Channel has broader applications than as simply a networking protocol. It can connect LANs, midrange computers, mainframes, disk arrays, and server farms as part of one giant network.

# THE STANDARD AND ITS SUPPORTING GROUPS

The American National Standards Institute (ANSI) ANSI X3T9.3 started work on the Fibre Channel standard in 1988. At that time, the main support for the protocol came from its supporting group, the Fibre Channel System Initiative (FCSI), headed by IBM, HP, and Sun Microsystems. The mission of the FCSI was to develop a high-speed open connection standard for Fibre Channel workstations and peripherals. This mission was accomplished early on. During its existence, the FCSI was a major influence in the design of the protocol, developing profiles and specifications that offered interoperability between existing architectures and Fibre Channel.

Since its ratification by ANSI in 1994, the Fibre Channel standard has been through many enhancements. For example, in 1991 the standard was modified to include support for copper and multidrop configurations. The most changes came in 1995, when the Fibre Channel Systems Initiative and Fibre Channel Association announced that the ANSI X3T11 committee overseeing the technology had adopted 2Gbps and 4Gbps data rates, a 400 percent increase over the previous 1Gbps ceiling. Shortly thereafter, the Fibre Channel System Initiative pronounced its job complete and passed its mantle as the standard bearer for Fibre Channel to the Fibre Channel Association (Austin, Texas), which has approximately 100 member companies. The Fibre Channel Association will pick up where FCSI left off. For information, contact the Fibre Channel Association, a 100-member consortium of Fibre Channel vendors, in Austin, Texas, at (800) 272-4618; e-mail FCA-info@amcc.com (see Appendix C).

# HOW DO THEY *Do* THAT?

Fibre Channel transports data in much the same way a router does. It reads the destination addresses of incoming packets, encapsulates the packets, and sends them across the fabric. Underlying data formats, packet structures, or frame types are not important to Fibre Channel devices.

As mentioned, Fibre Channel establishes point-to-point connections between devices. These connections are like switched circuits, and multiple circuits can exist simultaneously. The circuits are duplex connections that can provide 100MBps of transmission speed in both directions simultaneously. When a device wishes to transmit over a switching device or network, it simply requests a connection to that device. If the network is busy, the port tries to make the connection later.

The current Fibre Channel standard supports four transmission speeds: 133Mbps, 266Mbps, 530Mbps, and 1.062Gbps. Fibre Channel network equipment that supports 266Mbps and 1.062Gbps is now shipping from various vendors such as Ancor Communications, Inc., of Minnetonka, MN.

The Fibre Channel frame, as shown in Figure 11-2, supports a data payload of 70 to 2,112 bytes with a 24-byte frame header (preceded by a 4-byte Start of Frame delimiter). It is this relatively large payload supported by a very low overhead that allows such high end-to-end throughputs: 25MBps for 266Mbps Fibre Channel and 100MBps for 1.062Gbps Fibre Channel—speed close to that of the backplanes of some server systems.

The Fibre Channel architecture comprises five layers, designated FC-0 through FC-4, as shown in Figure 11-3.

## Fibre Channel Layer 0 (FC-0): The Physical Interface

Layer FC-0 is the layer that defines the physical and media interfaces and the media. This is the layer that describes the electrical characteristics of the media, and includes the transmitters, receivers, connectors, and cables, upon which the Fibre Channel network runs.

The FC-0 layer also defines a system unique to Fibre Channel: the open fibre control system, which affects the Fibre Channel running over optical fiber. The open fibre control system is sort of a "back off and resend" fail-safe system that is required because the power of the optical laser used in Fibre Channel exceeds ANSI safety standards for optical lasers. You see, Fibre Channel connections often break due to this excessive laser power. When that happens, the open fibre control system in the receiving device detects the open link, then sends a lower level laser pulse than that defined by the Fibre Channel standard. The lower level laser pulse continues until both ends of the connection receive it. After the physical connection has been restored, the network connection resumes a few seconds later. Figure 11-4 shows a sample FC-0 link with open fibre control.

**Figure 11-2.** The composition of a Fibre Channel frame

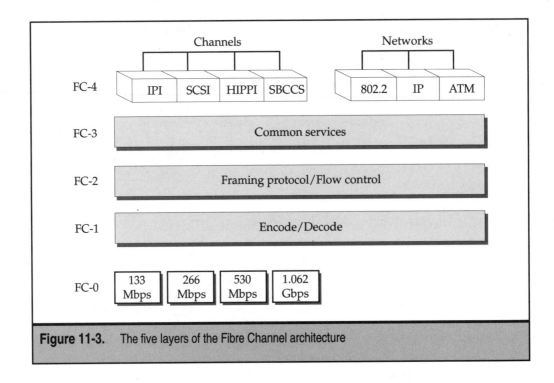

**Figure 11-3.** The five layers of the Fibre Channel architecture

## Fibre Channel Layer 1 (FC-1): The Transmission Protocol

FC-1 describes the transmission protocol layer; that is, the layer responsible for establishing the rules for transmitting each data packet. It defines the special data encoding scheme, called 8B/10B encoding, that Fibre Channel employs for high-performance data transmission. This scheme encodes each consecutive 8 bits of data

**Figure 11-4.** An FC-0 link with open fibre control mechanism

(i.e., each byte) into a 10-bit transmission character. Transmitting these uniformly sized 10-bit characters enables the protocol to synchronize data transmission, thereby providing a recovery and retransmission mechanism when errors are detected. Furthermore, Fibre Channel uses a special character, called a comma character, to ensure byte and word alignment. The block diagram in Figure 11-5 shows the 8B/10B encoding scheme.

**NOTE:**   8B/10B encoding is also used in Gigabit Ethernet.

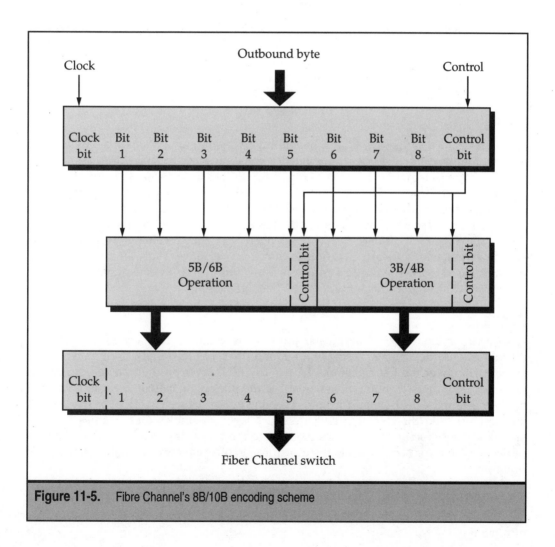

**Figure 11-5.**   Fibre Channel's 8B/10B encoding scheme

# Fibre Channel Layer 2 (FC-2): Signaling Protocol

FC-2 is the signaling protocol layer. It defines the method of moving data between end devices on the network, called node ports or N_ports, through the Fibre Channel switching device, called fabric ports or F_ports. The N_ports have a management system known as the Fibre Channel Link_Control_Facility that manages the physical and logical links between them. The FC-2 layer is concerned with defining the objects that will be managed by the Link_Control_Facility. These objects are called ordered set, frame, sequence, exchange, and protocol. Flow control, congestion management, and class of service designations are also handled at this layer.

## Ordered Set

An ordered set is a delimiter, or *flag*, used by Fibre Channel to signal events in low-level link functions. For example, the Start of Frame delimiter is an ordered set. The structure of an ordered set is a combination of four 10-bit characters, both data and special characters. This signaling helps Fibre Channel establish a network link when devices are first powered on. It also enables a few basic recovery actions.

## Frame

As we mentioned earlier, the Fibre Channel frame begins and ends with a 4-byte frame marker, followed by a 24-byte frame header containing addressing information. Next comes a large Data field that can contain up to 2,112 bytes (2,048-byte payload and an optional 64-byte header). The Data field is followed by 4 bytes for a cyclical redundancy error check and, finally, the 4-byte end of frame marker. (Refer to Figure 11-2.)

In classes of service that guarantee delivery, which we will define and discuss in detail shortly, each frame is acknowledged by the receiving N_port. These acknowledgments also provide notification of nondelivery of the frame to the transmitting N_port. The FC-2 layer also defines "Busy" and "Reject" signals that notify the transmitting N_port that a frame hasn't been delivered.

## Sequence

A sequence is the unit of data transfer in the Fibre Channel. It is a frame or group of related frames describing a single operation that has been put into packets for transmission over the Fibre Channel fabric. The FC-2 layer on the transmitting end is responsible for disassembling these sequences and packaging them in the frame size that has been set up by the transmitting and receiving ports—as well as all intervening ports on the fabric. On the receiving end, the FC-2 layer assembles these frames into the operation they describe, then passes them on to the higher layers of the Fibre Channel protocol. If an error occurs during the transmission of a sequence, the entire sequence is retransmitted.

Each sequence is assigned a Sequence Identifier, which appears in a field in the header of each frame sent over the fabric. As well, each frame within the sequence is numbered with a Sequence Count Identifier, which also appears in the frame header information.

This use of sequences allows Fibre Channel both to send large blocks of data without dividing it into smaller frames and to support other channel protocols, such as IP and HIPPI, transparently.

## Exchange

An exchange is a group of sequences that make up a single operation. An operation usually involves several tasks. For example, sending a packet of data can involve connection initiation, connection acknowledgment, packet transmission, and acknowledgment of packet receipt. Each of these tasks is a separate sequence, but together make up one exchange. Only one sequence at a time can be active in an exchange, although multiple exchanges can be active simultaneously.

The relationship among ordered sets, frames, sequences, and exchanges is illustrated in Figure 11-6.

## Classes of Service

With Fibre Channel, flow control and delivery acknowledgment depend upon the class of service designated for the network traffic in question. Currently, three classes of service are defined within the FC-2 layer. These classes range from Class 1 service, which provides a dedicated connection with confirmed delivery of packets, to Class 6 service.

**CLASS 1 SERVICE**    In Class 1, data packets are delivered in the same order in which they are transmitted, and each frame's delivery is confirmed by an acknowledgment from the receiving device. If congestion causes a frame to be dropped, a busy frame is returned to the sender, which then resends the frame. This type of service is well suited to applications that require high-speed, guaranteed packet delivery such as full motion video.

**Figure 11-6.**    How the components defined in the FC-2 layer work together

The Class 1 service also contains a service mode called Intermix. Intermix allows you to set priorities among data traffic. In Intermix, you can multiplex all classes of service over a single wire, but only Class 1 connections get guaranteed bandwidth. Frames sent within the other classes are only transmitted when bandwidth in excess of that needed for the Class 1 connection is available. This is similar to Fiber Distributed Data Interface's prioritization mechanism.

**CLASS 2 SERVICE**   In Class 2 service, no dedicated connection is established. Instead, bandwidth is shared rather than dedicated as it is in Class 1 service. The protocol uses multiplexing to send multiple frames over the wire simultaneously. The frames aren't necessarily received in the same order they are sent, and in fact may take different paths because Class 2 service allows packets to make use of the shortest path available at the time of transmission.

However, delivery of frames is guaranteed in Class 2. As well, just as in Class 1 service, in Class 2 service the sending device will get a "busy frames" signal if the receiving device can't process an incoming frame, so the sender knows to retransmit the frame. Class 2 service is therefore best suited for use in networks that aren't transmitting time-sensitive data.

**CLASS 3 SERVICE**   Class 3 is a connectionless packet-switched service like Class 2, but it does not provide guaranteed frame delivery. Thus, devices operating in Class 3 service require buffers on both the transmitting and receiving stations to avoid lost packets. Therefore, Class 3 is best suited for data that requires high-speed, time-sensitive transmission, but in which a dropped frame is useless if not received in time. Videoconferencing and teletraining are such applications.

**CLASS 4 SERVICE**   Class 4 is Fractional Bandwidth Connection-Oriented Service. It offers a bidirectional buffer-to-buffer and node-to-node reliable service (that means, guaranteed frame delivery). It provides high-speed virtual connections with guaranteed quality of service for the traffic in that connection. Therefore, it is perfect for no-delay frame delivery for real-time systems such as multimedia applications.

**CLASS 6 SERVICE**   Class 6 Service is known a Simplex Connection Service. In this respect, it's a lot like Class 1 service, although it also offers multicast functionality and frame preemption. It is used mostly for video broadcast or mass data transfer applications.

# Fibre Channel Layer 3 (FC-3): Common Services

The next layer of the Fibre Channel architecture, FC-3, defines common services such as support for multicasts and hunt groups. These functions are

    ▼  **Multicast**  Multicast delivers a single transmission to a group address that defines multiple destination ports.

- ■ **Hunt groups**   This operates much like a telephone hunt group in which an incoming call can be answered by any one of a predefined group of phones. A hunt group is useful when connecting high-speed devices. It is a predefined group of ports attached to a single node, such as a set of ports belonging to a mass storage device. Frames addressed to a hunt group are delivered to any available port within the hunt group.

- ▲ **Striping**   Striping is a method of parallel transmission, similar to that of parallel printing. Fibre Channel can use multiple connections simultaneously to deliver a packet of data, striping the data across the connections to deliver it faster.

## Fibre Channel Layer 4 (FC-4): Upper Layer Protocol Mapping

The FC-4 layer is the top layer of the Fibre Channel architecture. This layer defines the upper layer protocols (ULPs) that are interfaces to transport protocols, communications protocols, and other channel protocols. These ULPs allow Fibre Channel to support these other protocols transparently.

# CABLING CONSIDERATIONS

Fibre Channel is in many ways a cable installer's dream, because of the following:

- ▼ It is media independent. As we mentioned earlier, it supports single-mode fiber, multimode fiber, coaxial cable, and Type-1 shielded twisted-pair cable.

- ▲ Its huge maximum network spans on fiber media mean that it will operate on existing fiber runs.

However, the short supported distances on copper media—especially at high bandwidths—require that you review your cable plant carefully to make sure that existing cable runs don't exceed the maximum distances allowed by the Fibre Channel protocol.

# BRAVE NEW TOPOLOGY

Fibre Channel supports shared and switched connections just like most network protocols. However, one of the keys to Fibre Channel's versatility is its ability to support a topology that other protocols don't support well or can't support at all. That topology is a point-to-point connection with no intervening devices, which is called Fibre Channel Arbitrated Loop (FC-AL).

Fibre Channel Arbitrated Loop has been receiving a lot of attention lately. This topology lets you connect multiple devices in a ring without using hubs or switches. This makes it a flexible and cost-effective solution for localized high-bandwidth applications. The loop can support up to 127 ports that share bandwidth. An example of FC-AL is shown in Figure 11-7.

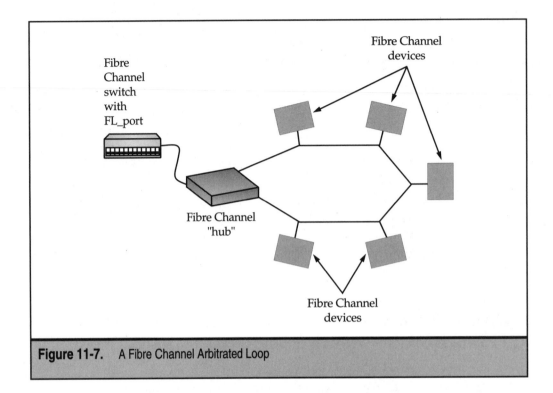

**Figure 11-7.** A Fibre Channel Arbitrated Loop

In FC-AL, a port is granted access to the loop based on its port address, with the lowest port address getting access first. When this port completes its transmission, the device with the next lowest port address is given access to the loop, and so on. Only one pair of ports, a sending port and a receiving port, can be active in the loop at any one time. A loop can also be attached to a Fibre Channel fabric to enable ports on the loop to communicate with ports on the fabric.

# INSTALLATION AND CONFIGURATION

As we mentioned earlier, because of its large network span, Fibre Channel usually requires no physical changes to an existing user's Ethernet or token-ring-based network. As a result of its use of sequences and exchanges, Fibre Channel works with common channel protocols such as IP, SCSI, and HIPPI, so your applications will probably require no modifications, either.

I'd like to point out, however, that when you are dealing with an extremely high performance protocol like Fibre Channel, the computing power of the network devices could quickly become a bottleneck. For this reason, we recommend that all devices attached to the Fibre Channel loop and/or fabric have high-performance processors and high-throughput bus architectures.

# Interoperability

At first glance, Fibre Channel appears ultra-interoperable. As we mentioned, Fibre Channel can support most channel protocols such as IP and HIPPI transparently. What's more, Ethernet, FDDI, and even ATM frames or cells can be transmitted over the Fibre Channel fabric thanks to the encapsulation techniques used to create sequences and exchanges.

Furthermore, Fibre Channel is a fairly mature ANSI standard, so its specifications are well defined and readily available. This may be one of Fibre Channel's greatest assets: it is an open, consistent interface. However, as of this writing, no vendors were shipping Fibre Channel adapters for routers. Without router support, Fibre Channel is a poor choice for backbones or other segments that have a wide variety of data paths and types of traffic.

# Scalability

Fibre Channel is extremely scalable both in distance and number of networked devices. The Fibre Channel protocol supports up to 16 million nodes on a single fabric. Furthermore, because of its data prioritization and guaranteed delivery mechanisms, performance for critical applications will not drop significantly as devices are added to the network.

Also, Fibre Channel supports a network span of up to 10km. The maximum network span depends upon the type of medium used and the transfer rate implemented. Table 11-1 shows the distances supported by the various media.

| Media | Transmission type | Speed | Distance |
|---|---|---|---|
| **Electrical** | | | |
| Coax/Twinax | ECL | 1.0625 gigabit | 24 meters |
| | ECL | 266 megabit | 47 meters |
| **Optical** | | | |
| 9 micrometer single mode fiber | Longwave laser | 1.0625 gigabit | 10 kilometers |
| 50 micrometer multimode fiber | Shortwave laser | 1.0625 gigabit | 300 meters |
| | Shortwave laser | 266 megabit | 2 kilometer |
| 62.5 micrometer multimode fiber | Longwave LED | 266 megabit | 1 kilometer |
| | Longwave LED | 132 megabit | 500 meters |

**Table 11-1.** Distances Supported by Various Media

Taken together, this means that Fibre Channel is so scalable, aggregate data rates into the hundreds of gigabits per second or even terabits per second are feasible.

## Manageability and Fault Tolerance

Fibre Channel supports a unique means of network management. Instead of having each node on the network perform its own management functions such as routing, configuration management, time synchronization, and fault management, Fibre Channel has assigned these functions to special management servers operating in the fabric. While this points to a single point of failure within the fabric, it does on the other hand free the nodes to concentrate on delivery of high-bandwidth transmission. For management reporting and monitoring, Fibre Channel supports Simple Network Management Protocol (SNMP), and most vendors implement SNMP management information base data with their network adapters and switches.

## Performance

Fibre Channel is the highest performance protocol available right now in terms of raw bandwidth, throughput, and latency. As we mentioned, Fibre Channel can offer as much as 1.062Gbps bandwidth, with a real throughput (in full duplex) of 200MBps. Furthermore, switched Fibre Channel has extremely low latency. This is because Fibre Channel dedicates separate circuits to traffic, thereby minimizing buffering and consequently latency at the switch.

# ADVANTAGES: FIBRE CHANNEL VS. ATM

Fibre Channel's only real rival in the area of performance is Asynchronous Transfer Mode (ATM), and much ink has been shed over the relative advantages of these two technologies. We will discuss ATM in detail in Chapter 16, but I would like to highlight the main points of differentiation between them:

▼ **Ease of migration and integration**  As we have discussed, Fibre Channel supports most existing applications, communications protocols, and transport protocols transparently. On the other hand, ATM requires sophisticated LAN emulation techniques to work with existing LANs, and these LAN emulation technologies are currently proprietary.

■ **Maturity**  Fibre Channel is fairly mature ANSI standard. All of ATM's standards have not yet been finalized.

■ **Voice traffic**  Fibre Channel is able to carry voice traffic easily and cost effectively right now. ATM, as we will see, will require significant work on its ATM adaptation layer-1 protocol to accommodate voice traffic in a cost-effective way.

▲ **Raw throughput**  Fibre Channel offers more raw throughput than ATM does.

However, before we take this comparison of the two protocols too far, I think we should consider that they are really designed to serve different segments of the high-speed networking market. Fibre Channel is really designed for a local environment comprised of high-speed devices needing access to other devices. It supports user nodes almost incidentally. ATM, as we will see, is fundamentally designed to integrate wide area and local connections seamlessly, and in many ways provides better support for user connections.

# DISADVANTAGES

Fibre Channel has two big drawbacks: it lacks good wide area integration capabilities, and there aren't a lot of people out there who know much about it. Therefore, it's best to implement Fibre Channel only for the local environment, and only if you already have (or are willing to invest in) the expertise to install and maintain it.

## Recommended for:

▼ High-bandwidth, localized applications, such as medical imaging and computer-generated animation

▲ Distributed parallel processing

## Not Recommended for:

▼ Backbones, because of lack of integration with existing routers

▲ Wide area

# CHAPTER 12

## isoEthernet

Many of you have probably not heard much about isochronous Ethernet, more widely known as isoEthernet. That's because isoEthernet has fairly limited industry support. To be honest, even in the applications where isoEthernet excels, there are a lot more cost-effective alternatives. However, because the support that it does have is from some very large and influential companies, such as National Semiconductor and IBM, isoEthernet is nevertheless still a contender in the high-speed networking arena. In addition, isoEthernet is viable because it can be integrated with ISDN public networks and is capable of upward migration to ATM.

## THE SECOND COMING OF ETHERNET

Not a high-speed networking protocol *per se*, isoEthernet is instead a technology that lets you revitalize your existing 10Base-T network by letting you take multimedia, wide area, and telephony traffic out of the LAN infrastructure and support it on a separate channel.

## THE IEEE 802.9A (ISOETHERNET) STANDARD

Introduced in 1992 by National Semiconductor, isoEthernet is similar to the more familiar 10Base-T. It offers 10Mbps Ethernet support on shared, twisted-pair copper cable and it adheres to all of the cabling rules of 10Base-T. It varies from 10Base-T, however, in that it dedicates some circuits to time-sensitive traffic, such as video. The IEEE 802.9a spec is similar to standards such as 802.3 Ethernet and 802.5 Token Ring in that it defines the media access control (MAC) and physical layers of the standard. In addition, 802.9a specifies a signaling layer based on ISDN protocols and using existing 10Base-T infrastructure. Therefore, it can be implemented in a legacy network without replacing cable or equipment.

**NOTE:** For purposes of discussing isoEthernet, I will use the terms Ethernet and 10Base-T interchangeably. Please note, however, that Ethernet and 10Base-T are not the same, and employ slightly different frame structures.

## IN THE BEGINNING, THERE WAS ETHERNET

To fully understand the difference between isoEthernet and 10Base-T, it's probably best to start with a discussion of isochronous services in general. The term "isochronous services" means that the network is capable of delivering data packets at precise time intervals. Real-time data such as voice requires isochronous connections. As a result, the public switched telephone network is a well-known example of an isochronous network. It is timed upon precise 8kHz clock signals. A digital phone line consists of a serial 64Kbps data stream with one byte every 125 microseconds. Known as bearer channels, or

"B channels" for short, these 64Kbps digital phone lines are multiplexed serially with other B channels to form 128Kbps data streams that support more calls of greater bandwidth than a single B channel alone could. For example, a T1 link provides 23 B channels, which can be multiplexed to support simultaneous voice conversations and video transmissions.

Because the telephone network is circuit-switched rather than packet-switched, it provides isochronous connections between calling parties that remain dedicated for the duration of the call. Before any voice data is transmitted, a connection is established between the sending and receiving stations, and a portion of bandwidth is dedicated to this connection. Therefore, the circuit-switched telephone network supports multimedia communications well.

Local area networks using Ethernet, on the other hand, use a packet-based transmission method that doesn't require a connection to be established before the packets are transmitted. Instead, the packets are all of a uniform structure, containing origination and destination addresses in the header information that allow the network to route each packet to its destination. This means that packets from various origination addresses can travel together over the same cable. It also provides adequate LAN bandwidth to all parties. However, because the bandwidth isn't dedicated, all transactions contend with one another for bandwidth, and therefore transmission delays are unpredictable when network traffic is heavy. This makes packet-based transmission undesirable for time-sensitive traffic like voice.

# ENTER ISOETHERNET

The new IEEE 802.9a isoEthernet standard was designed to overcome this basic incompatibility between packet-based LAN transmission and time-sensitive data, and to do so without interfering with existing Ethernet packet traffic or requiring expensive replacement of equipment, management systems, and cable plants. By intertwining the ISDN standard for WAN communications throughout the Ethernet LAN, the standard goes a long way toward meeting this goal.

There are three main features of isoEthernet that separate it from other desktop technologies:

▼ A new encoding scheme to increase bandwidth

■ Time division multiplexing to separate isochronous traffic from packet-based network traffic

▲ The 8kHz master clock to implement timing

## Two Networks in One

The isoEthernet standard really calls for two separate networks running over the same unshielded twisted-pair wiring. In addition to the 10Mbps channel allotted for 10Base-T traffic, there is also a separate 6.144Mbps channel dedicated to providing isochronous services. This channel is divided into 96 channels of 64Kbps each—in other words, 96 ISDN bearer channels ("B channels"). This makes for a total of 16Mbps of bandwidth squeezed out of the same 10Mbps 10Base-T infrastructure.

## Where Do They Get the Extra Bandwidth?

To understand how IsoEthernet squeezes an extra 6Mbps out of ordinary 10Base-T, you first need to understand something about baseband signaling in Ethernet. Baseband signaling is the process of transmitting data in digital form over a baseband LAN. The job isn't a straightforward one, despite the fact that computers produce data already in digital format. This is because the encoding method used by computers is different than that used by LANs.

Computers use a digital signaling method called *unipolar nonreturn to zero* (NRZ) signaling. In NRZ, a positive voltage is used to represent a binary 1, and no voltage is used to represent a binary 0. The signaling method is called "nonreturn to zero" because the signal goes from 0 to some predefined positive voltage level and doesn't return to 0 between successive binary 1's (represented by the presence of voltage), as shown in Figure 12-1. If two successive 1 bits occur, two successive bit positions then have an identical voltage level. If two successive 0 bits occur, then they both have the same 0 voltage level. Because there is no voltage change to delineate between bits in the case of successive bits of the same value, it could be difficult to determine where—and whether—one bit ends and the next begins. Therefore, NRZ signaling depends upon precise clocking to determine the beginning and ending of each bit.

To avoid expensive and high-overhead clocking in baseband LAN equipment, Ethernet and other LAN protocols have done away with unipolar NRZ signaling in favor of *Manchester encoding.* In Manchester encoding, an equal amount of positive and negative voltage represents each bit, and a timing transition always occurs in the middle of each bit. Therefore, a low-to-high voltage transmission represents a binary 1, and a high-to-low voltage represents a binary 0. This coding technique provides a good timing signal for clock recovery from received data due to its timing transitions. Figure 12-2 illustrates Manchester encoding.

**Figure 12-1.** Unipolar nonreturn to zero signaling

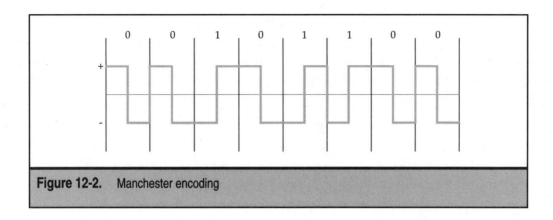

**Figure 12-2.** Manchester encoding

As you can see from Figure 12-2, Manchester encoding is only 50 percent efficient. Therefore, the 10Mbps of Ethernet data is carried via a 20Mbps signal on the medium. While Manchester coding was chosen in 1979 for Ethernet because it was easy to implement, silicon integration technology has advanced sufficiently to make it as easy to implement a more efficient line-encoding technique. As shown in Figure 12-3, isoEthernet replaces the Manchester encoding with a 4B/5B block-encoding scheme that is 80 percent efficient. Thus it provides 16Mbps in the same 20Mbps line rate used by 10Base-T. As in regular 10Base-T transmission, 10Mbps is available for Ethernet, and an

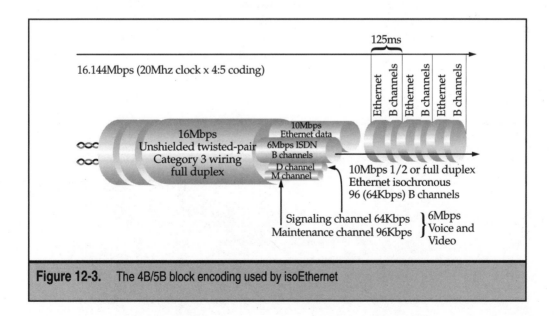

**Figure 12-3.** The 4B/5B block encoding used by isoEthernet

additional 6Mbps becomes available for isochronous data transmission like video and voice transport.

**NOTE:**   Since isoEthernet provides only 6Mbps for isochronous video transmission, to provide an acceptable delivery rate, the video applications must be highly compressed.

## Two Networks, Four Channels

Contained within isoEthernet are four service channels, as illustrated in Figure 12-4. These channels are called the *circuit channel*, the *data channel*, the *maintenance channel*, and the *packet channel*.

### The Circuit Channel

The circuit, or "C channel," is the switched 6.144Mbps, isochronous channel that contains 96 full-duplex, 64Kbps ISDN B channels designed to transmit digital voice and video.

### The D Channel

To ensure proper signaling and call-control services of the isochronous connections, a separate 64Kbps, full-duplex data channel, or "D channel," is in place. This channel performs the same functions as the ISDN D channel. It can also transfer such packet data as ITU-T X.25.

### The M Channel

The maintenance channel, or "M channel," is a full-duplex, 96Kbps channel that provides low-level control and status information to the remote end of the link.

### The P Channel

The packet channel, or "P channel," is the standard Ethernet 10Base-T line. Unlike the switched isochronous channels, the 10Mbps pipe is a shared medium. A 10Mbps P channel

**Figure 12-4.**   The four channels contained within isoEthernet

carries normal data packet traffic unchanged from current 10Base-T Ethernet. It can be passed transparently to other 10Base-T or isoEthernet nodes sharing the same network.

## Time Division Multiplexing

As illustrated in Figure 12-5, isoEthernet uses time division multiplexing (TDM) to isolate local multimedia applications from a company's normal LAN packet data flow, thereby maximizing the performance of both. In TDM, the transmission channel is divided into time slots, and each transmitting device is assigned one of the time slots for its transmissions. The time slots are assigned so that each transmitting device gets an equal amount of time; however, multimedia devices are usually assigned more time slots than other types of devices to make sure that they get enough bandwidth for acceptable delivery rates.

By plugging a stackable isoEthernet hub into the wiring closet, you provide a separate channel for bandwidth-gobbling voice, video, and multimedia files. Separating time-sensitive traffic from the packet-oriented traffic takes a tremendous amount of pressure off the standard packet-oriented network and limits the contention for bandwidth inherent in 10Base-T networks. Thus, isoEthernet prevents multimedia traffic from disrupting data traffic and eliminates the delays that make 10Base-T unsuitable for voice and video transmission.

## Clockers

IsoEthernet is the only desktop protocol that implements the 8kHz clock—used by the public telephone network—at the desktop. This is a much simpler and less expensive timing mechanism than other high-speed protocols. ATM, for example, requires buffering and adaptation protocols to support synchronous traffic.

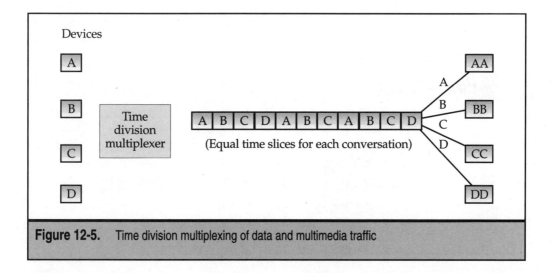

**Figure 12-5.**   Time division multiplexing of data and multimedia traffic

# THE BENEFITS OF ISOETHERNET

In applications that involve wide area support that must reach smoothly to the desktop, isoEthernet has many advantages over asynchronous high-speed protocols. Here are a few examples.

## IsoEthernet and Wide Area Support

IsoEthernet makes wide area network support simple. It lets you connect the isochronous hub to a switched public service, and thereby gives you direct access to WAN services from the desktop. Therefore, a single wide area service can support many locally linked users via the 6Mbps isochronous channels. IsoEthernet provides direct desktop integration with the following services:

▼   T-1

■   E-1

■   ISDN basic rate interface

■   ISDN primary rate interface

▲   ATM devices that support standard Q.931 signaling

## IsoEthernet and Videoconferencing

Videoconferencing is one application in which isoEthernet shines. The international standard for videoconferencing is the International Telecommunications Union's H.320 standard for full-duplex audio and video compression. The compression/ decompression (codec) techniques defined in this standard require an 8kHz clocking signal to maintain synchronization at both ends of the connection. WAN protocols support this clocking signal; however, most packet LANs don't. However, because isoEthernet provides the 8kHz clocking, it operates with the public switched telephone network in the WAN and delivers vidoeconferencing to the desktop without additional buffering adaptation techniques.

## Manageability

IsoEthernet provides voice, video, and data over existing 10Base-T cable without requiring any changes to routers, network management systems, servers, and existing packet switches. The packet channel of isoEthernet uses the same frame type as standard 10Base-T. Therefore, all your existing 10Base-T management tools will work just fine on isoEthernet.

## Scalability

The maximum network span is 100 meters. The isochronous portion allows better scalability because the bandwidth is dedicated, not shared among an increasing number of users. Furthermore, isoEthernet can also operate in "all isochronous mode," which allows end stations to achieve a maximum isochronous bandwidth of 15.872Mbps. Thus, the 15.872Mbps isochronous channel would contain 248 64Kbps ISDN B channels to service bandwidth-busting video server applications.

# Cost

IsoEthernet equipment is expensive, probably because there aren't a lot of vendors producing isoEthernet devices and competing for consumers' dollars. National Semiconductor is really the only vendor supplying isoEthernet network adapters, and these are priced at about $500 each. This is a far cry from their original stated goal to provide isoEthernet NICs at only $10–$15 per unit. When you add to this the fact that you're not getting the 100Mbps bandwidth that other local area protocols provide, you quickly conclude that it's usually not cost effective.

# Security and Fault Tolerance

IsoEthernet doesn't offer any more security or fault tolerance than shared 10Base-T. Therefore, it's probably not a good choice for a backbone protocol. In fact, many supporters of isoEthernet suggest using FDDI-II or ATM as a backbone for isoEthernet.

# Performance

IsoEthernet is a good performer, but not a great performer. It delivers better multimedia performance than regular shared 10Base-T, but not really any better than switched 10Base-T. It certainly doesn't outperform 100VG-AnyLAN in voice and video transmission.

However, one environment in which isoEthernet's performance excels is desktop WAN integration. Because traffic doesn't have to pass through routers and gateways—being encapsulated, translated, and bridged en route—to reach from the wide area to the desktop, isoEthernet delivers unrivaled performance. Furthermore, isoEthernet enables the transmission of PBX-quality voice over 10Base-T cabling, which packet-based protocols simply can't deliver.

# Ease of Installation/Maintenance

IsoEthernet is fairly easy to install, but don't think you'll just be snapping it into your existing network. IsoEthernet runs over 2-pair Category 3 UTP cabling with a distance limit of 100 meters. Therefore, currently wired corporate sites don't have to rework their cabling system. IsoEthernet can also run on Category 5 cabling. However, it will require new adapters and repeaters as well as an isochronous-capable backbone such as FDDI-II or ATM.

As with most new networking protocols, isoEthernet requires the installation of new hubs and network adapters to implement isochronous connections. However, because isoEthernet integrates Ethernet and ISDN circuits on the same adapter and across the same wire, it's easy to install in existing cable plants. Therefore, you can usually connect your current NICs, routers, and hubs into an isoEthernet card and continue working in 10Base-T as before.

In a voice system, the only new equipment necessary is hubs, software, and network-interface cards. The hubs connect to the WAN or private branch exchange (PBX) and the existing LAN on one side, and to 10Base-T or isoEthernet devices on the other, as shown in Figure 12-6. This configuration allows you to transmit voice, video, and data over Category 3 cable to the desktop.

Transmitting real-time voice and video on the isoEthernet network requires attaching an isochronous Ethernet NIC to a *compression/decompression adapter* (codec), as shown in Figure 12-7, which converts analog voice to digital signals. Unfortunately, there are no hardware codecs available that can use all of the 6.144Mbps isochronous channels. Hopefully, continued development of the market for isoEthernet will remedy this.

# DISADVANTAGES OF ISOETHERNET

Despite its benefits, isoEthernet has many serious shortcomings. One of the most critical is the lack of applications that are designed to take advantage of isochronous channels' wide area connectivity or real-time voice and video support.

**Figure 12-6.** An isoEthernet implementation supporting voice traffic

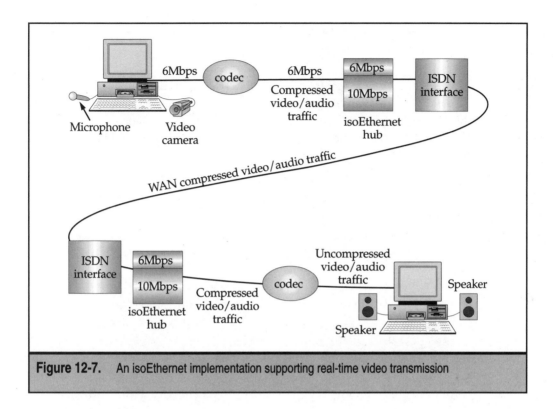

**Figure 12-7.**    An isoEthernet implementation supporting real-time video transmission

# FUTURE TRENDS

Despite its limited use, work is continuing on the 802.9 standard. Some new innovations we can expect to see added to the standard in the near future are

▼   100Base-T (Fast Ethernet) support

■   802.9b: simplified interhub signaling

■   802.9e: integrated ATM support at 16Mbps

■   Support for switched 10Base-T connections

■   802.9c: specification of the managed-objects conformance statement for compatibility testing

■   802.9d: specification of the protocol-implementation conformance statement (PICS) for compatibility testing

▲ 802.9f: remote line powering (a technique allowing remote powerdown of the isoEthernet network)

# The Isochronous Network Communication Alliance

A group of LAN, telecommunications, and compression-product manufacturers have joined together to form the isochronous network communication Alliance, or incAlliance. As stated in the press release announcing the formation of the group, their five main purposes are

▼ To demonstrate high-quality, real-time, interactive multimedia- and computer-telephony integration products and services and promote them as key business tools

■ To educate the industry on differences and requirements between voice, video, and data communications for LAN/WAN implementations and how these services can be integrated and synchronized

■ To foster industry growth through joint applications development and interoperability testing to ensure robust, yet affordable, total system solutions

■ To inform customers of the availability of new isochronous networking technologies such as isochronous Ethernet (isoEthernet) as key enablers for delivering interactive communications solutions in the networked enterprise to the desktop

▲ To provide a vision and roadmap for upgrading networks without causing forklift upgrades and through adherence to and support of open LAN and WAN industry standards

The incAlliance can be contacted at 2640 Del Mar Heights Road, Suite 134, Del Mar, California 92014, telephone (619) 792-7964, fax (619) 792-7967.

## Strengths:

▼ Excellent wide area integration

■ Supports time-sensitive traffic over existing cabling

■ Requires little replacement of equipment

▲ Easy to install

## Weaknesses:

▼ Lack of third-party hardware suppliers

■ Lack of application support

■ Expensive

▲ Limited security and fault tolerance

## Recommended for:

▼ Multimedia

■ Collaborative workgroups

■ Telemedicine

■ Remote training

■ Wide area to desktop integration

▲ Computer telephony integration

## Not Recommended for:

▼ Backbone

▲ Networks without time-sensitive traffic

# PART III

## How to Speed Up: Wide Area Solutions

# CHAPTER 13

## Integrated Services Digital Network

The evolution of the ISDN species has been a long and difficult process. You have no doubt been hearing about Integrated Services Digital Network (ISDN) for nearly a decade or more. From its conception, it was proclaimed by the telecommunications pundits as the public telephone and telecommunications interface of the future. But for years no practical, productive, or cost-effective implementations materialized. As a result, both users and providers began attributing new definitions to the acronym ISDN, the kindest of which was probably "I Still Don't [K]Now."

Today, however, ISDN is booming. It is available in most large metropolitan areas now, and the service providers there report a backlog of installation requests—mostly to residences. Because ISDN integrates data, voice, and video signals into a digital (as opposed to analog) telephone line, it can provide an efficient and cost-effective way to connect office LANs with high-bandwidth digital services, and to provide home "telecommuters" with the same digital services they are accustomed to having at their offices. Furthermore, ISDN has developed international standards for providing many digital services, making it easier for data networks to span countries and continents.

## THE PRIMORDIAL MIRE

The origin of the ISDN species is the narrowband ISDN standard. The first ISDN standards defining end-to-end digital interfaces appeared in 1984, handed down by the Consultative Committee for International Telegraph and Telephone (CCITT), now known as the ITU. The CCITT issued additional defining standards in 1988. ISDN was considered a major advance for a couple of reasons. First, it specified digital network services that would be delivered over the existing integrated digital telephone networks. Second, it offered a top performance of 2Mbps in the local link, and either 64Kbps or 128Kbps over the wide area. At the time narrowband ISDN began to emerge, analog modem speeds topped out at 9,600bps.

While ISDN never became the wide area high-bandwidth digital service of choice for local area network connectivity, it is certainly no dinosaur. It's now considered a cost-effective way to provide the following:

▼   Remote access to users who dial into their companies' LANs

■   A suitable link for some LAN-to-LAN connections

■   High-bandwidth interoffice fax traffic

▲   High-speed access to the Internet

ISDN is a flexible service that automatically switches among different devices attached to it. For example, it will provide digital services to a phone, a fax machine, or a PC, all of which can be attached to the same ISDN interface. ISDN can also be used as a local access link into frame relay and X.25 networks.

# ANATOMY OF THE ISDN SPECIES

ISDN is a service composed of two types of channels: *bearer channels* and *signaling channels*. ISDN providers have combined these two channel types to construct two different types of ISDN service offerings: the *Basic Rate Interface* and the *Primary Rate Interface*. We will define each of these channel types and rate interfaces, then discuss the signaling techniques that they use to make integrated voice and data transmission possible.

## Channel Types

As we mentioned, ISDN uses two types of channels, one type for transmitting data and the other for handling the management signaling and call control. These two types of channels are called bearer channels and signaling channels, respectively.

### Bearer Channels

Bearer channels, or B channels, do one thing: they carry data; hence, the name "bearer." These channels bear user information across the ISDN network. The B channels are 64Kbps circuit-switched channels of the same type used to handle a regular voice telephone call, although the ISDN B channels are digital channels rather than analog channels like Plain Old Telephone Service (POTS) uses. The B channels are set up, then taken down when the call is complete. They can connect any two ISDN sites.

### Signaling Channels

ISDN also specifies a second type of channel, called a signaling channel, or D channel. The D channel is separate from the B channels, providing *out-of-band* signaling to set up, control, and tear down calls. Because all this call control signaling is done on a separate channel, the calls are set up much faster than if the signaling information had to share bandwidth with the actual data. For example, the D channel provides the network with the number of the party to call while the data is waiting on the B channels to be transmitted. Therefore, as soon as the call is set up, data transmission can begin. The D channel signaling is a function of the Physical, Datalink, and Network layers relative to the OSI protocol model, as shown in Figure 13-1.

Different operations are performed at each layer of the OSI Reference Model. Here's a brief description of how D channel signaling protocols work within the OSI Reference Model.

### Physical Layer Functions

ISDN's Physical layer protocol sets up a 64Kbps, circuit-switched connection. It also supports the physical interface for the *network terminal adapter*, which will be discussed a little later in this chapter, which supports the connection of multiple devices simultaneously. Finally, this protocol manages circuit testing and monitoring functions.

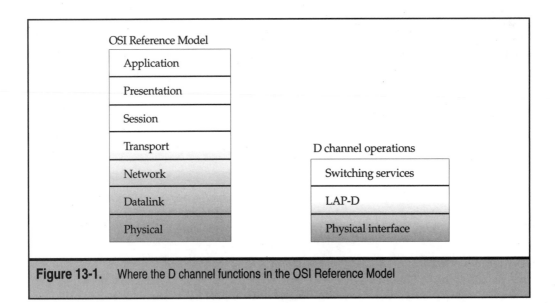

**Figure 13-1.**    Where the D channel functions in the OSI Reference Model

## Datalink Layer Functions

ISDN's Datalink layer protocol sets up the virtual paths through the networks for data frames. This protocol also manages call control and signaling functions via the Link Access Procedure for D Channel (LAP-D), which is the procedure that works across the signaling, or "D channel."

## Network Layer Functions

ISDN's Network layer protocol handles all circuit-switching and packet-switching services. The Network layer creates the addressing and route-determination information that the Datalink layer uses to set up virtual paths.

# IT'S ALL IN THE PACKAGING

As we mentioned, ISDN carriers have developed two standard service offerings, called *rate interfaces*, that combine the bearer channels and the signaling channel in different densities. These are called the Basic Rate Interface (BRI) and the Primary Rate Interface (PRI).

## Basic Rate Interface ISDN

The Basic Rate Interface (BRI) usually consists of two 64Kbps B channels for data transmission, plus one 16Kbps D channel that provides signaling for the B channels. With the proper equipment, you can bond the two B channels of the BRI together to get a maximum bandwidth of 128Kbps. Therefore, the BRI is appropriate for use in connecting small offices, small-to-medium-sized local area networks, or for telecommuters working from home who want to connect to their company's LAN.

Notice that we said the BRI usually consists of two 64Kbps B channels. Some ISDN providers offer BRIs with only one B channel and one D channel, or with only one D channel. In fact, the smallest unit of ISDN that can still be called ISDN is the D channel. The D channel provides the out-of-band signaling that really defines ISDN and makes the service what it is.

## Primary Rate Interface ISDN

The Primary Rate Interface (PRI) channels are available to ISDN subscribers who need more bandwidth than a BRI can provide. They are based on the DS1 rate of 1.544Mbps and include 23 B channels and one 64Kbps D channel to do the signaling. The B channels can be bundled in one of the following configurations, referred to in local exchange carrier terminology as H services:

- ▼ H0 channel:  384Kbps (6 B channels)
- ■ H10 channel: 1.472Mbps (24 56Kbps B channels)
- ■ H11 channel: 1.536Mbps (24 B channels)
- ▲ H12 channel: 1.92Mbps (30 B channels)

The lines can be used as a high-speed trunk for transferring large files and other continuous data streams or be subdivided with a multiplexer to provide channels for multiple devices. By providing a range of service options, the PRI can be configured to handle compressed video, video telephones, and teleservices.

# ISDN'S FUNCTION IN THE WIDE AREA FOOD CHAIN

ISDN is a significant departure from the other wide area data services discussed in this book. ISDN and its attendant equipment actually perform much of the processing and data signaling that used to be the exclusive responsibility of the carrier's central office equipment. Transferring these functions from the central office to your PC is one of the causes of much of the difficulty and confusion in ordering, configuring, and troubleshooting ISDN. Therefore, we should probably spend some time talking about the functions in question: what they are, where they have traditionally been done, and how ISDN changes all of that.

A *Plain Old Telephone Service* (POTS) call, the kind of analog call that we have placed and received nearly every day of our lives since we were able to dial, doesn't require much from the equipment at our houses. As Figure 13-2 shows, all of the processing of voice and data takes place at the local exchange carrier's central office switch. Our analog phones simply contact the telephone company's switch and tell it whom we want to call.

**Figure 13-2.**    A Plain Old Telephone Service call

The telco's switch does all the rest. In essence, our analog phones are not much more than amplifiers with dials.

An ISDN call, on the other hand, requires that the equipment on the customers' premises be much more sophisticated. ISDN telephones and PC adapters must be able to process information and determine what kind of signal—voice, data, fax, etc.—is being received, and respond by routing the data to the appropriate device.

Figure 13-3 shows the route of an ISDN call from your premises through the public switched network and to its destination. Your call is first set up when your equipment sets up a connection with the central office switch using Digital Subscriber Signaling System 1 (DSS1).

Once the call is set up between your site and the central office via DSS1, it's time to set up the next leg of its journey. For better or for worse, the signaling needed to route the call within the public switched network is not DSS1. Instead, the public telcos use a system called Signaling System 7 (SS7), which can handle both digital and analog calls, to route calls between central offices. Therefore, at the telco your DSS1 instructions are converted to SS7 signals. SS7 is a packet-mode switch that manages call control, including call setup and teardown.

When your call reaches the last central office on its route, it is then converted back to DSS1 format for transmission from the last central office to its final destination—the party with whom you wanted to communicate in the first place.

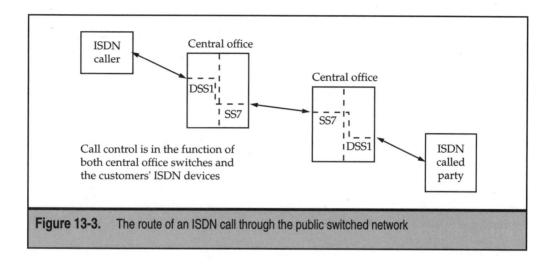

**Figure 13-3.**    The route of an ISDN call through the public switched network

Your ISDN equipment is required to interact with both DSS1 and SS7—something your POTS telephone was never required nor designed to do. It is this interaction with two large and complex external signaling systems that brings about many of the configuration nightmares associated with ordering, installing, and using ISDN.

## Great Moments in Evolution: SPID-ing in the Ocean

Although you can probably have a long, happy, and productive career as an ISDN user without knowing the details of DSS1 and SS7, there is one requirement of DSS1 that will affect you immediately and continue to do so for as long as you use ISDN. This requirement is a Service Profile Identifier (SPID). SPIDs are identifying numbers assigned to your ISDN line at the time it is set up by the local exchange provider. Be sure to write this number down and keep it in a safe place, because configuring your equipment will undoubtedly require entering a SPID. You see, the SPID identifies the individual logical processes connected to the ISDN interface, and prevents contention among different processes on the ISDN bus in the event that incoming calls are received while a device is actively using the B channel. This is the procedure in DSS1 that lets you connect several devices to one ISDN line. Furthermore, the SPID, together with another parameter required by DSS1, the terminal identifier (TEI), identifies the actual ISDN equipment connected to the ISDN interface. A single TEI might have multiple SPIDs associated with it. Negotiating among the SPIDs is difficult and complicated—so much so that some ISDN providers have found it easier to support bus contention, and thus allow you only one SPID per bearer channel.

# THE GOAL OF EVOLUTION: WHAT THESE SERVICES CAN PROVIDE

Services provided by ISDN operate at higher protocol levels than simple phone connections. After all that negotiating among your computer's ISDN adapter, DSS1, and SS7, they should. These services use the B channels for transmission and the D channel for signaling. We describe them briefly here.

## Bearer Services

In the most basic sense, ISDN bearer services don't really do anything that other protocols don't do. These are the services that carry data from end to end. They come in two types:

▼ Circuit mode

▲ Packet mode

### Circuit Mode vs. Packet Mode

Circuit mode is pretty much the same as the circuit switching we have discussed in various chapters throughout this book. In circuit mode, a connection is established between the caller and the called party, and the circuit remains dedicated to that conversation until one of the parties disconnects. The two parties are the only ones who can use the connection for as long as they maintain the call. Even if no data is being transmitted, while the call is in session, all the bandwidth associated with that circuit is dedicated to that call. This can be very wasteful, since many conversations are largely "dead air." See Figure 13-4.

Packet mode solves the problem of unused, dedicated bandwidth. Packet mode breaks a single conversation up into small pieces, gives each of these pieces an address and a sequence number, and sends them on their way over the wire—along with packets from many other conversations. Because each packet has its own address, it can share bandwidth with other packets without scrambling data transmissions. Furthermore, each packet could take a different route to the called party, as shown in Figure 13-5.

Packet-mode transmission isn't nearly as wasteful as circuit-mode transmission, because several conversations are using the same connection. Therefore, when one conversation isn't transmitting anything, the other conversations sharing the connection can use that idle bandwidth to transmit more of their data. Ultimately, this means that the carrier needs less packet-switching equipment than circuit-switching equipment to support the same number of conversations.

**Figure 13-4.**  A circuit-mode transmission

ISDN bearer services offer both circuit-mode and packet-mode services. Circuit mode uses B channels to transmit data and the D channel to control the call. Packet mode can use both the B and the D channels to transmit data.

Generally, circuit-mode services are best for voice traffic and packet-mode services are best for data traffic, but this isn't always the case. ISDN packet-mode bearer services offer a virtual circuit service that can handle analog traffic, such as voice, quite well.

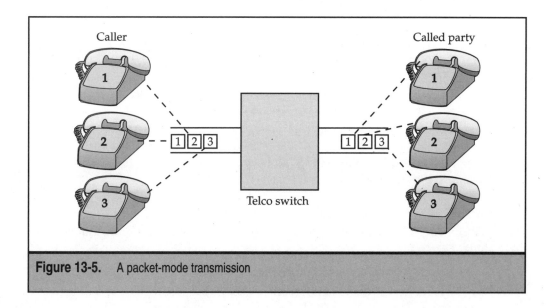

**Figure 13-5.**  A packet-mode transmission

## Supplementary Services

These supplementary services are exactly that: services *in addition* to the bearer services that provide added functionality. Supplementary services vary from ISDN provider to ISDN provider, so this is just a representative list of the types of services you may find available:

▼ **Calling Line Identification Presentation**   This is similar to Caller ID that is now widely available for incoming calls on most public telephone systems. It identifies the number of the incoming caller.

▲ **Multiple Subscriber Number**   This service assigns a different telephone number to each device attached to your ISDN interface. For example, suppose you have a telephone, a modem, and a fax device all on one ISDN interface. With Multiple Subscriber Number service, each of these would have its own telephone number. Then, when a call comes in for the telephone, the telephone rings. When a call comes in for the fax, the fax answers—you get the idea.

**NOTE:**   In the ISDN world, telephone numbers are known as directory numbers, or DNs.

### Call Offering

These are services such as call transfer and call forwarding that let you control where the call goes after it rings your number:

▼ **Call Transfer**   Anyone who has worked in an office with a PBX is familiar with this one. When you answer a call and then find the call needs to be sent to someone else, you can transfer it to the right person.

■ **Call Forwarding Busy**   This service lets your calls be directed to another number if they come in while you are on your phone.

▲ **Line Hunting**   Known in the PBX world as a *hunt group,* call hunting defines a group of telephones that can answer any call coming in to any telephone in the group. This enables an incoming call to ring—one phone at a time—at each telephone in the group until it is answered.

### Call Waiting and Call Hold

Thanks to the out-of-band signaling of the D channel, ISDN adds a new dimension to these familiar services.

▼ **Call Waiting**   Unlike the familiar POTS, when a call comes in on your ISDN line, your conversation isn't interrupted. This is because signaling is done on the separate D channel ("so *that's* why the D channel is so cool"). This is especially handy when you're using your modem—incoming calls won't break your data connection. That's right—you can keep Call Waiting on while using your modem.

▲ **Call Hold**   ISDN lets you put multiple calls on hold simultaneously without tying up a separate connection for each call. That means you'll have a tough time "busying out" your phones.

### Multiparty Services

ISDN also offers a variety of multiparty services such as conference calling.

## Teleservices

Teleservices are sophisticated services that ISDN can provide because ISDN operates at higher levels in the OSI Reference Model than POTS. Although currently not widely used in this country, they are often considered the future direction—and the real value—of ISDN. Some of these teleservices are as follows:

▼ **Telefax**   Group 4 fax capability that uses digital information at 64Kbps

■ **Teletex**   Provides end-to-end messaging between two devices using standard character sets

■ **Videotext**   Enhances Teletex services by adding a text and graphics mailbox

▲ **Videotelephony**   Provides television transmission service over ISDN

# MAKING ISDN HAPPEN

Now that you know what ISDN is and what it can provide, how do you get it? Although it's gotten a good deal easier over the last year or so, acquiring and configuring the equipment and services for ISDN can often be far from simple. Here's a road map and checklist for making sure you and your local exchange carrier have all the right stuff for ISDN.

## The Local Exchange Carrier's Part

The first, most critical, and least controllable issue in getting ISDN service is whether your local exchange carrier (LEC) is able and willing to provide it. Here's what you need to find out.

### The LEC's ISDN Switch

Does your carrier offer ISDN? If your carrier doesn't have an ISDN-ready switch in your area, it doesn't offer ISDN. If it does offer ISDN, you'll need to find out how ISDN is implemented on the switch so you can configure your devices to communicate with it.

The key to how ISDN is implemented on the LEC's switch is contained in two pieces of information you must get from your LEC:

▼ Which ISDN protocol (NI-1 or NI-2) they use

▲ What type of ISDN switch they have

When you configure your ISDN equipment, you will need to enter either or both of these pieces of information.

**NATIONAL ISDN-1 (NI-1) AND ISDN-2 (NI-2) PROTOCOLS**    The NI-1 protocol is the BRI protocol used by the Regional Bell Operating Companies (RBOCs). It is the first step in establishing a consistent ISDN definition for the United States. As such, it enables all NI-1-compliant devices to connect to any switch that supports the NI-1 protocol. A newer version of the protocol, NI-2, is emerging.

If your ISDN device and your providers' switch support either the NI-1 or NI-2 protocols, then that's all the compatibility information you'll need. However, it usually isn't that simple. Note that NI-1 is used mostly by the Regional Bell Operating Companies. Other LECs may not use this protocol, so in order to configure your ISDN device to communicate with their switch, you'll need to know the manufacturer of the switch.

## Media

The next issue is the wiring from the LEC's ISDN switch to your premises. If you're lucky, your local access is fiber-optic cable, and you can skip to the next section. However, it's more than likely that your local access loop is copper. In this case, your twisted-pair local access wire must be no more than 18,000 feet (a little under 3.5 miles) in length. If it exceeds this length, your telephone company may be able to install a *mid-span repeater* between the central office and your premises. A mid-span repeater regenerates the ISDN signal and doubles the distance allowed between the central office and your premises.

Even though your local access loop meets these specifications, it may not be ready for ISDN. That's because your local cable pair may have connections running off it. These connections are called bridge taps, and they aren't supposed to be there—but sometimes when the telephone company is installing a new customer, they run a line from the new customer's premises and join, or tap, into an existing unused local loop left behind by a former customer, as shown in Figure 13-6. The former customer's tap is disconnected at the former customer's site, but still joined to what is now your local loop. Such taps can cause signal distortion that doesn't usually affect analog signals, but wreaks havoc with ISDN. Therefore, any bridge taps must be removed.

Next, the LEC will have to check your line to remove any devices that were installed to condition analog lines. Conditioning means adjusting lines to reduce signal distortion. Unfortunately, techniques that reduce signal distortion for analog signals can actually cause distortion in digital signals.

Finally, your LEC will test your line to see if it meets ISDN specifications. If it does, you're good to go. If it doesn't, the phone company will have to install another line.

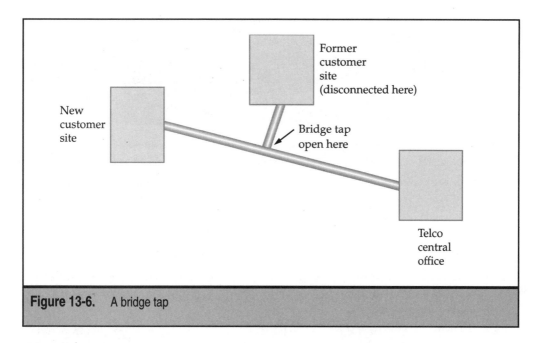

**Figure 13-6.**    A bridge tap

# The Home Front

Assuming your LEC is able to provide ISDN service to your premises, the next step is to select the proper equipment to use that service. There are two major pieces of equipment you will require: a network terminal adapter (NTA) and either an ISDN adapter or bridge.

## Network Terminal Adapter

An NTA is a device that connects your data or telephone equipment to the local exchange carrier's ISDN line. In the United States, the NTA is purchased and installed by the customer, while in other countries it is owned and maintained by the local exchange carrier.

The NTA connects both *terminal equipment* (TE) and *terminal adapter* (TA) equipment to the local loop. TE devices are equipment: telephones and computers that are ISDN compliant. TAs are interfaces: adapters that connect non-ISDN equipment to the ISDN service.

In the United States, the NTA is connected to the local exchange carrier's ISDN service via the U interface that is described next. The customer's equipment is connected to the NTA via an S/T interface, also described later in this section, that allows up to eight devices to connect with and be addressed by the NTA device.

Figure 13-7 illustrates the NTA device and the eight possible connection points for TE and TA devices. Note that not all NTA devices are the same. Some may have only two connectors, one for data equipment and one for a phone. Additional devices are then daisy-chained together.

**Figure 13-7.**    NTA device with eight connection points

**INTERFACES**    Your NTA equipment provides three different types of interfaces to support connected devices. These are described here:

▼    **U interface**    This interface transmits full-duplex information on a single wire pair. This means information travels in both directions simultaneously. The U interface supports only one device.

■    **S/T interface**    This interface breaks the ISDN signal into two paths: transmit and receive. Each signal is now carried on a separate pair, and you are allowed to connect multiple devices.

▲    **R interface**    This interface allows you to connect a POTS telephone to your ISDN service. The telephone will function, but it won't provide all the features that an ISDN telephone connected to an S/T interface would.

## ISDN Adapters

ISDN terminal adapters, also commonly known as *ISDN modems,* come in internal and external models just as analog modems do. And these two models have the same benefits and liabilities as their analog cousins: internal modems support higher internal data transfer rates, while external modems provide more diagnostic information and control.

**SERIAL PORT CONNECTIVITY**    If you select an ISDN terminal adapter that connects to your computer through a serial port, you will need to be sure to install a serial port driver that supports ISDN's higher bandwidth. Otherwise, the serial port will become a serious bottleneck, and all that extra bandwidth for which you are paying will be useless; for example, the highest serial port data rate supported by Microsoft—considerably below ISDN's common 64Kbps. There are several high-speed drivers for serial ports available both as freeware and on the commercial market, including TurboExpress Port 920 from Pacific CommWare.

**INTEGRATED NETWORK TERMINAL ADAPTERS**   Most ISDN terminal adapters have integrated NTA devices. This may save you a little expense as well as time and trouble when configuring your ISDN devices for the first time. However, it can also limit the number of devices you can connect to your ISDN line to the number of S/T ports the adapter vendor supplies—usually much fewer than provided by external NTAs.

**MULTIPLE B CHANNELS**   Most, though not all, ISDN terminal adapters support more than one B channel. If you plan to pay for more than one B channel, be sure your network terminal adapter supports it. As well, be sure the equipment you select can bond multiple B channels if you hope to take advantage of the 128Kbps or higher bandwidth possible by combining bearer channels.

## ISDN and Telephones

Your ISDN service will require ISDN telephones unless your terminal adapter has an R interface. The R interface supports analog equipment—like standard telephones. You can also buy separate adapters that will convert existing analog telephones to ISDN telephones. However, keep in mind that standard analog telephones can't take advantage of some special ISDN services such as Caller ID.

## ISDN Equipment for LANs

Installing ISDN equipment for LANs requires a bridge or router with an ISDN interface, as shown in Figure 13-8. Among the router vendors currently offering ISDN interfaces are Cisco and Ascend. The ISDN router is connected directly to the ISDN wire, so it must be configured not only to route traffic to the appropriate segments, but also to interoperate with the ISDN network. This involves many of the same tasks as configuring a stand-alone PC, including entering the correct SPIDs and DNs.

# Configuration and Installation

Now that ISDN connectivity is becoming cheap and readily available, organizations of all sizes are flocking to install it for the increased bandwidth and therefore increased functionality it offers over garden-variety 56Kbps lines. However, as you have probably surmised from reading this chapter, implementing ISDN isn't nearly as simple as installing those 56Kbps lines was. It takes a lot more than a mere telephone call to the local exchange carrier. In fact, it's fairly safe to say that right now, to be a sane, successful ISDN user, you must also become somewhat of an ISDN expert. You'll have to make yourself understand what's involved in implementing ISDN before you commit to a full-scale installation. To help you do this, I've put together a cheat sheet of issues that you must address before, during, and after the installation of ISDN.

**Figure 13-8.** An ISDN wide area network

## First: Ordering What You Want

Ordering ISDN from your local exchange carrier (LEC) is like walking into an ice cream parlor and ordering gelato. Even if somebody behind the counter understands what you said, they may never have heard of it before. And even if the clerk has heard of gelato, he or she may not really know what it is, much less that he or she can provide what you want. Even if you find a clerk who understands that gelato is ice cream, and that he or she can sell it to you, you may still not be any closer to getting the flavor you want than when you walked in the door.

Not every local exchange carrier offers ISDN, and not every company that does can offer the type of ISDN that you need. Different switches are *provisioned*, or configured, to provide different types of ISDN service. Therefore, the first thing you have to determine is which ISDN features you want, then ensure that your local exchange carrier can provide them.

## What Are You Hungry for?

What is the real reason you need more bandwidth? Do you want to do videoconferencing? Do you want to send more faxes faster? Or do you simply want to speed up file transfers? Do you want to use ISDN to transmit voice? Data? Both? What's the maximum bandwidth you will need: 64Kbps? 128Kbps? More?

Make a list of all the bandwidth-gobbling applications you may want to implement over the next year or so. This will be absolutely vital to selecting the ISDN service you need.

## What's on the Menu?

As we mentioned, ISDN comes in two packages, or rate interfaces. The Basic Rate Interface (BRI) provides two 64Kbps B channels that carry transmission signals and one 16Kbps D channel that carries signals that control the calls on the B channels. The Primary Rate Interface (PRI) provides 23 64Kbps B channels and one 16Kbps D channel. The rate interface you choose depends entirely upon the number of connections and amount of bandwidth you need.

## How Many Channels?

Many veteran ISDN users think that the smallest ISDN component that still retains the properties of ISDN is the BRI: two B channels and one D channel. This isn't true. The real molecule of ISDN is a single D channel. So, for a BRI, you could have two B channels and one D channel, or one D channel and one B channel, or simply one D channel. This gives you some ability to scale your ISDN connection to meet your needs. Furthermore, as we mentioned, the PRI comes in several different bandwidths, as shown here:

▼ 384Kbps (6 B channels)

■ 1.472Mbps (24 56Kbps B channels)

■ 1.536Mbps (24 B channels)

▲ 1.92Mbps (30 B channels)

## ISDN à la Mode

Once you have decided how many channels you want to order, you need to find out which mode of data transmission you will be using on each channel. As we described earlier in this chapter, ISDN services are either circuit mode or packet mode. At this writing, ISDN offered ten different circuit-mode services and three different packet-mode services (and counting), each designed for transmitting a different type of data. Generally, circuit-mode services are preferred for voice and other analog transmissions, while packet-mode services are better suited for data.

**TIP:** New services are being added to ISDN all the time, so ask your ISDN order taker to explain in detail each type of bearer service they offer so you can select the most appropriate for each channel.

## If There's Room for Dessert. . .

Additional services are available for ISDN, just as they are for regular telephone services. As we described earlier in this chapter, some of the additional services available are Videotext, Teleconference, Caller ID, Call Waiting, and Call Forwarding.

*TIP:* Don't forget your long-distance carrier and Internet access provider. If you can't find a long-distance carrier in your area that can handle ISDN, there's really no point in implementing it for long distance, now is there? Ditto for your Internet access provider, if you were planning to use ISDN primarily as a high-speed access service.

## Confusion Sets In

Now—and only now—it is time to call your local exchange carrier to order ISDN. Be prepared for "IS what?" or other expressions of confusion and/or disbelief from your LEC. You may be told to call a variety of different numbers, and be switched to many different operators before finding the appropriate department. If you are told that ISDN is not available, be sure to ask them:

1. Why, and

2. When it will be available.

The reason for asking why is because LEC order takers have been known to tell callers that ISDN isn't available rather than admit they have no idea what ISDN is. So if you get an answer like, "It's a proprietary technology," or "The standards haven't been finalized," or even "ISDN is another company—you'll have to contact them," you'll know you haven't found the right person.

When you finally find the right person, and when that person tells you that ISDN is available in your area, you can start describing the type of ISDN service you need.

**56/64KBPS**    Your order taker may tell you that the ISDN service available is 56Kbps. While this isn't really ISDN, it isn't necessarily bad. This 56Kbps service is ISDN, adapted to work on an LEC's existing T1 systems, and it's frequently offered in places where full 64Kbps ISDN isn't yet available. The popular ISDN protocols can accommodate 56Kbps service until full 64Kbps ISDN service is available, so there's no need to avoid it simply because it's not "the real thing."

**LINE SETS**    Furthermore, while you're talking to your order taker at the LEC, he or she may use a term such as *line sets*. A line set is a term used by the National ISDN Users' Forum (NIUF) to describe the different combinations of B (from 0 to 2) channels with the D channel and the kinds of information (circuit-mode data, packet-mode data, and/or voice) that you want to transmit on these channels. For example, Line Set 1 has no B channels and one D channel on which you can transmit packet mode data. Line Set 6 has one B channel on which you can transmit voice and one D channel on which you can transmit packet-mode data. The various combinations of channels and call types are identified by number, currently Line Set 1 through Line Set 29. To avoid having to memorize all the line set numbers and their corresponding descriptions, just tell the order taker how many B and D channels you want, and what kind of information you want to transmit on them. Then, the order taker can find the correct line set number that describes this configuration.

The order taker should also ask you about *feature sets.* As we mentioned earlier, a feature set is another NIUF term that describes a combination of either circuit-mode or packet-mode data services and/or call management services. There are at least ten different feature sets, detailing everything from data throughput rate to call forwarding options. Have your order taker provide you with the latest information on available feature sets, then choose them after you've had a chance to study them.

Finally, after you have selected the number of channels, call type(s) supported on those channels, and the features and interfaces you want, you will have completed the ordering process. Your LEC should send you a letter or form confirming your order and specifying the services contained in it. This letter should also include the telephone number(s) of your new ISDN connection(s) (which are known as *directory numbers,* or DNs in the ISDN world), as well as something called your Service Profile Identification number, or SPID. *Write both of these down and keep them in a safe place!* You will need them when configuring your ISDN equipment.

## Cabling Considerations

ISDN cabling uses eight pins, as shown in Figure 13-9, and therefore requires RJ-45 connectors. Furthermore, ISDN cabling is straight-through, not crossed the way standard POTS cabling is. Therefore, it will require special ISDN cables to connect your ISDN adapters and/or bridges to the ISDN jack.

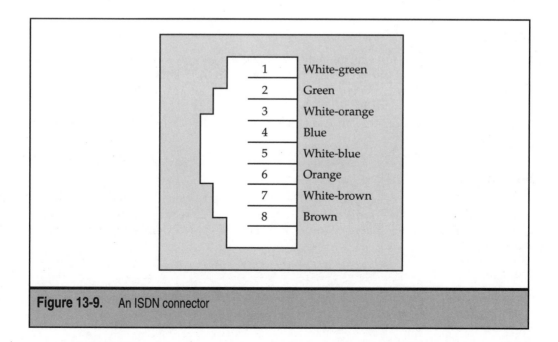

**Figure 13-9.**  An ISDN connector

## Performance

ISDN isn't really such a high-speed performer. The maximum bandwidth available from an ISDN BRI is 128Kbps, and that's only providing that your BRI includes two B channels and your equipment and service providers all support bonding the two channels together. The maximum bandwidth available through a PRI is 1.92Mbps, through what is called an *H12 channel* that consists of 30 B channels and one 64Kbps D channel. Again, the equipment and all the parties—the local exchange carrier, the access software provider, and the called party—must support the bonding of the B channels.

The Broadband ISDN standard, which we will discuss later, will support data transmission rates of up to 622Mbps. However, this standard is not yet finalized, so the cap on ISDN remains at the Narrowband ISDN rate of 1.92Mbps.

## Management and Fault Tolerance

While ISDN by its very nature provides you with many different call management and control services—some of which were described earlier in this chapter in the section entitled "The Goal of Evolution"—management of the ISDN service itself is wholly in the hands of the local exchange carrier. Optimizing and troubleshooting ISDN service is therefore a tedious and often fruitless exercise involving multiple telephone calls to a service provider and long waits for repair people to respond.

As for fault tolerance, remember that your ISDN provider may have only one ISDN-ready switch per area. If so, when something goes wrong with that switch, you're out of service until it is repaired.

## Scalability

ISDN is probably the most scalable wide area high-speed protocol available. With the proper equipment and services, it can be scaled from a simple 14.4Kbps modem connection to 1.92Mbps. However, as we've described earlier in this chapter, configuring your equipment and services to support this scalability is no simple matter, and sometimes it's simply not possible to get the needed cooperation among vendors to make it a reality.

## Availability and Pricing

As we mentioned, ISDN is currently available in most major metropolitan areas, and its availability is spreading rapidly. As ISDN becomes more readily available, prices for ISDN PC cards are falling sharply. You can now get an ISDN modem with a built-in NT-1 for around $200.

Pricing for ISDN services varies widely. In certain areas, during special promotions conducted by the local exchange carrier, ISDN installation rates are free. In other areas during peak pricing times, ISDN installation can be as much as $400 per line. Monthly rates vary just as much, ranging from $30 per line per month to over $100.

**TIP:** Several LECs across the country have raised their ISDN rates from the bargain basement to the outlandishly expensive. The reason given is that the demand for ISDN far exceeded initial projections, and that the market isn't nearly as price sensitive as they had first thought.

# THE FUTURE: BROADBAND ISDN

The ITU-T is currently working on specifications for the Broadband ISDN model, shown in Figure 13-10, which will deliver up to 622.08Mbps full-duplex data transmission. These high data rates will support sophisticated two-way interactive transmissions, store-and-forward multimedia broadcasts, and multimedia messaging and retrieval services.

The B-ISDN standard is also the basis for Asynchronous Transfer Mode (ATM), which we'll discuss in Chapter 16. ATM and B-ISDN appear to be the direction in which the whole voice and data networking are going.

# ADVANTAGES

ISDN is an affordable, scalable high-speed protocol. In areas where it is available, it can be fairly inexpensive to implement and expand.

**Figure 13-10.** The Broadband ISDN model

# DISADVANTAGES

ISDN has some major disadvantages to overcome. As we described in painful detail earlier in the "Configuration and Installation" section, simply ordering ISDN services requires a level of expertise most busy network managers don't have time to develop. Becoming an expert on the installation and configuration of ISDN devices, especially in different LEC areas, is usually out of the question for most network managers. That means hiring integrators and consultants, and that means a lot of extra expense.

Furthermore, gaining the cooperation of the various vendors and providers can be difficult. For all its fairly long history, ISDN is still unfamiliar to the technical staffs of many providers. It may be some time before the local exchange carriers can train their employees to provide the level of service in ordering, selection, installation, and troubleshooting that most network managers require.

Narrowband ISDN's maximum bandwidth is also limited well below that of other promising high-speed wide area protocols, so it may only be a stopgap measure on the way to protocols such as DSL and ATM.

## Recommended for:

▼   Internet access

■   Multimedia

▲   Combined voice and data traffic

## Not Recommended for:

▼   Voice-only traffic (there are simpler, cheaper options)

▲   Data-only traffic (again, simpler and cheaper options)

# CHAPTER 14

## Switched Multimegabit Data Service

Switched Multimegabit Data Service (SMDS) is not actually a protocol, but rather a "metropolitan area service." In essence, it is a method of transmitting ATM cells over a shared bus. First deployed in 1992, SMDS gained momentum when the Regional Bell Operating Companies (RBOCs) and other local exchange carriers began feeling the heat of competition from interexchange carriers (IXCs) in local markets, and felt the best defense against that competition was a high-speed data transmission facility. As a relatively low-cost and definitely high-speed switched data service, SMDS seemed the perfect solution, and many local exchange carriers (LECs) in large metropolitan areas began offering the service.

Today, SMDS is currently offered only by local exchange carriers (although whether and how the Telecommunications Act of 1996 ultimately affects this remains to be seen). Quite frankly, SMDS really hasn't caught on, and it isn't increasing in popularity. Therefore, many LECs are hesitant to offer it. So don't be surprised if it isn't available in your area. SMDS provides transmission rates in the T1–T3 range on demand, so customers pay only for the bandwidth they use. Obviously, this can be more efficient and cost-effective than leasing dedicated point-to-point lines if those lines are not fully utilized.

# WHAT IS . . .?

Switched Multimegabit Data Service is a marriage of the features of a shared-medium LAN and ATM. It is based on the IEEE 802.6 protocol, which defines the transmission of ATM cells over a shared bus. However, SMDS cells aren't identical to ATM cells: they use an 8-bit Access Control field, while ATM uses a 4-bit generic Flow Control field. This is due to the fact that SMDS is a shared-medium, connectionless service, and therefore requires a more detailed address than the switched, connection-oriented ATM (which we will discuss in detail in a later chapter).

SMDS was developed by Bellcore and is based on the IEEE 802.6 metropolitan area network standard. It is a cell-based, connectionless, packet-switched network that focuses on transmitting data—and data only. SMDS cells are switched from source to destination through one or more SMDS switches. These switches are connected by high-speed trunks, such as DS1 or SONET transmission systems, as shown in Figure 14-1.

**NOTE:** Although SMDS supports shared media, Bellcore's adaptation concentrated on point-to-point implementation. You can understand this when you consider that nearly all of the transmission facilities handled by the LECs to that time were exclusively point-to-point in nature, not shared media or rings.

## Cell-Based?

Cell-based means that the basic unit of data transfer is a fixed-length cell rather than a variable-length packet. Packet switching, which utilizes bandwidth only when data traffic is present, was developed to handle bursty data traffic. However, packet-switching

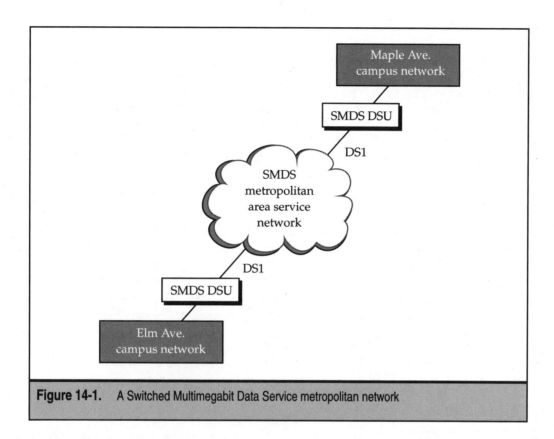

**Figure 14-1.**   A Switched Multimegabit Data Service metropolitan network

systems don't perform adequately for real-time, two-way traffic such as interactive video. Cell switching overcomes this limitation because it employs cells, which are fixed-length packets rather than variable-length packets. Each SMDS cell consists of a 48-byte payload and a 5-byte header, as shown in Figure 14-2. Because these packets are identical to ATM packets (in fact, they *are* ATM packets), SMDS is considered by many to be a stepping-stone to ATM connectivity.

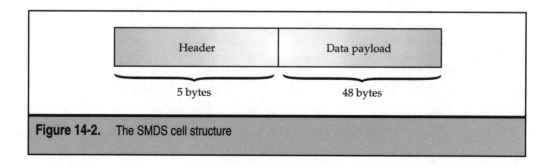

**Figure 14-2.**   The SMDS cell structure

# Switched?

SMDS is not a shared bandwidth service. Rather, each port on an SMDS switch is dedicated to one user. An SMDS switch sets up a virtual connection between a transmitting node and a receiving node. This connection is made on the basis of the destination address of each cell, and it lasts only as long as it takes to transfer one cell. These data transfers can take place in parallel and at full network speed. Because the cell is transmitted only to the port associated with that specific destination address, no other port receives the cell, which provides both low traffic and, as an extra bonus, high security.

# Connectionless?

Like ATM, SMDS defines a service at the user-network interface. But, unlike ATM, which is a connection-oriented service, SMDS is a connectionless service. Connectionless means that no connection is established between the transmitting and receiving computers before data is transferred. Packets are simply transmitted on the medium as soon as the SMDS interface receives them. Therefore, there is no delay for call setup or teardown.

In SMDS, the switch takes essentially connectionless data cells and maps them into a virtual circuit for transit through the network. The station's network adapter substitutes an 8-byte SMDS address for the 6-byte address used by legacy LAN protocols. The transfer may be in cells or in packets, as we will see shortly, but it always appears connectionless to the end user.

# The Architecture

As we mentioned, SMDS is based on the IEEE 802.6 metropolitan area network (MAN) standard. This standard specifies a high-speed network protocol that runs on a shared dual fiber-optic bus. The SMDS network is a dual bus design that forms an open ring, as shown in Figure 14-3. Physically, it looks like a star, and in this respect it is somewhat similar to token ring, which is a logical ring topology that forms a physical star because all cables are connected at a central hub. If the SMDS bus is cut, the open portion is automatically closed to "heal" the ring, which makes it something like FDDI.

# Standards Compliance

SMDS is not only compatible with the IEEE 802.6 MAN standard on which it is based, but also with the broadband ISDN (B-ISDN) model, illustrated in Figure 14-4. As a result, SMDS supports a fixed-length cell size of 53 bytes, as well as the ATM Adaptation layer protocols 3 and 4. SMDS also provides some services that aren't described in the MAN standard, such as management and billing, which we will discuss later in this chapter.

**Figure 14-3.**   The SMDS dual fiber-optic bus architecture

## Data Exchange Interface

Because SMDS supports the transmission of data only, most of the data sent on the SMDS network is received from legacy LANs in the form of packets. To avoid having to convert these packets into cells on every segment, the SMDS data exchange interface (SMDS-DXI) was developed. SMDS-DXI supports routing over SMDS services. SMDS-DXI is based on

**Figure 14-4.**   The B-ISDN model

packets rather than cells. It uses standard high-level datalink control (HDLC) framing, so unlike cell-based interfaces, it needs no additional hardware to transmit packet-based traffic.

SMDS-DXI makes implementing SMDS easy and inexpensive, because the HDLC hardware necessary to support SMDS-DXI is easy to obtain, relatively inexpensive, and time-tested. SMDS-DXI also supports the low-speed access of legacy protocols, giving network managers more flexibility over bandwidth choices, and thus more control over costs (remember, in SMDS, users pay only for the bandwidth they use).

# WHERE . . .?

Switched Multimegabit Data Service is a metropolitan area service. Therefore, it is currently available only from LECs. As discussed earlier in this book, *local exchange carriers* are companies such as the RBOCs, GTE, and others that handle local telephone and telecommunications connections. Until recently, these companies were restricted by federal law to handling local communications, providing *point-of-presence* (POP) facilities for long-distance carriers, and offering wide area communications services only within their local service areas, known as local access and transport areas (LATAs). However, recent legislation has permitted them to compete with long-distance carriers and eventually to discontinue providing POP facilities to their competitors in this.

As carriers prepare for ATM, some are installing SMDS as a stepping-stone to ATM. MCI and GTE, for example, are offering SMDS. AT&T, on the other hand, seems to be a proponent of the "pure" ATM network. Because SMDS uses the same cell-switching technology as ATM, carriers can offer SMDS service running on ATM switches. In fact, many carriers are installing ATM switches that implement all of the fast-packet technologies, including not only SMDS, but also frame relay and X.25 interfaces.

# HOW . . .?

SMDS is a *fast-packet* technology, meaning that the protocol doesn't handle error checking and flow control itself. Instead, it leaves these procedures up to the end nodes. The belief is that current telecommunications transmission technologies and facilities transmit data with very few errors, so the complex and sophisticated error-checking mechanisms of earlier protocols are no longer necessary. If a packet is missing, the receiving node is responsible for requesting a retransmission. Asynchronous Transfer Mode and frame relay are also fast-packet protocols that do not include error checking as a network function.

## Access Method

The IEEE 802.6 metropolitan area network standard specifies access to the shared-media dual fiber-optic bus via the *distributed queue dual bus* (DQDB). DQDB divides the bus into vacant time slots that any connected station can fill with data cells for transmission. All attached stations can access the bus at any time until the bus is saturated. Theoretically, the DQDB access method supports up to 512 nodes and operates at 150Mbps on a network that can span up to 160km. The DQDB transmitting node can transmit packets of up to 9,188 bytes. These packets are disassembled into smaller 53-byte cells (48-byte data payload with 5-byte header) to fit into the SMDS slots. After transmission, they are reassembled at the receiving end.

# WHY . . .?

As a switching technology, SMDS has advantages over building private networks with dedicated digital lines such as T1 or even ATM. These advantages include ease of installation and configuration, scalability, and cost.

## Installation and Configuration

As shown in Figure 14-5, customers installing an SMDS network only have to set up one line into the LEC's SMDS network. In a T1 environment, users would have to set up lines between all the sites that need interconnection. Its connectionless nature provides any-to-any connections between a variety of sites without the delays involved in call setup and teardown procedures. Therefore, SMDS offers LAN-type communication over metropolitan areas. Once information reaches the SMDS network, it can be switched to any site or sites.

Furthermore, the connectionless nature of SMDS makes it easy to add and drop sites in just minutes. Adding or dropping sites in an ATM network, with its connection-oriented protocol, would require reconfiguring address tables over the entire network.

## Manageability

SMDS offers some nice management features that many other protocols, such as ATM, don't. For example, SMDS provides usage-based billing as well as a feature that controls network access to prevent nodes from monopolizing the network. It also has an address screening facility that heightens security by limiting communication to a group of addresses, and lets you build a private logical network over the public SMDS network. SMDS also provides usage statistics and other network management data directly to the end users. Finally, SMDS lets you construct data packets on top of the basic ATM cell structure, letting you take advantage of both packet features and fast cell switching.

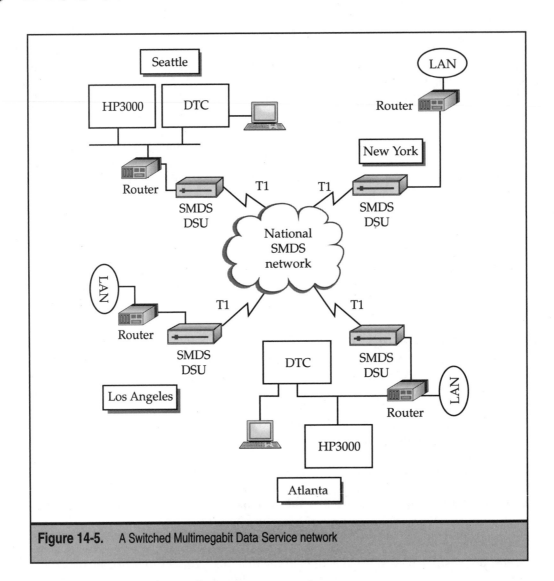

**Figure 14-5.** A Switched Multimegabit Data Service network

## Scalability

Switched Multimegabit Data Service is widely and easily scalable. Because it is easy to add and drop connections—and because you only pay for the bandwidth you use— SMDS can provide flexibility and connection options to accommodate quickly changing needs.

Furthermore, SMDS isn't just a MAN service. Despite its emphasis on the metropolitan area, SMDS is also a WAN service that can span long distances. This means that it's theoretically easy to expand an SMDS network to span the city or the nation.

However, at the time of this writing, MCI is the only long-distance carrier offering SMDS, and the availability varies among LECs.

SMDS also has a wide range of access speeds, from 56Kbps to 45Mbps, which gives you many options for building high-speed segments. For example, you could build a 45Mbps backbone, then link lower traffic sites to the backbone at 56Kbps. And remember, you're only paying for the bandwidth you use.

## Interoperability

Switched Multimegabit Data Service provides a fairly high level of interoperability with existing network infrastructures. It supports most existing network environments, including TCP/IP, Novell's IPX, AppleTalk, DECnet, SNA, and OSI. Furthermore, as we mentioned in our discussion of the DQDB access method, it allows a data unit of up to 9,188 bytes. Thus, SMDS can encapsulate entire packets from most LANs.

Perhaps most significantly, the SMDS Interest Group and the ATM Forum working together have developed specifications for SMDS and ATM service internetworking. However, if you are considering using SMDS as a means to migrate to ATM, you should note that SMDS supports the ATM Adaptation layer-3/4. As you will discover in Chapter 16, most LAN emulation is based on ATM Adaptation layer-5. This means that when it comes time to integrate your existing local area networks into your high-speed backbone, you may have to convert to ATM to take advantage of LAN emulation. There is a complete discussion of LAN emulation and the issues surrounding it in Chapter 16, "Asynchronous Transfer Mode."

## Performance

As we mentioned, SMDS supports a wide range of network and access speeds. It currently provides for user access at DS1 (1.544Mbps) and DS3 (45Mbps) rates. Network access requires a dedicated line running at a DS1 or DS3 rate.

## Cost

Over the metropolitan and wide area, in which transmission media are relatively expensive to purchase, install, and maintain, the economics of shared media, which SMDS offers, are compelling. The cost of the service is usually a flat monthly fee based on the bandwidth of the links. Furthermore, SMDS offers easy expansion abilities by simply paying for another port connection charge and the related usage fees.

However, the buyer should beware: Because the local exchange carriers are the primary providers of SMDS, there is usually no competition for the service in any given area. Therefore, you may want to weigh the cost of SMDS against other services.

***TIP:***   It's hard to predict network usage. Therefore, to keep SMDS usage fees from playing havoc with your budget, try to find a carrier that offers a flat monthly usage fee or a monthly cap on SMDS usage charges.

# DISADVANTAGES

While SMDS seems like an easy-care, cost-effective solution for the "waitin' on ATM blues," it does have some significant disadvantages. Weigh these carefully before taking the plunge.

## Limited Multimedia Support

As we mentioned at the beginning of this chapter, the LECs began implementing SMDS to help them compete in the long-haul data transmission market. Therefore, they didn't spend much time developing voice and video support for the service. As a result, SMDS can only transfer data. It doesn't offer deterministic transmission like frame relay or guaranteed sequenced-packet delivery like ATM.

## Limited Usage

Currently, there are just a couple hundred or so companies in the United States that are actively implementing SMDS. Even though the SMDS market is expanding very rapidly, such a small market may not be able to guarantee sufficient revenue to keep a lot of vendors in the market, which ultimately limits your choices in SMDS equipment and services, as well as increasing your costs. Although many SMDS vendors and industry analysts are predicting that this number will grow substantially, there are just as many naysayers who believe that SMDS has missed its opportunity as ATM products become cheaper and more plentiful.

## Limited Vendor Support

As we mentioned, SMDS is far from universally available. It isn't offered by some LECs. Furthermore, as of this writing, MCI is the only long-distance carrier offering nationwide SMDS.

# THE FUTURE

To be perfectly candid, SMDS has an uncertain future. While it is a relatively cost-effective means to transmit data at high rates, its somewhat restricted availability and data-only orientation have limited its usefulness. There is also some confusion over which direction it will go in terms of development. Some users would like to see vendors concentrate on enhancing DXI, making it more of a support service to connection-oriented protocols. Others would like to see vendors and carriers put more energy into developing multimedia support, making SMDS a direct competitor with connection-oriented services. However, in both areas, SMDS has more than enough well-established competition to challenge its widespread adoption.

## Recommended for:

▼   Customers who need to switch among many sites

■   Linking LANs within a single metropolitan area

▲   Metropolitan area networks that plan to implement ATM in the future

## Not Recommended for:

▼   Real-time terminal-to-host applications

▲   Wide area networks, because of currently severely limited wide area support

# CHAPTER 15

## Frame Relay

Frame relay is a spawn of Integrated Services Digital Network (ISDN). It is the packet-switching data service portion of ISDN, which has been unbundled and offered as a separate service. While relatively low-speed, frame relay's improved packet-switching architecture offers some features that may appeal to the network manager seeking to speed up a wide area data connection.

# SON OF ISDN

Before frame relay emerged as a protocol in 1989, it was actually part of the ISDN standards. As the packet-switching component of ISDN, frame relay was designed to provide a very high-speed packet-switching data transmission service to provide connectivity between devices such as routers that required high throughput for short durations. Then, the developers of frame relay realized that the principles behind the protocol could be applied outside the realm of ISDN. As a result, frame relay was developed as an independent protocol for stand-alone use.

# WHAT IT IS

Much like X.25, frame relay is a packet-switching protocol that connects two local area networks (LANs) over a public packet-switched network. In essence, a frame from one LAN is placed in, or encapsulated in, a frame relay frame. It is then transmitted through the frame relay network to the destination LAN. Frame relay uses statistical multiplexing techniques to load data from multiple sources at the customer site on a single line to the frame relay network. Statistical multiplexing essentially provides the LAN with bandwidth on demand, meaning that the network can get the bandwidth it needs when it needs it without having to reserve the bandwidth in advance and hold it unused until it is needed.

Each frame relay packet contains addressing information that the network uses to route through the telephone carrier's switches. Frame relay can be implemented using either private networks or a public carrier service. By placing responsibility for managing the network infrastructure in the hands of the frame relay service provider, using a public data network lets frame relay subscribers minimize service and equipment costs.

Frame relay offers improved performance over X.25 because it has very limited error detection and correction routines, which we will describe in detail later in this chapter. The result of the streamlined packet delivery mechanism is data transmission speeds of up to 45Mbps.

# HOW IT WORKS

Like the X.25 protocol, frame relay divides the user data stream into packets that are transmitted over the carrier network and reassembled at their destination. However, frame relay does it much faster than X.25. What follows are the nuts and bolts of how frame relay transmits data—and transmits it so quickly.

## Frame Relay vs. Packet Switching

Like X.25, frame relay is based upon the principle of packet switching, which makes it well suited to data applications. In frame relay, data is divided into variable-length frames that contain destination addresses. These frames are then forwarded into the frame relay network, which delivers them. On its surface, this looks exactly like packet switching. In fact, the real difference between frame relay and packet switching lies under the hood: packet switching operates at Layer 3 of the OSI Reference Model, shown in Figure 15-1, while frame relay operates at Layer 2—and even then it doesn't implement all of the Layer 2 functions. This means that frame relay is a simpler protocol than X.25 and other packet-switching protocols, implementing less error checking and correction but offering more speed.

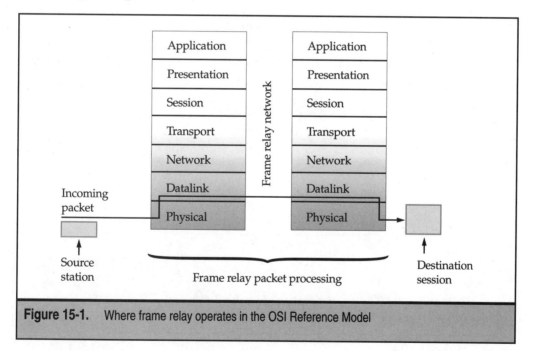

**Figure 15-1.** Where frame relay operates in the OSI Reference Model

To understand frame relay's advantages and how it achieves them, let's take a look at how X.25 and other Layer 3 packet-switching protocols work, then compare them to frame relay's simpler operation.

## Packet Switching and How Little It Means to You

Figure 15-2 shows a sample X.25 packet. As you can see, the packet includes a field containing Network layer information. A packet contains six major components:

▼ **Start of Frame delimiter**   This is an 8-bit sequence that signals the beginning of a packet. The Start of Frame Delimiter and End of Frame Delimiter are crucial to determining when a packet begins and ends, because X.25 packets are not fixed in length.

■ **Link layer field**   This field contains information to handle packet errors and flow control. The Link layer functions manage error correction and recovery as well as detecting whether there are sufficient buffers in the destination packet switch to receive the packet.

■ **Network layer field**   This field contains all the information necessary for the packet to establish an end-to-end connection between the transmitting and receiving stations. The Network layer is responsible for setting up and tearing down a connection for each packet transmitted, as well as providing some flow control procedures.

■ **User data field**   This is the data "payload" of the packet. It's usually 4KB or smaller in size.

▲ **Frame check sequence**   This is a 2-byte field containing a checksum to determine whether the packet has been damaged or corrupted during transmission. A checksum is calculated on an arriving frame and compared with the FCS field, which was calculated by the sender. The packet is discarded if there is a mismatch and the end stations must resolve the missing packet.

As you can see from reviewing the packet structure of an X.25 network, this protocol involves a lot of packet processing. Not only is an end-to-end connection established for

| Start of Frame delimiter | Link layer functions | Network layer functions | Data field | Frame check sequence | End of Frame delimiter |
|---|---|---|---|---|---|

**Figure 15-2.**   A sample data packet

each and every packet sent, but the packet is checked for errors by both the Link layer protocols and the Frame Check Sequence. As well, both the Link layer and the Network layer provide extensive flow control, which controls the rate at which devices transmit packets into the X.25 switch. If the receiving switch is unable to accept any packets from the transmitting station because it's congested, the receiving switch won't acknowledge receipt of the packets. Furthermore, it issues a "send no more packets" message to the transmitting device. When the congestion within the receiving switch clears, it will send the relevant "OK to send again" message to the originating device. This guarantees that the receiving switch will never have to discard data for reasons of lack of buffer capacity and offers one more level of data transmission reliability. The protocol's developers considered this level of packet processing necessary because of the relatively unreliable transmission links available at the time.

These extensive error-checking and flow-control mechanisms do indeed ensure packet delivery. However, they also slow the transmission of packets and therefore reduce the performance of the network as a whole. Luckily, two things happened that have helped make these mechanisms less important. The first was the advent of much more reliable high-speed transmission systems that delivered packets with much fewer errors and corruption. The second was the development of applications within the end-user stations that were designed to detect and recover packet errors. As a result of these two innovations, network designers were eager and able to do away with these cumbersome—and now unnecessary—error-checking procedures.

## Frame Relay to the Rescue

Frame relay was developed on the assumption that the transmission media is reliable and relatively error-free, and that the end-user applications can detect and recover from packet errors. Therefore, frame relay discards packets that contain errors. Also, if a frame relay switch's input buffers are full, it discards incoming frames until the congestion clears up. In short, frame relay makes little attempt to detect errors and congestion, and no attempt whatsoever to correct them.

So what does it do? A frame relay switch has three core functions:

▼   Route incoming frames to the correct outgoing port.

■   Check the Frame Check Sequence field to determine whether the frame contains an error. If so, it discards the frame.

▲   Check to see if its buffers are full. If so, it discards incoming frames until the congestion clears up.

That's it. No connections are established, no flow control is maintained—no Level 3 functions are performed at all. If you look at the frame relay frame structure shown in Figure 15-3, you can see that the frame doesn't even contain fields for the information necessary for the switch to perform these functions.

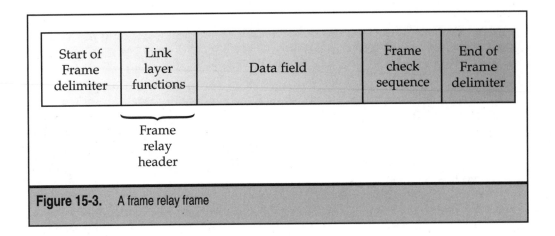

**Figure 15-3.** A frame relay frame

## Frame Format

The frame structure for the frame relay packet is pictured in Figure 15-3. Very similar to the X.25 packet, the frame relay packet has the following components:

▼ **Start of Frame delimiter**    This is an 8-bit sequence that signals the beginning of a packet.

■ **Link layer field, also called the frame relay header**    This field contains addressing information and what little flow control management frame relay does. The Link layer field also detects whether there are sufficient buffers in the destination packet switch to receive the packet. This field has two subfields:

     ■ **Datalink connection identifier (DLCI)**    This is the address of the logical connection that is multiplexed into the channel.

     ■ **Discard eligibility (DE)**    This indicates whether the frame can be discarded in the event of network congestion. We'll discuss the use of the DE subfield later in this chapter.

■ **User data field**    This is the data "payload" of the packet. It's usually 4KB or smaller in size.

▲ **Frame check sequence**    This is a 2-byte field containing a checksum to determine whether the packet has been damaged or corrupted during transmission.

## Frame Relay Network Devices

So, how do these almost-but-not-quite-X.25 frames travel over the frame relay network? A station sends data packets to a router, which sends them across the port connections comprised of either permanent virtual circuits or switched virtual circuits to a frame relay switch or router, which reads the destination address contained in the DLCI subfield of the frame relay header. The network device then routes the frame to the proper destination over the frame relay network. At the other end of the network, the frame relay information is stripped off and the data is reassembled in its native packet format, which can then be processed by the receiving station.

# Frame Relay Connections

Frame relay supports several different types of connections, all of which work together to form the frame relay network mesh.

## Port Connections

A port connection is a physical access point onto the frame relay network that defines the maximum amount of data sent onto the network across all PVCs at any time. A single network interface can support multiple ports. The port connection is the interface to the public or private frame relay network, and at the time of this writing is generally available at 56/64Kbps, 128Kbps, 256Kbps, 384Kbps, 512Kbps, 768Kbps, 1.024Mbps, and 1.536Mbps. The port connection dynamically allocates data across the permanent virtual circuits.

Frame relay uses a multiplexing technique (which we will discuss later) that allows a large central site to be connected to a public frame relay network with a single router port and a single high-speed connection to the network. Because the circuits are not dedicated to a specific site the way point-to-point services are, multiple transmissions to many different sites can take place simultaneously.

## Permanent Virtual Circuits

A permanent virtual circuit (PVC) is a path through the frame relay network that connects two points. A PVC is dedicated bandwidth that guarantees a level of service, called a committed information rate (which we will discuss later in this chapter), to a particular station. The network manager orders PVCs from a frame relay service provider, who configures them according to the network manager's specifications. Permanent virtual circuits remain active and available to the subscribing network at all times.

# Switched Virtual

As we mentioned, the frame relay protocol has no flow-control mechanism. Therefore, frame relay networks have no procedure for slowing or stopping data transmission when the network is congested. There is a means of notifying stations when the network becomes overburdened, but if the station's application isn't designed to respond to the notification by suspending transmission, the station will just keep sending data onto an already jammed network. Therefore, when a frame relay network gets congested, it starts discarding frames.

The network can select frames to discard in one of two ways:

▼   Arbitrary selection

▲   Discard eligibility

In arbitrary selection, the frame relay network simply starts discarding packets when it gets congested. This is certainly effective, but it doesn't distinguish between packets that were sent under the auspices of the customer's committed information rate (CIR) and packets that were sent as part of a burst over and above the CIR. What's worse, though, is that it doesn't distinguish between vital data transmissions and transmissions that contain idle chitchat. That's why many frame relay users prefer the second method of selecting frames to discard.

End users designate the discard eligibility of frames within transmissions by configuring their routers or switches to set flags within the frame relay data frames. For example, a customer may configure its router to flag all administrative traffic DE ("discard eligible"), but not flag all manufacturing-related transmissions. Then, should the network become congested, frames from the administrative traffic would be discarded—to be retransmitted by the application later when the network is not so busy—while all manufacturing traffic would continue. Using the DE flag lets you determine which information is most important to you and ensures that it receives a higher transmission priority than less important data. It is entirely the responsibility of the receiving workstation to determine whether packets have been discarded and to take steps to initiate a retransmission.

# Getting What You Pay for . . .

As we mentioned, frame relay has no flow-control mechanism. Therefore, users can theoretically send as much data as they want over the frame relay network. This means that the protocol has no means of preventing a single bandwidth-hungry station from monopolizing the entire bandwidth for the same flat fee. This is why frame relay carrier services have developed the CIR.

When you order frame relay service and its attendant virtual circuits from a frame relay provider, you will be asked to specify a committed information rate. The CIR is the minimum bandwidth that your carrier will guarantee to be available to your PVC 24 hours a day, 7 days a week. The committed information rate is not tied in any way to the speed of your physical connection. Therefore, you could have a 1.544Mbps physical connection but only a 64Kbps CIR. You determine what your CIR should be by estimating your normal network traffic (or your budget—the higher the CIR, the higher the cost of the frame relay PVC).

## And Getting More

If your network traffic exceeds your committed information rate, you're not necessarily out of luck. Frame relay can theoretically accommodate bursts in excess of the allocated bandwidth. Therefore, if the frame relay network receives a transmission from your network that bursts beyond your CIR, the frame relay network will attempt to open additional circuits to complete the transmission. When the network is not congested, sometimes you can send data bursts as large as twice your CIR.

Don't count on being able to exceed your CIR on a regular basis, however. Bursting above the CIR can occur only when the network isn't congested. We'll explain why later in the section on statistical multiplexing. Still, you should be able to plan on sending some traffic bursts, which means that frame relay network designers must build networks with sufficient capacity to handle the CIR plus a reasonable amount of bursts in excess of the CIR.

To provide some guidelines to frame relay network designers, most frame relay carrier services have adopted two additional guaranteed rates. These are the committed burst rate (CBR) and the excess burst rate (EBR). The CBR is the maximum amount of data rate that the network provider agrees to transfer under normal network conditions. The EBR is the maximum data rate over and above the CBR that the carrier's network will try to sustain. EBR data is automatically flagged DE.

## Management and How Little There Is of It

The frame relay protocol really has no integrated management. Therefore, what little management information the network devices require to control the connections between end stations and the network mesh is provided out of band, meaning this information travels over a separate virtual circuit. The management system that provides this information is known as the local management interface (LMI).

The LMI is very much a "bare bones" management system, providing only four basic functions:

▼  Establishing a link between the end user and the network interface

■  Monitoring the availability of frame relay circuits

■  Notifying network stations of new PVCs

▲  Notifying network stations of deleted or missing PVCs

## Statistical Multiplexing and Bandwidth on Demand

As we mentioned, frame relay was designed to handle bursty traffic efficiently and even elegantly. Therefore, much of the traffic you see on a frame relay network is bursty in nature, which means that much of the time these devices are transmitting little if any data at all. Rather than waste money on idle bandwidth for a large number of bursty connections, frame relay gives network managers the ability to connect multiple bursty connections to the same segment. The strategy is that on only a very few occasions will two or more connections send a burst of traffic at the same time, and when some of them do, there is enough buffer capacity in the frame relay switch to capture the frames and transmit them as bandwidth frees up.

Statistical multiplexing is the technique for interleaving of data from several devices onto a single transmission line. Figure 15-4 is a simplified illustration of how statistical multiplexing works. Each device with data to transmit is allowed a transmission slot on

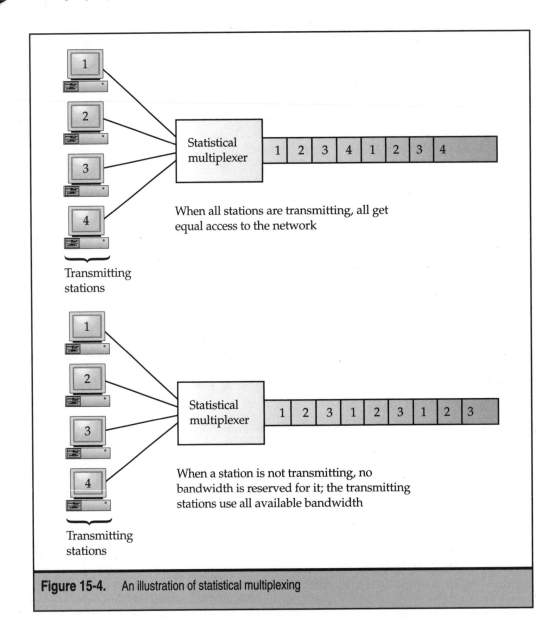

When all stations are transmitting, all get equal access to the network

Transmitting stations

When a station is not transmitting, no bandwidth is reserved for it; the transmitting stations use all available bandwidth

Transmitting stations

**Figure 15-4.** An illustration of statistical multiplexing

the network. If the device has nothing to transmit, however, its slice of bandwidth is allocated to a station that does have data to transmit. This is how frame relay accommodates bursting in excess of a subscriber's committed information rate—it makes use of bandwidth currently unused by other stations on the network.

# Installation and Configuration

When you are preparing your order for frame relay service, there are a few issues you need to work out before placing the call to the carrier service. These are as follows:

▼ **Access method** This is the speed of the connection between your site and the carrier's frame relay network. You have several options, and the speed you select will determine the type of access line required:

■ 56/64Kbps over switched 56 or ISDN lines

■ 128Kbps over ISDN lines

■ 384Kbps to 1.544Mbps over fractional T1 or T1 lines

■ **Physical location of the frame relay devices at your site** As we mentioned earlier, you'll need a router with a frame relay WAN port. Furthermore, your carrier will need to install a frame relay assembler/disassembler (FRAD) on your premises, as shown in Figure 15-5.

▲ **Committed information rate, committed burst rate, and excess burst rate** You will need to determine your network's traffic requirements—or your budget limitations—before you begin ordering the service.

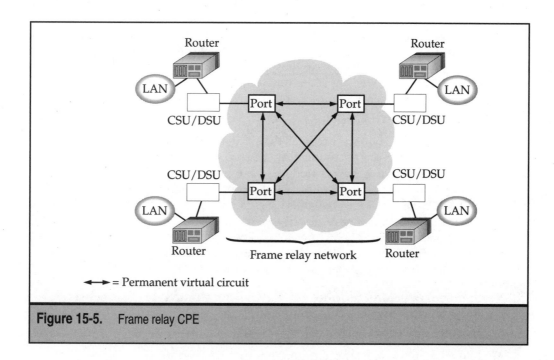

**Figure 15-5.** Frame relay CPE

To configure your router for frame relay, all you have to do is enter the datalink connection identifier (DLCI) information furnished by the frame relay service provider in your router's configuration tables. While you will be responsible for the LAN-to-router connection and router-to-FRAD connections, your local telephone company will be responsible for the FRAD-to-central-office connection. Furthermore, your local telephone company and your frame relay carrier together will be responsible for the central-office-to-frame-relay-network connection. Clearly, this leaves a lot of room for finger pointing, so be sure you're comfortable with the expertise of the carriers—and be patient.

## Availability and Pricing

Most wide area carriers in major metropolitan areas offer some flavor of frame relay service. However, destination cities and pricing vary a great deal, so make sure you verify that the carrier you are considering indeed offers frame relay services to all the locations you want to connect.

As we mentioned, frame relay can be very cost-effective, especially when compared with leasing multiple point-to-point connections. Generally, frame relay is very cost-effective for companies that have multiple sites in multiple geographically distant locations. Most leased-line connectivity is priced through federally regulated tariffing, which provides a fixed monthly fee plus an additional mileage fee. Frame relay, on the other hand, is usually priced on a flat fee, based on the port access speed and committed information rate. The monthly rates for frame relay service are in the neighborhood of $125 for 56Kbps service up to around $650 for 1.544Mbps service. However, you should be aware that these services come with a fairly hefty one-time installation fee of around $1,500 per port. If these rates are significantly lower than the costs involved in establishing a point-to-point dedicated line network to connect the same locations, then you should definitely consider implementing frame relay.

## Management and Fault Tolerance

One of the beauties of using frame relay is that, if you are using the services of a public frame relay carrier, your physical management responsibilities are very limited. Adds and changes to your services require nothing more from you than a call to your carrier. Fault tolerance is also the responsibility of the carrier, and frame relay offers automatic rerouting of PVCs when a connection fails.

On the other hand, as we have already mentioned, frame relay as a protocol isn't known for its manageability. There are only a few management features offered with frame relay, and those are implemented via out-of-band signaling. However, here are a few optional services available that may make your life easier:

▼ **Simple flow control** provides XON/XOFF flow control for those network devices that require flow control.

■ **Multicasting** allows stations to send frames to multiple destinations.

▲ **Global addressing** lets applications emulate LAN addressing.

Frame relay also offers the security benefit of having only private lines access the frame relay mesh. There are also some optional security features you can implement from your carrier, such as password protection and a feature that logs stations off the network after a predefined period of inactivity.

## Interoperability

Frame relay offers good interoperability now, and also holds the promise of quicker and easier interoperability when switched virtual circuits (SVCs) are supported by the public carriers. SVCs could connect ISDN to frame relay networks, and they may eventually give users the ability to dial up frame relay connections.

You may want to consider routing nonlocal area network protocols over frame relay as well. It may seem a bit strange at first, but frame relay is often much more cost-effective than other wide area transmission protocols, so it's worth a look. To route non-LAN protocols over the wide area, you'll need a device called a frame relay assembler/disassembler (FRAD). A FRAD takes data packets from other protocols—such as SNA, asynchronous, and even X.25—and breaks them into pieces, encapsulates the packet pieces in a frame relay frame, and sends them over the frame relay WAN to its destination. At the other end, the frame relay headers are stripped off the packets, and they are reassembled as packets in their original protocol, where they can be processed by the receiving stations. Figure 15-6 illustrates this.

### A FUNI Way of Interconnecting

Most ATM switch manufacturers have announced support—or at least an intention to support—frame relay and ATM connectivity. The ATM Forum has offered a proposal,

**Figure 15-6.** A FRAD in action

known as Frame-to-User Network Interface (FUNI), designed to set standards for connecting 56Kbps to 1.544Mbps circuits to ATM networks using a frame structure much like frame relay's. However, we've yet to see any actual FUNI installations, so the success of this proposal is yet to be seen.

### Interconnecting the Carriers

Different frame relay carriers implement the service in different ways, and as a result many of them are unable to interoperate. Not only do they often use different switches, but they also may implement different congestion control and signaling methods. The Frame Relay Forum has set about to resolve some of these interoperability issues by developing a set of interconnection specifications called the Network-to-Network Interface (NNI) standards. Theoretically, if all carriers use frame relay equipment that adheres to these standards, the interoperability problems will cease to exist.

## Performance

Frame relay is generally available at CIRs from 56Kbps to 1.544Mbps. As well, it supports much higher burst rates—up to 45Mbps. Furthermore, frame relay has low network latency of about 20ms.

## Scalability

Scalability is the hallmark of frame relay. The ease of adding more bandwidth via the committed information rate, along with the ability to send bursts of traffic well over the CIR, make frame relay one of the most flexible wide area protocols around. At the same time, thanks to frame relay's use of statistical multiplexing, providing this flexibility doesn't result in wasted idle bandwidth.

# CAN YOUR VENDOR DO THIS?

Whether you're selecting a vendor to implement a frame relay WAN from scratch, or to provide a specific device for your existing frame relay WAN, there are certain questions to answer fully. Although every frame relay network is different, and every expansion and upgrade within each network is unique, there are basic questions that are relevant to every frame relay project. To help you get started with the vendor selection process, we've provided a sample list of five questions to put to each prospective vendor. We've divided these questions into issues of experience, interoperability, performance, and management. Please note: for those of you implementing a frame relay network for the first time, we've assumed you have done your homework and are CERTAIN that frame relay is the correct protocol choice given the traffic, type of data, speed, transmission reliability, and internetworking characteristics of your network.

## The Experience Question

Has your vendor ever done this before? Are the technicians who have done it still on staff? This may seem silly, but it could be the most important question of all. You don't want to subsidize on-the-job training for your vendor's technical staff. Get references and check them thoroughly. Ask for the names of the technicians who performed the work. Make sure that those technicians are still employed by the vendor. Ask to interview them. Consider writing the name(s) of the experienced technician(s) into your bid acceptance.

## The Interoperability Question

Are you a member of the Frame Relay Forum? If not, does your equipment meet the frame relay standards? This is really relevant to equipment vendors. Ask them to provide examples—complete with references—of other vendors' equipment with which they have successfully internetworked. Be sure to check the references thoroughly. The last thing you need is to be bound to a single vendor because their frame relay implementation is "almost" in compliance with the standards set by the Frame Relay Forum.

## The Performance Question

What is the maximum line speed supported now—and 12 months from now? Obviously, 2.048Mbps should be the minimum. And for now it can be the maximum. Your vendor should have—or at least have plans for—support for speeds up to 45Mbps. And it wouldn't hurt to check the cost of upgrading to these higher speeds.

What are the switching speeds, expressed in frames per second, between: a) trunk ports; b) access ports; c) access and trunk ports? Get speeds for frame sizes varying from 128 bytes to 2,048 bytes. This question helps you ensure that the equipment can switch frames as quickly as it can receive them. For example, connected to a 2.048Mbps line, your router will receive about 2,000 128-byte frames per second. So if you have a device that can be configured to support more than one 2.048 line, yet can switch at a maximum of 2,000 frames per second, the router is actually a bottleneck.

*TIP:* You can expect the best performance on the trunk-to-trunk ports, so make them quote their access port-to-trunk port switching speed, too.

## The Management Questions

How does the router handle congestion management? How does it handle recovery? Congestion and overflow comprise the number one management issue for frame relay, so this is a key question. Ask whether the equipment complies with the IT-U and/or ANSI standards for congestion management, and if so, how. Explore whether the vendor's implementation uses the discard eligibility bit to let the equipment or the user set the discard priority of frames. What management facilities do they offer? Frame relay is not famous for its inherent manageability. Therefore, it pays to spend some quality time learning the management facilities offered by the proposed system or equipment. The number one feature you should require is congestion notification, since—as we noted above—congestion management will be your overriding concern with frame relay.

Another critical management issue is routing. The system should provide both manual and automatic routing, because although you will prefer manual routing for priority traffic, it would be silly to try to define manual routes for every frame of every priority. And, as with most systems, your frame relay system should provide useful troubleshooting and diagnostics utilities. You should also expect the system to provide comprehensive statistics on traffic levels, speeds, and discarded frames. You can use this information not only for network administration purposes, but also for billing information if your network has a chargeback system. Finally, if security is an issue, have the vendor describe security features in detail to see whether they meet your needs.

Searching for a frame relay vendor can be like a treasure hunt without clues. It can be frustrating and tedious. However, the stakes are high, so it's well worth the effort it requires. Although this list is by no means comprehensive, these questions will give you a map to follow while hunting for the right vendor for the job.

# THE GOOD NEWS

Frame relay services require less hardware than dedicated circuits. With dedicated circuits like 56Kbps and T1, because of their point-to-point orientation, you need two channel service units (CSUs) and two routers for each circuit—one per connection. So, for a configuration like the one shown in Figure 15-7, you will need five CSUs and five routers at each site.

With frame relay, on the other hand, you will need only one router and one CSU at each site, as shown in Figure 15-8.

Frame relay services typically cost less, yet give you more bandwidth. A dedicated circuit gives you the stated amount of bandwidth and no more. However, a frame relay circuit can support bursts of bandwidth well above your CIR.

It's faster and easier to reconfigure a frame relay network than a dedicated circuit network. Adding a new location to a dedicated circuit network requires that the end user purchase new equipment and order new lines, which can take anywhere from a few days to a few weeks to organize. Adding a new location to a frame relay network is simply a matter of adding an access port and configuring new PVCs, both of which are done by the carrier and can often be completed in a couple of days.

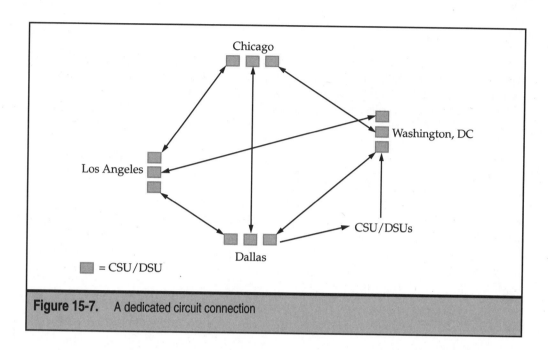

**Figure 15-7.** A dedicated circuit connection

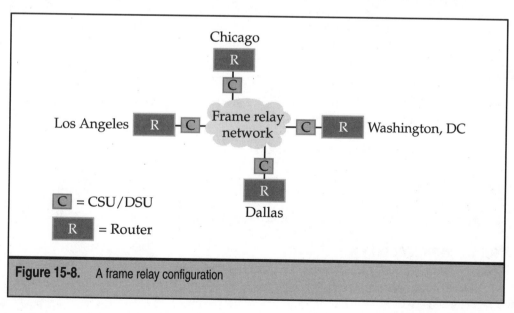

**Figure 15-8.** A frame relay configuration

# THE BAD NEWS

When frame relay was proposed to the standards committees in 1988, it was quickly defined and approved. It was subsequently implemented and supported by many local and interexchange communications carriers. By late 1991, frame relay was both widely available and widely implemented by users. At the time, the Federal Communications Commission didn't consider frame relay a basic service, and therefore it wasn't tariffed—that is, the FCC didn't require carriers to publish and abide by a set rate for frame relay service. Instead, the price of frame relay services was negotiated privately and separately between the carrier and each frame relay customer. This negotiated price was then written into a contract between the two parties. Shrewd customers were sometimes able to negotiate very favorable pricing through this procedure.

In October 1995, however, the FCC changed its mind. It now feels that frame relay is so widely used that it now constitutes a basic service. As such, the FCC is requiring frame relay carriers to tariff the service. Although this may be more equitable, it also eliminates the possibility of getting a bargain, because prices of tariffed services are much less flexible than those of untariffed services.

## Voice and Frame Relay

Originally, people didn't think voice (or video) could run over frame relay due to the protocol's variable-length frames. However, many vendors, including Micom Communications, are now offering mutliplexors that put both voice and data on frame relay bandwidth with very acceptable performance.

## Frame Relay Forum

The Frame Relay Forum is an association of frame relay users, vendors, and service providers based in Mountain View, California (510-608-5920). The organization is made up of committees that create implementation specifications and agreements for the purpose of developing frame relay standards.

### Recommended for:

Connecting LANs over the wide area
  Database applications and other applications that generate bursty data traffic

### Not Recommended for:

Video traffic, because of frame relay's variable-length frames
  Voice traffic, because of frame relay's variable-length frames
  Delay sensitive applications

# CHAPTER 16

## Asynchronous Transfer Mode

Anyone who has read a network trade magazine or attended a technical conference in the last three years has heard about ATM. Asynchronous Transfer Mode seems to be the great networking hope of both the near and distant future; some vendors have even called ATM this decade's most significant networking technology. ATM promises to integrate LAN functions, wide area functions, voice, video, and data into a single uniform protocol and design. It also promises uniformity and scalability that will ultimately simplify network design and management. Therefore, nearly all complementary technologies are engineering "ATM readiness" into their own development.

All the hype notwithstanding, ATM offers some benefits that no other wide area networking protocol has offered:

▼ **Speed**   ATM supports transmission rates of up to 622Mbps.

■ **Scalability**   ATM allows increased bandwidth and port density within existing architectures.

■ **Dedicated bandwidth**   This guarantees an application's consistency of service, which is not available in shared technologies.

▲ **Universal deployment**   ATM offers the potential of an end-to-end solution, meaning it can be used from desktop to local segment to backbone to WAN.

So, if ATM is so significant, what exactly is it? How will it improve your network? How much will it cost? When should you implement it? Because ATM will no doubt have an important role in your network before the end of the century, we will spend a great deal of time exploring exactly what ATM is, why it is so significant, where it is now in its development, where it is going, and the issues surrounding its implementation—both in its current form and in the future.

# HOW IT STARTED

ATM began as part of the Broadband Integrated Services Digital Network (B-ISDN) standard developed in 1988 by the Consultative Committee for International Telegraph and Telephone (CCITT). An extension of narrowband Integrated Services Digital Network (which defined public digital telecommunications networks), B-ISDN provides more bandwidth and enables more data throughput than narrowband ISDN. The B-ISDN Reference Model is shown in Figure 16-1.

As you can see, ATM lies directly on top of the Physical layer of the B-ISDN Reference Model. However, it doesn't require the use of any specific Physical layer protocol. Therefore, the Physical layer could be FDDI, DS3, SONET, or others. We'll talk more about the reference model and its implications for ATM later in this chapter.

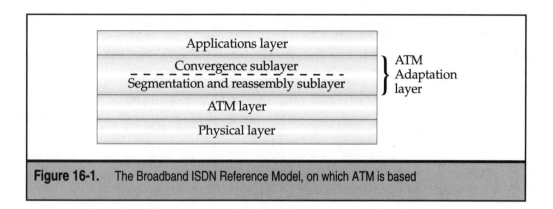

**Figure 16-1.**   The Broadband ISDN Reference Model, on which ATM is based

# WHO STARTED IT

As mentioned earlier, ATM was originally defined by the CCITT, a part of the United Nations charged with developing and recommending international standards for telecommunications technology and operations. This body is now more commonly known as the International Telecommunications Union (ITU), of which the CCITT is a committee. The International Telecommunications Union is currently formalizing standards for ATM.

In 1991, the ATM Forum, a consortium of vendors, carriers, and users, was formed to expedite industry agreement on ATM interfaces in North America. The ATM Forum is a driving force in the establishment of industry-wide ATM standards.

# ATM: THE SHORT ANSWER

In brief, ATM is a cell-switched, connection-oriented, full-duplex, point-to-point protocol that dedicates bandwidth to each station. It uses asynchronous time division multiplexing (TDM) to control the flow of information over the network. ATM operates at bandwidths ranging from 25Mbps to 622Mbps and beyond, although most of the development time (and marketing fanfare) is currently going into 155Mbps ATM. Among the benefits offered by ATM are

▼ Excellent scalability

■ Legacy network integration

■ Bandwidth on demand

■ Ability to handle the entire range of network traffic—voice, data, image, video, graphics, and multimedia

▲ Adaptability to both LAN and WAN environments

# IF ATM IS THE ANSWER, WHAT WERE THE QUESTIONS?

Like all the high-speed protocols discussed in this book, ATM was developed as an alternative to existing transport protocols such as Ethernet and token ring that were obviously limited in bandwidth and scalability. However, ATM was also designed to handle multiple types of data simultaneously and with increased efficiency. Therefore, ATM had to be able to transmit a wide variety of bit rates and support bursty communications, since voice, data, and video traffic all exhibit bursty behavior.

*NOTE:* Most people don't think of circuit-switched voice traffic as bursty, but it is. In fact, a circuit-switched voice conversation utilizes far less than half of the available bandwidth.

## What Is a Cell?

Packet switching, which utilizes bandwidth only when data traffic is present, was developed to handle bursty data traffic. However, packet-switching systems don't perform adequately for real-time, two-way traffic such as interactive video. ATM overcomes this limitation because it employs cells, which are fixed-length packets, rather than variable-length packets. Each ATM cell consists of a 48-byte payload and a 5-byte header, as shown in Figure 16-2.

Fixed-length ATM cells offer many advantages over variable-length packets:

▼ **Hardware switching capability**   Because it is simple, predictable, and reliable to process fixed-length cells, ATM switching can be done at the hardware level, rather than requiring expensive and processing-intensive software to manage flow control, buffers, and other management schemes.

■ **Guaranteed levels of service**   Networking and switching queuing delays are more predictable with fixed-length data cells. Therefore, switches can be designed to provide guaranteed levels of service for all types of traffic, even for delay-sensitive services such as voice and video.

**Figure 16-2.**   ATM cell structure

- ■ **Parallel processing**   Fixed-length cells allow cell-relay switches to process cells in parallel, for speeds that far exceed the limitations of bus-based switch architectures.

- ▲ **Voice processing capability**   Although ATM cells require bandwidth only when traffic is present, they can still provide the equivalent of a TDM time slot for continuous traffic. As a result, ATM can handle real-time continuous traffic such as digitized voice, and bursty traffic such as LAN transmissions, equally well.

The ATM cell is used to carry data transmitted between switches. A 48-byte segment of the user data payload is placed in a cell along with a 5-byte header, forming the 53-byte ATM cell. The cell header carries information necessary for switch operation.

# What Is Switched?

ATM does not employ shared bandwidth. Rather, each port on an ATM switch is dedicated to one user. An ATM switch sets up a virtual connection between a transmitting node and a receiving node. This connection is made on the basis of the destination address of each cell, and it lasts only as long as it takes to transfer one cell. These data transfers can take place in parallel and at full network speed. Because the cell is transmitted only to the port associated with that specific destination address, no other port receives the cell, which provides both low traffic and, as an extra bonus, high security.

## ATM Switching and Virtual Connections

To communicate over the ATM network, applications must first establish a virtual connection (VC) among switches. A VC is a transmission path for an ATM data cell. The VC extends through one or more switches, establishing an end-to-end connection for the transmission of application data via ATM cells. VCs can be established in two ways. First, a permanent virtual circuit (PVC) can be manually configured by a network manager. A PVC is dedicated bandwidth that guarantees a level of service to a particular station. Network managers would configure PVCs for mission-critical applications that must always receive high priority or for permanent connections such as among routers and bridges. The second means of establishing a VC is the switched virtual circuit (SVC). An SVC is a VC set up "on the fly" as it is needed by the application.

The cell header also contains two address fields, the virtual path identifier (VPI) and the virtual channel identifier (VCI), which together total 3.5 bytes and define the virtual circuit identifier, which is the route of the cell to a particular switch. These fields are updated by each switch in the path.

**VIRTUAL CIRCUIT IDENTIFIERS**   Virtual circuit identifiers tag the cells for a particular connection, then the switches transfer the data in a VC by hardware-based switching, triggering the VC connection tag in the cell header.

The problems of congestion and "VC routing" among multiple switches are still outstanding in the standards process. Congestion management is important because a small level of cell loss (e.g., 0.1 percent) gets magnified to a dramatically large frame loss (e.g., 20 percent). This is unacceptable, and several alternative congestion management policies are under active study and evaluation.

All ATM cells are the same size, unlike frame relay systems and local area networks, which have variable packet sizes. Using same-size cells allows the following:

▼ **Guaranteed bandwidth** Variable-length packets can cause traffic delays at switches in the same way that cars must wait for long trucks to make turns at busy intersections.

■ **High performance** Large volumes of data can flow concurrently over a single physical connection.

■ **Hardware switching** In the short term, this yields higher throughput, and over time the technology can continue to exploit improved price/performance as processor power increases and incremental costs decrease.

▲ **Data prioritization** ATM can deliver a deterministic response, which is essential to carry "latency-sensitive" communications, such as motion video and audio, or mission-critical, interactive data traffic. I think this device is extremely helpful in organizing information and emphasizing important points.

## What Is Connection-Oriented?

"Connection-oriented" means that a connection must be established between the transmitting and receiving computers before data is transferred. Each intermediate switching point must be identified and informed of the existence of the connection. Each packet is routed independently, and therefore each must carry a complete address of the ultimate destination.

## What Is Full Duplex?

Full duplex allows transmission over one pair of wires and receipt over the other pair simultaneously, which provides nearly full utilization of both pairs and sustainable high data rates. By supporting full-duplex operation, ATM doubles the effective bandwidth of ordinary half-duplex transmission that is employed by most network protocols.

## What Is Point-to-Point?

As mentioned earlier, ATM networks must establish a connection between the sending and receiving stations before transmitting a cell. This connection between two stations is the only concern of the ATM switch. Unlike a router, an ATM switch doesn't try to define this one-to-one connection in the context of all possible connections on the network. Instead, the ATM switch selects the route between the sending station and the receiving station, then informs the intermediate switches along this route to ensure that the resources for transmitting the cell are allocated through the network.

Once a cell's transmission route is established, the ATM switch then assigns a connection number to each point-to-point link along this route. Connection numbers are chosen independently for each of the point-to-point links in the transmission path. A path may be formed from a number of such links, with the links joined by switches. This means that a single cell carries a potentially different connection number on each different link of the connection path. A switch changes the connection numbers of each cell as it transfers the cell from one link to another. This change of connection numbers at the junction of two links means that the connection number fields only need to be big enough to distinguish the connections carried by a single link.

This point-to-point connection orientation of ATM and the changing of the connection numbers at each switch hop allow ATM to use small connection numbers rather than the large addresses required by most protocols. This makes ATM more efficient, because small connection numbers conserve space in cells and thus bandwidth, and also faster, because it makes for small lookup tables in switches.

# What Is Dedicated Bandwidth?

Efficient bandwidth use is not the only issue addressed by ATM technology. In fact, different traffic types require different delay behavior, delay variation, and loss characteristics. ATM provides different qualities of services to accommodate these differences. ATM allocates bandwidth to each active station. The station requests the appropriate amount of bandwidth for each connection, and the network automatically assigns this bandwidth to the user. In reality, the bandwidth isn't actually dedicated per se. It is shared by other users, but the network ensures the requested level of service. The network can do this because it controls the number of simultaneous conversations on the network.

To access the network, a station requests a virtual circuit between the transmitting and receiving ends. During connection setup, the end station can request the quality of service it needs to suit transmission requirements, and ATM switches will grant the request if sufficient network resources are available. The guaranteed level of service of cell-based switched access is particularly useful for transporting real-time, interactive communication such as voice or video. ATM uses a protocol called user-to-network interface (UNI) to establish dedicated levels of bandwidth to stations and applications.

## User-to-Network Interfaces (UNI)

ATM's UNI protocol provides multiple service classes and bandwidth reservation, established during call setup of a switched virtual connection. The UNI defines the interoperability between the user equipment and the ATM switch port. A public UNI defines the interface between a public service ATM network and usually supports a SONET or DS3 interface. A private UNI, on the other hand, defines an ATM interface between an end user and a private ATM switch, and would most likely have a copper or fiber-optic cable interface.

While the ATM Forum has successfully stabilized the UNI protocol, there are a couple of key issues that network managers should consider when choosing products. The UNI protocol in the products they select must coordinate the bandwidth allocated locally among other switches and internetworked LAN segments. It must also support a variety of network operating systems to guarantee multiple classes of service. Both of these issues affect the interoperability of the ATM network, and so the network managers should select products that support the network's current design and equipment.

# HOW IT ALL WORKS TOGETHER

The combination of cell switching and point-to-point connections, with their resulting small connection numbers, lets ATM break the core networking task into two separate components—route determination and data forwarding (better known as routing and switching)—each handled with a different technology. To fully illustrate this separation of functions, let's first look at how a cell is transmitted across an ATM network.

## Route Determination

Route determination is a computer-intensive function, typically software-based, that requires dynamic knowledge of the global network topology. Route determination in ATM is performed by establishing virtual connections, and the route determination occurs only once per data transfer session. ATM chooses a path for the cells of the connection (routes the connection) during establishment of the connection; all cells of the connection follow the same path. After connection establishment, only simple cell transfer operations are performed—operations that implement routing decisions made at connection establishment time. This keeps data transfer simple and efficient, but it requires a separate system for connection setup. The connection setup part of ATM is, and must be, based on connectionless protocols. The main difference between ATM and traditional networking solutions is that traditional networking must solve both components of the networking problem simultaneously. Thus, every packet in a traditional network carries the globally significant routing information, and every packet must be processed by routers before the data can be forwarded. This continual evocation of the route determination function is a very wasteful use of an expensive resource, and becomes the network bottleneck due to the expense of wire-speed capable routers.

To illustrate the routing problem that the ATM architecture solves, let's consider a network backup. Suppose you must back up 2 gigabytes of data residing on a server on a routed network. The backup program will probably create 10 million 200-byte packets, because 200 bytes is the most common transfer unit size permitted in routed networks. Each of these 10 million packets will be assigned a network-wide routing address, and each router along the path processes these 10 million packets separately—even though they are streaming continuously along the same route. This means that each router along the path must examine the Network layer header of each packet, then compute the route again for each packet separately, despite the fact that the route is identical for all 10 million packets. What a waste of processing power!

The scenario is very different with ATM. The ATM switch establishes the route only once with a virtual connection (VC). The switch then assigns a connection identifier to tag the route. Switches on the route are informed of the bandwidth requirements of the VC and are instructed to interpret the connection identifier appropriately. After that, all cells with that connection identifier are hardware-switched along the route, permitting the route determination function to service new requests rather than continually servicing the request of an established session. Thus, cells don't contain complex routing addresses. Instead, they are tagged with a small temporary connection identifier, which the ATM switches are instructed to map onto the route defined by the VC.

# Data Forwarding

Data forwarding, on the other hand, is a hardware-intensive function requiring gigabits of switching capacity. ATM's cell-based switching allows simple switching which, like Ethernet switching, can be performed entirely in hardware. It is performed by ATM switches operating on ATM cells, and the ATM cell definition has been optimized for implementing a gigabit-capable, hardware-based switching capability. Therefore, cells are hardware-switched along the path previously established by the VC for the session.

ATM is primarily a format for use by switches and includes no access arbitration protocol. Each port on a switch behaves in many ways like a station. The cell header information in a received cell is used to look up the forwarding information needed to route the cell within the switch. Error checking is performed in the cell header, and cells with errors are discarded. This cell header address information is changed at each switch to represent the route at the next switch. Addressing in the ATM cell is of local significance to a switch, in contrast to the MAC address, which identifies individual users either with locally or globally unique values.

# ATM Switches

ATM switches allow one desktop connection per port. Some ATM switches are nonblocking, meaning they have the capacity to support a backbone link equivalent to the sum of the input port speeds. In addition, nonblocking switches transfer traffic directly from input to output without a store-and-forward process. Buffering is used only if multiple inputs attempt to access the same output simultaneously. In spite of occasional buffering, ATM is still superior to the slow, store-and-forward operation of traditional routers.

Scalable hardware switching elements are the basis for the gigabit-speed backbone networks that can be built with ATM. Although gigabit switching seems far beyond the needs of today's 10Mbps desktops, nonblocking LANs are constrained to small numbers of ports without a gigabit switch in the backbone.

### ATM Switch Control Point

The ATM switching function really consists of two parts: the switch hardware, which performs the actual switching, and the switch control point, which manages the switching fabric. The ATM switch control point maintains the switch fabric by

▼ Managing requests for virtual connections (VCs)

■ Learning the ATM network topology

■ Maintaining the forwarding databases

▲ Enabling SNMP-based ATM network management

## Cabling Considerations

ATM's topology is a mesh of switches. This means that any point in the network can be reached from any other point via multiple routes involving independent connections among switches. ATM doesn't require any specific Physical layer protocols to accomplish this. ATM also has no distance limitations other than those imposed by the attenuation characteristics of the medium used. This simplifies the building of the cable plant, because there really aren't any rules to constrain the design. However, it makes documentation all the more important, because with no rules as guidelines, it would be nearly impossible to decipher an undocumented cable plant.

### ATM Media Support

Media independence is a driving principle of ATM. Many physical layers are specified, starting at 25Mbps, including several for 100 to 155Mbps, and going all the way up to 622Mbps. ATM at 155Mbps will include support for Category 3, 4, 5 UTP, Type 1 STP, fiber-optic cable, multimode fiber, and single-mode fiber local area networks.

### Wide Area Network Physical Interface

The 155Mbps WAN interface to the public network carriers will be based on the Synchronous Optical Network (SONET). As we mentioned earlier, SONET is an internationally supported physical layer transport scheme developed in the early 1980s.

## Setup and Configuration

ATM is different from any LAN protocol you have ever managed. While the installation and configuration processes aren't physically difficult, they are complex, requiring a detailed level of knowledge about ATM as well as a great deal of careful planning.

Therefore, be prepared to spend both money and time training, planning, and consulting before undertaking an ATM implementation.

## Scalability

ATM can add scalability to legacy protocol networks. For example, in Figure 16-3, the network is connected by three 24-port Ethernet switches, each having two 100Base-TX uplinks connected to the other two switches to form a mesh. Such a network could provide nonblocking service for 60 Ethernet users—less than currently connected. Furthermore, as the number of users and switches grows, more switch capacity must be dedicated to backbone links than to desktop interfaces.

Using a 1.55Gbps ATM switch in the backbone adds ten ATM ports, each at 155Mbps, as shown in Figure 16-4. Only one ATM port is required from each Ethernet switch to provide connectivity among all ports. Whereas the network in Figure 16-3 could support

**Figure 16-3.**    A 10/100 switched Ethernet network providing nonblocking service for 60 users

only 60 users, the network in Figure 16-4 can provide nonblocking service for 240 dedicated Ethernet users, with room to grow.

Scalable ATM LAN switches on the market today can support as many as 100 155Mbps ports in nonblocking configuration. In conjunction with dedicated Ethernet access devices, these switches provide the foundation for a nonblocking network of 1,000 dedicated Ethernet users. As the ATM market matures, nonblocking networks with 1,000 155Mbps ports—or 10,000 Ethernet ports—will be achievable.

A need for nonblocking networks or high-speed desktop connections isn't necessary to justify ATM. Although ATM is most beneficial when used in a nonblocking LAN configuration, it can also be deployed in a blocking configuration to maximize bandwidth usage.

In a blocking configuration, the sum of the user port bandwidths exceeds the backbone link bandwidth, and contention for backbone links can occur. Constructing a network with potential blocking can be a cost-effective solution for customers in the early stages of migrating to ATM. For customers who are installing ATM to the desktop, current workstation processing loads may not yet require full use of the available bandwidth. In this case, more users can be added to the network than the backbone can support in a nonblocking configuration. When bandwidth-hungry workstation applications are deployed, bandwidth and switching capacity can be adjusted to produce a nonblocking configuration.

When combined with proper traffic management techniques, a blocking ATM network is capable of exceeding the performance of a shared-media LAN. Traffic management allows conventional LANs with relatively low-speed users to benefit from ATM with cost-effective blocking configurations.

Support 240 dedicated 10Base-T users with nonblocking service

**Figure 16-4.** An Ethernet network with an ATM backbone

# Manageability

ATM backbones are easier to manage than those in most routed networks, because ATM eliminates a lot of the complexity required to configure large internetworks that have different addressing schemes and routing procedures. ATM hubs provide connections between any two ports on the hub, independent of the type of device attached to it. The addresses of these devices are premapped, making it easy to send a message, for example, from one node to another, regardless of the network type the nodes are connected to. In fact, simplified network management may be the primary reason for many users to migrate to an ATM-based solution, even prior to performance requirements dictating the transition.

## Virtual LANs

Setting up filters or constraints between different groups of users is awkward and time-consuming with conventional bridges and routers. Network managers think in terms of workgroups, not the physical location of users. Therefore, they shouldn't have to set up a series of filtering statements based on physical ports. The connection-oriented nature of ATM and the performance of hardware cell switching enables the creation of virtual networks.

Rather than configuring and reconfiguring routers every time end stations move, network managers can implement virtual LANs. A virtual LAN is a list of device media access control (MAC) or network addresses that are independent of a physical port, much like an access list used by some router vendors. However, virtual LANs have network-wide significance. A device can access any other device on the same virtual LAN. Virtual LANs can define filters among themselves, just like routers can.

Devices on different media can be members of the same virtual LAN. Furthermore, users can move end stations onto any segment within the virtual subnet without requiring address reconfiguration.

Virtual LANs enable network managers to group devices logically regardless of physical location and provide dedicated bandwidth and services to each, as shown in Figure 16-5. Users can plug into any port in the network, and the virtual LAN handles the rest.

In addition to address filtering, virtual LANs also provide the following:

▼   Simplified moves, adds, and changes

■   Bandwidth allocation

▲   Security features

## Simplified Moves, Adds, and Changes

One of the major problems network managers have in large, routed networks is the big administrative effort required to perform moves, adds, and changes. This is particularly

Segment D (Station Z and U)

Segment C (Station V)

Segment B

Segment A (Station Y and W)

**Figure 16-5.**    A virtual LAN configuration

true of Internet Protocol (IP) networks, where each physical LAN is associated with a logical subnet, as shown in Figure 16-6. If a user needs to move from one floor of a building to another, the workstation typically has to be reconfigured with a valid IP address on the new subnet.

To handle such moves, managers of legacy networks have to reconfigure routers manually. Virtual LANs, however, eliminate all of the manual address resolution and reconfiguration. Virtual LANs enable network managers to group devices logically regardless of physical location and provide dedicated bandwidth and services to each, as shown in Figure 16-7.

While networks obviously require routing capability, network managers would like to avoid having to manually reconfigure network address assignments every time users move from one network segment to another. Virtual networks let them do just that by identifying the physical address of a new device and associating it with a Network layer address based on prior assignment without human intervention to the system or the end station. Users can plug into any port in the network, and the virtual LAN handles the rest.

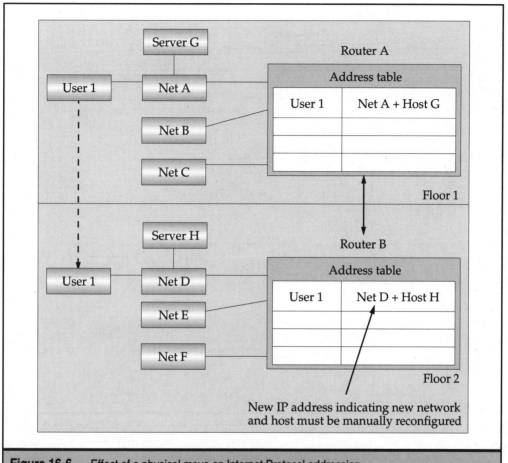

**Figure 16-6.** Effect of a physical move on Internet Protocol addressing

## Performance

ATM switches provide high-performance data forwarding: all information is converted to the common format of 53-byte cells. Unlike routers or packet switches, which are forced to process relatively large and variable-sized packets in software, ATM or cell relay switches always deal with data units of a uniformly small size. This allows key switching functions to be implemented in hardware. The result is very fast cell processing and switching and the capability to build large networks while maintaining acceptable

**Figure 16-7.** A virtual LAN configuration

propagation delays. This is critical for supporting multimedia applications such as video or voice where information has time dependency and must be transmitted with consistently low latency.

## Fault Tolerance

ATM is a mixed blessing in the area of fault tolerance. ATM allows redundant connections, which increases fault tolerance and, consequently, reliability. However, to enable a network fast enough to support multimegabit transfer rates, ATM provides no error detection and no retransmission, so let the buyer beware.

## Security

As we mentioned earlier, the connection-oriented nature of ATM brings additional potential advantages with respect to security. By using explicit call setup procedures, security can be implemented on a per-call basis as opposed to a per-packet basis, so users don't automatically have access to other resources. The network could intelligently determine which traffic should be passed based on source and destination identities. Furthermore, user authentication that restricts users from having access to all network resources can be implemented. The connection-oriented nature of ATM also ensures that traffic is only sent to the destination for which it is intended: there is no waste of network resources with unnecessary broadcasts, nor compromise of security. This behavior eliminates the need for broadcast or protocol filters to enhance efficiency.

### Security and Virtual LANs

Virtual LANs can increase security on ATM networks. Network managers can use policy-based virtual LANs to define filtering restrictions between groups of devices, providing tight security. Furthermore, ATM switches offer port-level security by allowing administrators to restrict virtual subnets to specific physical ports.

## Cost of Ownership

ATM is probably the most expensive technology discussed in this book. ATM products are likely to have a higher relative cost due to cell assembly and additional services. However, not only are ATM adapters and switches expensive, they are currently proprietary. This means that training and expertise will be vendor- and product-specific. If you change vendors, therefore, your costs will also likely include hefty training and integration expenses.

# THE ATM AND THE OSI MODEL

ATM reaches farther up the ISO-OSI model than most transport protocols, as shown in Figure 16-8. Therefore, to take full advantage of ATM as well as to integrate it into existing legacy-protocol networks, applications must be developed that support the higher-level implications of Asynchronous Transfer Mode.

## The ATM Layer

What we have discussed up to this point are actions that take place at the ATM layer, which corresponds somewhat to the Datalink and Network layers of the ISO-OSI model.

| | |
|---|---|
| Application | ATM Adaptation layer |
| Presentation | |
| Session | ATM Adaptation layer |
| Transport | |
| Network | ATM layer |
| Datalink | |
| Physical | Physical |

**Figure 16-8.**   The relationship among the ISO-OSI, B-ISDN, and ATM Reference Models

If ATM were like other protocols, these would be the only layers affected by ATM and we could end our discussion here. However, to ensure service levels by dedicating bandwidth to stations or applications, as well as to integrate networks of other transport protocols into an ATM network, we must explore the next higher level of the ATM Reference Model.

# The ATM Adaptation Layer (AAL)

The ATM Adaptation layer (AAL) sits above the ATM layer, as shown in Figure 16-9. This layer is where ATM translates user traffic from applications into ATM format. It is at this layer that ATM provides support for connection-oriented and connectionless applications, variable bit rate applications (like X.25 and local area network traffic, respectively), as well as for constant bit rate applications (like video and multimedia).

Actually the AAL is composed of two sublayers; the Convergence sublayer (CS) and the Segmentation and Reassembly sublayer (SAR). Here's how they work.

## Convergence Sublayer (CS)

The Convergence sublayer permits the relaying of voice, video, and data traffic through the same switching fabric. It interprets the data coming in from the higher-level application and prepares it for processing by the Segmentation and Reassembly sublayer. Obviously, the operations and functions performed by the CS vary depending upon the type and format of incoming data.

## The Segmentation and Reassembly Sublayer (SAR)

Before an application transmits data over an ATM network, the SAR sublayer segments data into 48-byte ATM data cells. Once the ATM cells reach their destination, the SAR sublayer reassembles them into higher-level data and transmits them to the appropriate local devices.

**Figure 16-9.** The Broadband-Integrated Services Digital Network Reference Model

## AAL-5

Because ATM can carry multiple traffic types, several adaptation protocols, each operating simultaneously, exist at the Adaptation layer. For example, local area networks often employ the AAL-5 Adaptation protocol, designed specifically to handle this type of variable-rate data traffic. In the AAL-5 Convergence sublayer, an 8-byte field, including data length and an error-detection checksum, is appended to a frame (or block) of user information (up to 64KB in length) coming from the higher-layer application. The AAL-5 frame is then separated into a stream of 48-byte data cells by the segmentation and reassembly sublayer, then sent along its way. At the receiving station, the SAR reassembles the cells into frames and the CS processes, then removes, the 8-byte data length and error-detection checksum field. The frame is then passed to the higher-level protocol.

AAL-5 is the foundation for LAN Emulation, a key technology in ATM integration and migration. We will discuss LAN Emulation in detail later in this chapter.

# ATM MIGRATION ISSUES

Installing ATM will probably require some dramatic changes in the design and equipment of your network. The concepts and rules of ATM are very different from those used in most local and wide area network protocols. For example, most LAN protocols are connectionless in nature, and therefore conflict on a very basic level with the connection-oriented ATM protocol. Another example is addressing. Because the ultimate goal of ATM is to be offered as a wide area public network, large addresses are going to be required to accommodate the millions of potential devices on a public ATM network. As a result, a scheme will have to be developed to resolve the smaller LAN addresses with the large ATM addresses. There is also a problem with standards and interoperability: ATM products from different vendors do not interoperate, and ATM LANs have only limited capability to interoperate with other LAN protocols. Connection setup and other issues stand in the way of internetworking between ATM and existing LANs. Knowing what issues to consider and what questions to ask will help ensure you make the right decisions for both the present and the future. Therefore, any integration and/or migration from legacy protocol networks to ATM's connection-oriented, dedicated, switched environment will require careful planning and execution.

## LAN Emulation

A major obstacle for the widespread acceptance of ATM in mainstream LANs is the integration of existing protocols such as Ethernet, token ring, and FDDI. As a point-to-point, connection-oriented protocol, ATM doesn't natively support the way legacy LAN protocols work.

The installed base of Ethernet isn't going to disappear soon. In fact, it will continue to grow for some time, particularly given its very low cost, standardization, new technology extensions such as switched Ethernet products, and huge installed base. Obviously, therefore, without providing an integration scheme for this large installed base, ATM will remain a niche technology for isolated pockets of high-end users.

> **NOTE:** There are approximately 40 million Ethernet nodes installed today, and about 10 million new ones being shipped every year.

LAN Emulation for ATM is the migration technology that allows end stations running existing applications—even those that require features unique to the legacy protocol—to be adapted to ATM services. LAN Emulation is a program that emulates conventional local area network operation. It provides a sort of bridge between legacy LAN protocols and ATM segments. LAN Emulation is tricky, because ATM is vastly different in many ways from the familiar LAN transport protocols of Ethernet and token ring. For example, as we mentioned, ATM is connection-oriented, while Ethernet and token ring are connectionless, meaning that packets go to all stations on the network and are acknowledged only by the station to which they are addressed. Also, ATM stations will have to provide support for broadcast and multicast operations that are so often used in Ethernet and token ring. In addition, ATM uses a 20-byte addressing scheme, while token ring and Ethernet both use 48-bit MAC addresses. Therefore, LAN Emulation has to resolve the differing MAC and ATM addresses.

## What Makes LAN Emulation Tricky

There are many issues that make LAN Emulation difficult to implement. Among these issues are the following:

▼ Address resolution

■ Broadcast and multicast support

■ Speed

▲ Connection setup

**SPEED** To provide the performance necessary for successful bridging between legacy and ATM networks, LAN Emulation devices have to have full wire-speed conversion and switching.

**CONNECTION SETUP** As we mentioned earlier in this chapter, ATM is a connection-oriented transport service. Legacy LAN protocols, on the other hand, are connectionless, meaning they send packets containing the full station address over the media without first establishing a connection with the receiving station. The receiving station monitors all the packets on the media and accepts those that are addressed to it. With only 5 bytes of header, an ATM cell cannot carry the full destination address for each cell. Therefore, adapting existing Network layer protocols that require the full destination address to ATM's connection-oriented cell switching is a major challenge.

One interface that has been developed to address this interoperability issue is the LAN Emulation user-to-network interface (LUNI). LUNI protocols allow the ATM network and its edge devices to control the virtual connections required for transmission and to emulate the connectionless nature of a LAN.

## ATM Edge-Routing Devices

An ATM edge-routing device converts packets from an Ethernet or token ring LAN to the cell structure of an ATM network and vice versa. To move traffic through the ATM network, devices at the boundary, or edge, of the network convert non-ATM traffic streams into cells. The addition of new traffic types requires only a new edge device, deployed where the demand for such traffic exists.

The ATM edge router is a radical departure from conventional routers. Conventional routers are symmetrical multiprocessor products designed to handle a balanced load of incoming and outgoing traffic. Each CPU is dedicated to one function, either route calculation and management, ATM connection setup and management, or data forwarding. Edge routers, on the other hand, are asymmetrical in design to create a switched fabric of small, modular routers that scale indefinitely by exploiting the enormous bandwidth and redundancy of a highly meshed ATM backbone.

Edge routers are also designed to overcome a problem in conventional routers: latency. The latency of the average multiprotocol router is relatively large (ranging from hundreds to thousands of microseconds). Furthermore, this latency is also unpredictable. However, edge routers are designed for deterministic latencies of 50 microseconds per device. This performance is a good match for ATM latencies, which are typically measured in tens of microseconds, which in turn are a good match for delay-sensitive data such as voice and video.

## An Overview of LAN Emulation

LAN Emulation is a collection of services that translate between the higher-level protocols of connectionless protocol services and the lower-level, connection-oriented ATM protocols, as shown in Figure 16-10.

**Figure 16-10.**   Translating between ATM and legacy protocols

As we mentioned earlier, the ATM Adaptation layer (AAL) sits above the ATM layer. The AAL formats data into the 48-byte ATM cell payload, a process known as segmentation. Once the ATM cells reach their destination, they are reconstructed into higher-level data and transmitted to the respective local devices in a process referred to as reassembly. Because ATM can carry multiple traffic types, several adaptation protocols, each operating simultaneously, exist at the Adaptation layer. AAL-5 is the adaptation protocol on which LAN Emulation is based.

LAN Emulation sits above AAL-5 in the protocol hierarchy. In the ATM-to-LAN converter at the network edge, LAN Emulation solves data networking problems for all protocols—routable and nonroutable—by resolving LAN and ATM addresses at the MAC layer. LAN Emulation is completely independent of upper-layer protocols, services, and applications.

Because LAN Emulation occurs in edge devices and end systems, it is entirely transparent to the ATM network and to Ethernet and token ring host devices.

## How LAN Emulation Works

Figure 16-11 shows how LAN Emulation works in a legacy LAN. Low-end PCs in an Ethernet environment access high-end servers with native ATM interfaces through a LAN/ATM switch. Because LAN Emulation makes ATM look like a classical LAN, standard bridging techniques allow the LAN/ATM switch to provide protocol-independent connectivity. No change is required in the legacy PCs, yet they experience

**Figure 16-11.**   LAN Emulation in practice

improved performance because of the high input/output capacity of the server, made possible through the high-speed ATM interface. In addition, they benefit from the dedicated bandwidth provided by the switched LAN implementation.

## Multiple Emulated LANs

The ATM Forum LAN Emulation standard also supports the implementation of multiple emulated LANs within a single ATM network. LAN Emulation is implemented through a client/server model. It works like this: a LAN Emulation client, such as workstation software, resolves MAC addresses into ATM addresses. Each client connects to the server by a virtual connection. Only those clients connected to the same server can learn about each other and communicate directly. Logically segmenting the network across multiple server functions—which can be stand-alone devices, software in end systems, or ATM switch modules—allows multiple emulated LANs to exist simultaneously on the same physical network.

Figure 16-12 shows the physical and logical view of multiple emulated LANs. In the physical view, the router runs two LAN Emulation clients—A2 for the accounting department and M2 for the manufacturing department. Each departmental server keeps track of its clients through a resident database. When accounting user Al sends a packet to manufacturing user Ml, the accounting server checks its database for a match. Finding none, it maps the MAC address to the router (A2/M2), which then forwards the packet to the manufacturing department server for delivery to Ml.

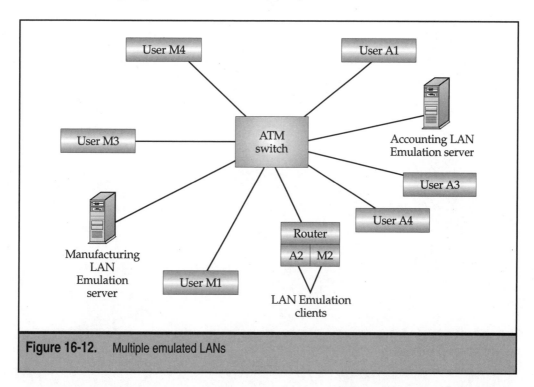

**Figure 16-12.**   Multiple emulated LANs

The logical view looks like the physical layout of today's LANs and is consistent with the goal of LAN Emulation. Departmental clients communicate directly with each other, directly with servers, and indirectly with other departments through a network router.

## LAN Emulation and Switched Virtual LANs

There are now products available, such as 3Com's Transcend suite of network management applications, that allow network managers to define multiple emulated LANs. When several different emulated LANs communicate through one or more switches on an ATM network, the result is a switched virtual LAN, as shown in Figure 16-13. Managing virtual LANs can be difficult, because managing physical connectivity

**Figure 16-13.**   Switched virtual LANs

isn't enough. You will have to be able to monitor and manage the logical interconnection across the LAN. With switched virtual LANs, routing is no longer a physical bottleneck, but a logical processing function that can be handled efficiently by the ATM switches.

Virtual switched emulated LANs offer the same benefits as garden-variety virtual LANs:

▼ Simplified moves, adds, and changes

■ Secure workgroups

■ Firewalls against broadcast storms

▲ Flow control to better utilize network bandwidth

It offers all of these benefits without requiring the purchase of new equipment or the recabling of network segments. Network administrators can manage segments just by redefining groups in the network management system and/or reconfiguring software in the end device and/or ATM switch.

# Routing Issues

Although ATM LAN Emulation greatly simplifies the creation of virtual workgroups, it doesn't change the role of routers on virtual LANs. Routers are still required to manage broadcasts and address resolution, as shown in Figure 16-14. As the network scales to higher-speed backbone links, the router must process traffic from these links at wire speeds in order to avoid creating a bottleneck.

## ATM and Conventional Routers

Even though many high-end routers now have ATM interfaces designed to forward packets at ATM speeds of 155Mbps, some legacy conventional routers just aren't designed to take full advantage of ATM's performance capabilities. Today's routers are optimized for a balanced load of incoming and outgoing traffic across a number of interfaces, unlike the ATM edge routers that we described earlier. A scalable ATM LAN architecture uses all of the functions of a router in a distributed manner. This enables the routing function to scale economically with the ATM network. A distributed router architecture separates the packet-forwarding functions from the routing functions. Routing functions are processor-intensive, but are performed on a relatively infrequent basis. Packet-forwarding functions, on the other hand, require little processing but high performance. In a distributed router, the packet-forwarding functions are performed by network access devices, as shown in Figure 16-15.

ATM switches are designed to perform many of the functions routers perform—to select an optimal network path, to provide an efficient LAN and WAN interface, and to provide internal security, flow control, and bandwidth management. As a result, routers are evolving into edge devices with the principal function of connecting multiple LANs to the ATM switch.

The easiest way for a router to use ATM is to use PVCs through the switched fabric. But this negates two of ATM's greatest strengths: dynamic connection and bandwidth allocation, as we discussed earlier in this chapter.

**Figure 16-14.**   Router bottlenecks in ATM networks

## ATM Virtual Routers

Although edge routers are the router of choice among ATM vendors these days, much of the industry is buzzing with talk of a new kind of ATM router called a virtual router. A virtual router works very differently from an edge router. It combines a central route server and a number of multilayer switches—hardware-based devices that are nearly as fast as a conventional switch that works on the MAC layer, but much smarter—that link existing LANs. The thinking behind this virtual architecture recognizes that conventional routers are a bottleneck because, as we mentioned earlier, they calculate routes on a packet-by-packet basis. In a virtual router, on the other hand, LAN interconnection is achieved by the multilayer switch.

The multilayer switch forwards on the basis of MAC or Network layer packet fields. But it doesn't handle the route discovery and topology updates. These functions are

**Figure 16-15.**    A distributed router architecture

managed by the route server. Each port on the multilayer switch can be assigned its own subnet address, just as with a conventional router. As well, just as with an edge router, multiple ports can share the same subnet address. The route server runs the routing protocols and maintains a picture of the ATM and internetwork topologies. The route server can even act as a broadcast server and resolve address queries. As far as the end stations are concerned, the virtual router performs all the functions of a physical router: protocol processing, bridging, routing, and filtering.

# EXPECT TO PHASE IT IN

ATM is currently a very costly technology, so widespread deployment throughout your network is probably prohibitively expensive. As well, most of your segments don't require its 155Mbps to 622Mbps bandwidth. Therefore, migration to a switched network should be considered a process, a series of evolutionary steps as new technologies are phased in. So, plan to implement it in phases: first the backbones (especially campus backbones), video-intensive segments, and even trunked voice traffic from the PBX switches.

A transition to ATM will require consideration of the protocol suites at both specific sites and the overall enterprise. In some cases, ATM will initially be limited to a few directly connected workstations, while the rest take advantage of ATM in the backbone, enabling high-speed access to shared resources such as servers. This means that legacy network access to ATM will be important.

An incremental approach to ATM migration combines the best of the various technologies by enhancing existing network investments in three ways:

▼    ATM deployment extends the life of the installed base of network equipment by boosting performance.

■    Combined with such capabilities as LAN Emulation, ATM enhances network management and operations by allowing virtual network configurations.

▲    Incremental upgrades keep investment and technical risks low while ATM technology matures.

Figures 16-16 through 16-18 show one way to phase in ATM. It begins with implementing an ATM backbone.

Next, the network plan progresses to add ATM workgroup segments employing LAN Emulation to enable all network users to communicate with one another.

Finally, a collapsed router backbone—a single, high-performance router—connects multiple segments into a logical network.

# Desktop Migration Issues

Although ATM is usually considered primarily a backbone solution, most ATM networks are currently workgroups in which workstations and servers are connected directly to an ATM switch. Though ATM workgroups are usually small in size and centralized geographically, thus simplifying implementation, there are still several issues to consider.

## Media Support

Review your existing network infrastructure. Most ATM products currently run over multimode fiber and unshielded twisted-pair Category 5 copper at rates ranging from 25Mbps to 155Mbps. Due to the attenuation characteristics of copper, the maximum distance for Category 5 cable runs is typically 100 meters. Multimode fiber, on the other hand, has a maximum cable length of 2,000 meters. Be sure your cable plan meets these requirements.

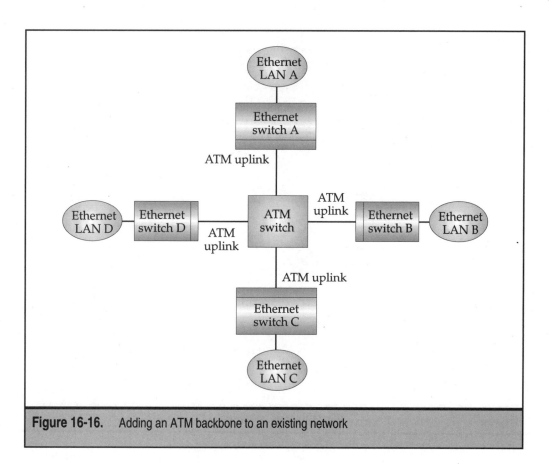

**Figure 16-16.**    Adding an ATM backbone to an existing network

## Application Support

Can your existing applications run over an ATM network? Because ATM is a lower-level protocol, this is usually not a problem. Most commonly, these applications are TCP/IP-based or based on PCs, Novell NetWare, or Microsoft Windows. However, are the applications you plan to use optimized to take advantage of ATM's dedicated bandwidth and data prioritization capabilities? To get the full benefit of ATM, whenever possible, choose applications that support these features.

### Computer Compatibility

In an ATM workgroup, each workstation must have an ATM network interface card (NIC). The NIC must be compatible with the bus type of the workstation, as well as with both the workstation and network operating systems. It is important that the NIC has been tested with both the type of workstation and the type of ATM switches you are using.

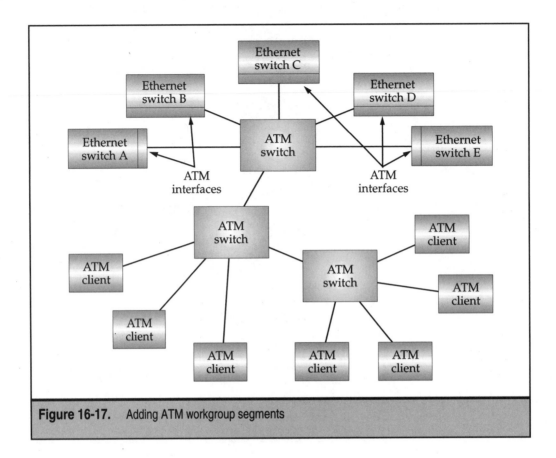

**Figure 16-17.** Adding ATM workgroup segments

## WAN Integration Issues

Although you can often integrate ATM into wide area networks without replacing any equipment, you will need some additional equipment, a thorough knowledge of applicable ATM interfaces, and a lot of careful planning.

There are four primary protocols required for successful internetworking over the wide area. They are:

▼ Public user-to-network interface (UNI)

■ Public network-to-network interface (NNI)

■ Intercarrier interface (ICI)

▲ Data exchange interface (DXI)

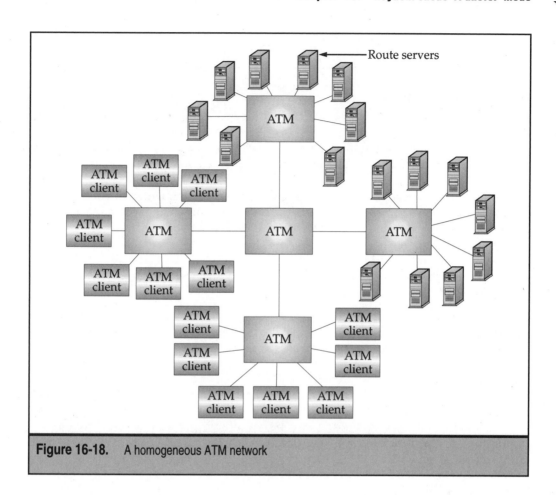

**Figure 16-18.**    A homogeneous ATM network

## Public User-to-Network Interface (UNI)

As we discussed earlier, ATM's UNI protocol provides multiple service classes and bandwidth reservation established during call setup of a switched virtual connection. The UNI defines the interoperability between the user equipment and the ATM switch port. A public UNI defines the interface between a public service ATM network, and usually supports a SONET or DS3 interface.

## Public Network-to-Network Interface (NNI)

As we also mentioned earlier, the NNI protocol provides virtual connection arbitration, congestion control, and topology management for private or public ATM network connections.

### Intercarrier Interface (ICI)

The ICI defines internetworking mechanisms on wide area ATM networks.

### Data Exchange Interface (DXI)

The DXI provides a standard ATM interface for legacy equipment. It supports routing over ATM because DXI is based on packets rather than cells. It uses high-level datalink control (HDLC) framing so, unlike cell-based interfaces, it needs no additional hardware to transmit packet-based traffic. Therefore, it is the protocol that allows you to connect to an existing ATM network.

To illustrate how each of these interfaces will affect the implementation of an ATM network, look at the network in Figure 16-19. This shows how a wide area ATM backbone might be integrated into an existing FDDI and 10Base-T network.

FDDI has an aggregate backbone bandwidth of 100Mbps, shared by all attached devices. The wide area ATM switch in this illustration has eight ports, each 155Mbps. Because those 155Mbps are dedicated to each attached device, the aggregate bandwidth is 8 multiplied by 155Mbps, or approximately 1.2Gbps.

**NOTE:** The actual aggregate bandwidth of this example will fall somewhere between 155Mbps and 1.2Gbps, depending on the traffic patterns and usage.

An ATM UNI was installed in both the FDDI router and the 10Base-T switch so both devices could be connected to the ATM switch. The WAN connection to the ATM switch is through a DXI to a service multiplexer, typically a special CSU/DSU. Thanks to its DXI, in addition to multiplexing traffic onto the wide area link, the service multiplexer performs AAL segmentation and reassembly, allowing non-ATM-capable devices to access the ATM network replacing hardware.

## Other Issues to Consider

Implementing a backbone with ATM involves many of the same issues and concerns as with any other protocol. Some of these are as follows:

▼ Security

■ Fault tolerance

■ Bandwidth requirements

▲ Management systems

## Availability of ATM Carrier Services

One of the big challenges you may face when implementing a wide area ATM network is finding a carrier service that both offers ATM all the way to the end user and is reasonably

**Figure 16-19.**    A wide area ATM network

priced. Although most digital service providers offer ATM, it isn't widely available yet because of a lack of strong, widespread demand at the end-user point of demarcation. Contracts may be available from service providers to ensure both availability and pricing, but obtaining one may require some persistence and negotiating skill.

Common carrier service providers acknowledge that ATM is definitely the future of wide area network communication. They understand that it erases the barriers between LANs and WANs, which are

▼  The drop in throughput between LAN protocols and public networks protocols

▲  Delays caused by store-and-forward WAN connection devices like routers

However, not all local exchange carriers (LECs) and interexchange carriers (IXCs) have installed integrated ATM/SONET digital networks to offer economical virtual private data network services. When they do, you can assume they will pass the heavy expense of installing these new networks on to the consumer. The good news is that ATM carries more traffic at reduced cost, which will eventually result in savings for the consumer. But that may be quite far off in the future, so be prepared for large ATM carrier service expenses for the wide area.

## THE PROMISED LAN

Overall, ATM holds excellent promise for nearly every network. It provides performance and functions never before available for:

▼  Electronic funds transfer

■  Voice annotation of memos

■  Interactive training videos

▲  Design and manufacturing development in which collaborative efforts involve complex data objects residing on a variety of different, geographically dispersed processors

ATM probably is the future of transport protocols and networking in general. However, the future is not now. As we mentioned earlier, many vendors have been quick to announce plans for ATM products and systems, but as of this writing, there simply aren't any end-to-end open, viable, interoperable ATM systems available.

# CHAPTER 17

## Digital Subscriber Line Services and Cable Modems

The new regulatory environment brought about by the Telecommunications Act of 1996 offers new business opportunities for telecommunications companies. Among these new opportunities is the ability for telephone companies and cable television companies to offer interactive information services over their existing networks—most notably for Internet access. This is already happening in some areas. The technologies that are making this happen are digital subscriber line (DSL) and cable modems.

While digital subscriber line services and cable modems are targeted mostly for home use in both technology and pricing, they may also be an important high-speed wide area networking service for telecommuters, small businesses, and businesses located in suburban areas. Of course, it's hard to determine from all the babble about these technologies whether, when, and how cost-effective these services will ultimately be. Therefore, I think it's in your best interests to read on.

# DIGITAL SUBSCRIBER LINE (DSL)

Digital subscriber line services are a recent product offering (generally under trial circumstances) from local exchange carriers that show a great deal of promise as high-speed Internet access services.

DSL services provide simplex (one-way) digital transmission over two pairs of wire—the same twisted-pair cable found in millions of telephone subscribers' homes today. DSL is an end-to-end technology, meaning the signal doesn't require conversion from analog to digital. Instead, DSLs use intelligent adapters at each of the circuits to split the existing twisted-pair cabling into two channels: upstream and downstream. The upstream channel transmits data from the subscriber's premises to the telephone company's network facility. The downstream channel transmits data from the telephone company's network to the subscriber's premises. All the while, the telephone service in the subscriber's premises remains virtually the same.

Besides using existing cable plant and networks, DSL has the benefit of bringing tremendous bandwidth to the subscriber's premises. Downstream traffic can be delivered at speeds of up to 60Mbps (using very high bit-rate DSL, described later) and upstream traffic can be transmitted at speeds ranging between 576Kbps and 1Mbps.

Furthermore, DSLs are simple to configure. This will come as a relief to anyone who has struggled with configuring and using Integrated Services Digital Network. A DSL is far easier to configure and use than ISDN.

Finally, because of all the advantages we've listed so far—using existing infrastructure and ease of deployment—DSL services should be fairly inexpensive, especially in terms of bandwidth for the buck. Some industry analysts expect DSL service prices to settle at about $40/month—for unlimited access—within a year or two after they are widely available.

However, therein lies the biggest drawback for DSL services. They aren't widely available yet. While GTE and other big players in the telecommunications industry have begun consumer trials of DSL services, at the time of this writing the trials were still underway and no resulting conclusions or projections about broad commercial DSL service offerings had been reported.

One of the other main drawbacks of DSL services is that they are distance-sensitive. This means that it is really good only for providing service over short distances. However, the signal can maintain its strength for up to 18,000 feet (with asymmetric digital subscriber line, depending upon the bandwidth it's supporting) from the central office without amplification or conditioning. However, this 18,000-feet maximum distance still allows telephone companies to reach over 85 percent of their service areas.

## DSL Equipment

DSL signal transmission requires a new device on both the user and the phone company ends of the line. This device functions more like a network adapter than a modem (because the DSL signal is digital from end to end), and right now is fairly expensive and scarce.

For example, ADSL adapters currently cost anywhere from $900 to $1,500 each, and are available from only a handful of manufacturers, including Westell Technologies and Amati Communications Corporation. However, many reports from the press and industry analysts predict that in 1999 we will be able to buy ADSL adapters for under $300.

## DSL Service Offerings

Because it is a digital signal, DSL services can divvy the composite two-way bandwidth pretty much any way the designers want to. This helps explain why digital subscriber line services come in a variety of different types:

▼ Asymmetric digital subscriber line (ADSL)

■ High-bit-rate digital subscriber line (HDSL)

■ Very high-bit-rate digital subscriber line (VDSL)

■ Symmetric digital subscriber line (SDSL)

▲ Rate-adaptive digital subscriber line (RADSL)

## Asymmetric Digital Subscriber Line (ADSL)

Asymmetric digital subscriber line is probably the DSL about which you've heard the most. It's been fairly popular with the press and industry analysts, and is currently the subject of a six-month trial in Irving, Texas by telecommunications service giant GTE. In this trial, GTE is monitoring the success its 30 subscriber participants are having in getting the new, high-speed service to work over GTE's existing cable plant.

ADSL was originally developed to deliver full-motion video from telephone companies to their subscribers' homes. Therefore, ADSL employs what is known as forward error correction. Digital video transmission applications currently can't employ error-control procedures on the Network layer. Forward error correction ensures that the line is free of noise and errors before the data is transmitted. However, forward error correction also makes ADSL very attractive for all data transmission, because it reduces data errors caused by line noise.

ADSL is called "asymmetric" because it doesn't provide equal bandwidth on both upstream and downstream channels. Taking into account that—for now, at least—most network users download more information than they upload, the original version of ADSL provides downstream bandwidth of 1.544Mbps (the same rate as a T1) and upstream bandwidth in the range of 64Kbps (the same rate as ISDN). However, current versions deliver downstream bandwidth of 6Mbps and upstream bandwidth in a range between 576Kbps and 640Kbps. What's more, ADSL network data transmission can take place simultaneously with voice telephone calls—over the same telephone pair. It does this via a multiplexing technique that reserves a third channel—4kHz of the bandwidth—for a voice telephone conversation.

Because ADSL is deployed over an existing network infrastructure, it's simple and inexpensive. Therefore, once commercially available, you should be able to implement it quickly just by installing an ADSL adapter and connecting to your telephone company's network (they'll have installed an ADSL at their POP).

Currently, there are two wholly incompatible ADSL signaling standards competing for dominance: carrierless amplitude modulation (CAP) and discrete multitone (DMT).

## Carrierless Amplitude Modulation (CAP)

CAP is the modulation technique used by cable TV companies. It employs phase and amplitude modulation (FM) methods, as shown in Figure 17-1, that transmit a lone signal down the cable at speeds of up to 1.5Mbps. The major proponent of CAP is AT&T, which gives it quite a bit of clout, indeed.

## Discrete Multitone (DMT)

DMT is the modulation technique endorsed by the American National Standards Institute (ANSI). It was developed more recently than CAP, so DMT product has just

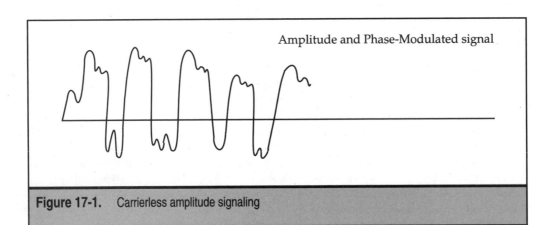

Amplitude and Phase-Modulated signal

**Figure 17-1.** Carrierless amplitude signaling

started appearing on the market. DMT signaling divides the total bandwidth into 4kHz channels—into 256 of these channels, as shown in Figure 17-2. These smaller channels each carry a portion of the transmitted data. All of the data carried by each of these small channels is reassembled at the receiving end of the channel.

ADSL using DMT lends itself to supporting 32-bit multitasking, multithreaded operating systems. Because all its channels are multiplexed on the fly into slower 4kHz channels, you should be able to perform multiple simultaneous real-time, online operations.

No doubt all these "standards wars" are a little scary. The last thing you need is a proprietary wide area network link, especially one upon which all your users rely (such as for Internet access). However, don't worry. To help bring about a lasting peace in the standards uprising, in 1994 the ADSL Forum was formed. Its charter is to promote ADSL standards and generally spread the ADSL gospel, and it now has 60 or more members from throughout the telecommunications industry.

Among the ADSL Forum's current priority projects is a bit interface for connecting ADSL directly to ATM. In fact, the dynamic bandwidth allocation of DMT will probably also enable ADSL to promote widespread use of ATM, easily allocating as much or as little bandwidth as necessary to accommodate switched streams of 53-byte cells. In fact, the ATM Forum has recognized ADSL as one of the supported Physical layer transmission protocols to run ATM over unshielded twisted-pair media.

## High-Bit-Rate Digital Subscriber Line (HDSL)

HDSL is probably the best known DSL service. As it was originally designed, HDSL employed two pairs of copper wire to transmit 1.544Mbps bandwidth in each direction. It could support these two-way T1-speed transmissions for a distance of up to 12,000 feet, and yet at a fraction of the cost of conventional T1 service. As such, HDSL shows some of its greatest potential in carrying cost-effective telephone service to hard-to-reach areas.

HDSL isn't without its problems, however. In addition to supporting only 2/3 the distance of ADSL, it also requires two pairs of cable.

**Figure 17-2.** Discrete multitone signal

**NOTE:** There is a version of HDSL that uses only one pair of copper wire, but it only supports two-way transmissions of up to 768Kbps. This is still sufficient for most data transfer needs, including most videoconferencing.

Another problem with HDSL is that it can't support voice traffic nearly as easily as ADSL does. To conduct a regular voice conversation over HDSL would require special converters and modems that ADSL just doesn't require.

## Very High-Bit-Rate Digital Subscriber Line (VDSL)

Originally conceived as a replacement technology for protocols that required fiber-optic cable and coaxial cable, VDSL offers downstream bandwidth in the range of 51Mbps to 55Mbps. It is very much like ADSL in that it divides the transmitted signal among multiple channels that dynamically allocate bandwidth, which can transmit ISDN or voice conversations.

Its upstream channel supports throughput of 1.6Mbps to 2.3Mbps to the network. However, VDSL can only carry these high bandwidth signals for a short distance—only for a range of about 1,000 feet to 6,000 feet—which means that there may be a very limited number of places where its deployment makes sense.

VDSL is experiencing the same struggle between CAP and DMT signaling that plagues ADSL. However, VDSL is nowhere close to being a standards-based technology. Right now, VDSL is far from being commercially available, standard or not. One reason is that currently the silicon circuitry for VDSL adapters is extremely expensive. There isn't yet a specification for mass producing VDSL silicon. However, the most promising entry in the race to develop low-cost VDSL chips is Amati Communications Corporation, which has a strategic relationship with NEC Corporation to develop a VDSL transceiver on one silicon chip.

## Symmetric Digital Subscriber Line (SDSL)

This is the version of ADSL that supports equal bandwidth in both upstream and downstream channels. Right now, SDLS supports a symmetric bandwidth of 384Kbps per channel. While this is much slower than the other varieties of digital subscriber line service, it's still more than sufficient for videoconferencing. As of this writing, however, no commercial trials of SDLS had yet begun.

Just as with ADSL, VDSL has competing, incompatible signaling standards vying for dominance. Originally, there were two additional signaling schemes besides carrierless amplitude signaling (CAP) and discrete multitone signaling (DMT), but recently the battle seems to have come down to these two signaling standards.

**NOTE:** Multiple contending signaling schemes are really more a problem for equipment vendors than for end users. Your telephone company will tell you which signaling type it supports, and you'll just go purchase equipment that supports that type of signaling. Still, multiple signaling schemes add to the complexity and confusion of implementing DSLs, as well as limiting the interoperability of DSL systems.

## Rate-Adaptive Digital Subscriber Line (RADSL)

Rate-adaptive digital subscriber line is a type of ADSL service that adapts itself to the network over which it transmits data. This means that RADSL adjusts its speed based on the quality of the signal and the distance over which that signal must be transmitted. RADSL supports a wide variety of fallback digital rates on one line, and it can adapt to any of those rates on the fly. Therefore, no matter how far you have to transmit a complex signal, RADSL will make sure it arrives intact.

Telephone companies originally developed RADSL to deliver movies to subscribers' homes. The downstream channel of RADSL can support transmissions of up to 7Mbps, while its downstream channel can transmit from the users' premises to the network at bandwidths up to 1Mbps.

Oddly enough, RADSL also suffers from the CAP vs. DMT struggle. It would seem on the surface that the adaptive nature of RADSL would lend itself almost exclusively to the multiple 4kHz channels of DMT. However, currently only a couple of vendors, Paradyne and Westell, are offering commercial RADSL, which is the major proponent of CAP encoding. Again, I'm confident that the capable offices of the ADSL Forum can help resolve these signaling standards conflicts and let RADSL vendors and subscribers get down to business.

# CABLE MODEMS

Cable modems are just that: modems that connect your computer or local area network to the community antenna television (CATV) cable network. Cable modems promise throughput rates of 40Mbps downstream and 2.5Mbps and higher upstream. Unfortunately, most CATV cable plants aren't two-way active. That means they can't support both upstream and downstream data traffic. After all, they were designed as a data delivery system, not as an interactive wide area link. In fact, to work around this one-way infrastructure, some cable modems such as the Surfboard from General Instruments use the coaxial cable infrastructure combined with a traditional telephone modem. The cable provides the downstream path, as it was designed to do, while the upstream data transfer is handled by the modem.

A cable modem by its very nature works differently from a digital subscriber line service. DSL services provide each user with a dedicated connection. Cable modem subscribers, on the other hand, will share an Internet feed (see Chapter 5 on the WAN and the Internet) with all other subscribers in their region. This Internet feed has bandwidth equal to one cable television channel, with data packets addressed to all subscribers traveling over the same channel. Each data packet contains a user ID in its header, and your cable modem will pick out only those packets addressed to you.

If you think this sounds like a local area network, you're right. In fact, a lot of the proposed cable modem and CATV Internet access systems use a transport protocol that is similar to 10Base-T in function.

Of course, this means that cable modems are going to have the same usage-based traffic problems that collision-based LAN transport protocols have. The more users on the network, the less bandwidth is going to be available to you. Therefore, even though your cable company may tell you that you have a 10Mbps wide area connection, you're only going to get a piece of that connection. And the more users that are connected to your channel and actively using it, the smaller the slice of the channel's bandwidth that is going to be available to you.

Furthermore, there is currently no standard cable modem format. And there probably won't be one for a while, because so many cable companies are going to have to upgrade their plants to support two-way connections that no one knows what the cable system of the future is going to look like.

# DSL VS. CABLE MODEMS

So which is the better option, a DSL service or a cable modem?

For those of you who are occupying buildings in a central business district, it seems pretty clear that you'll have DSL service available before cable modems are a real option. After all, CATV cable networks were developed and designed primarily to serve residential areas, so chances are your cable companies aren't concentrating on upgrading their networks in the business districts. Furthermore, don't forget that telephone companies won't have to upgrade their networks the way cable companies will.

However, both CATV operators and telephone companies will have to upgrade their facilities to become regular Internet service providers (ISPs). This means that they'll need routers and high-speed service facilities at all of their central offices.

Furthermore, DSL service, because it depends on only a standard cable pair, will let you pick and choose among DSL providers the same way you can now pick and choose among long-distance providers. The CATV cable modem service, however, is provided only by your local CATV operator—and only according to the transmission techniques they choose to offer.

On the other hand, if you are located in a suburban area where DSL and cable modem service are equal possibilities, remember that DSL service is several months, or even years (depending upon where you live), from widespread commercial availability. Cable modem service is being offered now—provided your CATV operator's infrastructure can handle two-way transmission. In that case, remember that upgrades to CATV plants will be expensive, and that expense will be recaptured from you, the users.

On the other hand, remember also that there are a lot more cable modem vendors than DSL adapter vendors, and more competition will likely keep prices lower.

Of course, chances are that wherever you are, either of these services is a long way off. They both have significant benefits, while they both have real and present delays and pitfalls. My rule of thumb is that DSLs will probably become a very viable and popular high-speed wide area service for businesses, while cable modems will be the darling of telecommuters and home businesses—until increased usage clogs the networks and makes performance unacceptably slow. Both, however, have the potential to speed up wide area network access—especially Internet access—so both bear watching.

# PART IV

## Network
## Construction Ahead

# CHAPTER 18

## How to Build Fast and Secure Intranets and Extranets

Ⅰf you listen to the buzz, you've probably heard that if you aren't running an intranet, you're not even in the networking game. And extranets are *the only way* to do business outside your enterprise. This may have many of you a little concerned. After all, what *is* this magical thing called an intranet that separates the players from the spectators in the networking arena?

# INTRANETS DEMYSTIFIED

Despite all the hype and mystery surrounding the term, an *intranet* is just a network. It's the *type of traffic* that runs over it that makes it different. An intranet is a local network that runs TCP/IP and other Internet-related protocols. An intranet also features Web servers to publish content and allow access to back-end systems. The client interface for an intranet is a Web browser, and its mail system is Internet mail. In other words, an intranet is local network that supports Internet network, messaging, and application protocols.

What an intranet offers is a cross-platform, open architecture with great interoperability for UNIX, Macintosh, and Windows clients. It lets you develop new applications and systems quickly and at relatively low cost. Properly designed, they can provide real-time multimedia, such as videoconferencing and live voice conversations. What it doesn't offer is magic.

## Making New Rules

So, if an intranet is defined by the type of data traffic and the applications deployed on servers throughout the network, rather than the design of the network infrastructure, why all the fear and trepidation over the network design? Well, intranets have brought about two changes that have a big impact on physical network design:

▼ Increased internetwork traffic

▲ Increased bandwidth requirements

### Increased Internetwork Traffic

The old 80/20 rule of networking has been turned inside out. When local area networks first emerged, 80 percent of all data traffic was local. In other words, almost all traffic was delivered to the same segment on which it originated. The advent of intranets has changed that, so that now at most 20 percent of data traffic is addressed to nodes on the same segment on which it originated.

### Increased Bandwidth Requirements

Not only the destination of traffic has changed, but also the nature of the traffic itself. The underlying application technologies in intranets and the Internet require much more bandwidth than the simple print and file services of LANs of yore. Intranets have made such things as videoconferencing and live newsfeeds a minute-to-minute possibility. And this has spurred demand for even more real-time, rich-graphic, multimedia information.

What enabled this technical revolution? More importantly, how do you design a network to support it?

# INTRANETS: ENABLING TECHNOLOGIES

To understand how these applications have started gobbling bandwidth, let's take a look at the technologies that make intranets what they are. Essentially, there are four technologies that enable an intranet environment:

▼ HTML

■ HTTP

■ Component technology

▲ Push

## Hypertext Markup Language (HTML)

*Hypertext Markup Language* (HTML) is the programming language used on the Internet to create Web pages. *Hypertext* is nonlinear text. This means that it lets you jump to a pointer or another source of information simply by clicking on it, rather than requiring you to scroll sequentially through a document until you arrive at the information you want.

Again, there is nothing magical about HTML. An HTML file is just a simple text file with embedded codes that are stored on Web servers. Upon initial access to a Web site, the Web server sends the client a default or *home* Web page in the HTML format. This page may have no links, or it may contain links to other pages at the same or other Web sites.

Coding HTML files is so easy—as easy as using word processor. In fact, you can create one using nothing more than a simple text editor and a few HTML codes. The codes largely consist of formatting instructions and pointers to other sources of information. When you open the source code of a Web page, you see HTML code. The next time you're on the World Wide Web, go to your favorite Web page. Click on Source from the View menu of your browser. For example, Figure 18-1 shows the Osborne/McGraw-Hill home page.

Figure 18-2 shows the source code for the same page.

The items enclosed in angle brackets are the embedded HTML codes, also known as *tags*. A tag marks the beginning of each format change. The end of a format change is indicated with a tag that contains a forward slash. For example, the title format of the page begins with <TITLE> and ends with </TITLE>.

Try this yourself. Type the following in a text editor or processor, then open it with any Web browser:

```
<HTML>
<HEAD>
<TITLE> Your Name Home Page</TITLE>
</HEAD>
```

```
<BODY>
<H1> Meet Your Name</H1>
You've probably always wanted to know someone like me, and now's your chance.
</BODY>
</HTML>
```

Of course, there are many development tools available for coding HTML documents. However, the principle is the same. Once you have created the text file with embedded codes and saved it, you can open it and view it with a Web browser.

## HTML Access and Network Performance

So, what's so dangerous about an HTML file? After all, text files with a few codes should pose no threat to a gigabit backbone! Well, HTML files, which have the filename extension "HTML" or "HTM," can display far more than text. They can contain sound, images, and/or other multimedia objects. And to further stress network traffic, these objects are not stored in the document itself. Rather, the HTML document contains a

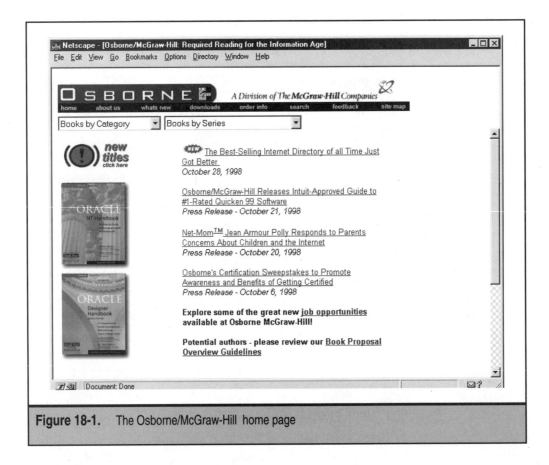

**Figure 18-1.** The Osborne/McGraw-Hill home page

```
<html>
<head>
<title>Osborne/McGraw-Hill: Required Reading for the Information Age</title>
</head>


<Frameset Rows="100, *" frameborder="no" border=0>


<FRAME SRC="topnav.html" name="topnav" scrolling="NO" NORESIZE border=0>

<Frame src="splash.htm" name="content" noresize border=0>

</Frameset>


<NOFRAME> This web site requires Netscape 2.0 or better or a similar frames
compatible browser. Please <A HREF="http://home.netscape.com">download the
newest version of Netscape</a>to view these documents.</Noframe>



</html>
```

**Figure 18-2.**   Source code for the Osborne/McGraw-Hill home page

pointer or reference to an image or sound clip or other multimedia object. These objects can reside in the same directory as the HTML document, or in a different directory, or even on an entirely different server! When a user accesses the HTML document, the pointer also pulls up the file containing the multimedia object.

So, an HTML page is much more than just a text file with some embedded codes. It is comprised of the HTML file as well as any external files containing multimedia objects—provided, of course, that the servers containing these objects are all online and accessible. This mean that servers containing HTML documents—especially heavily accessed ones—should be connected with a switched mesh of high-bandwidth connections.

## HTML Developments and Extensions

While many organizations are working to refine and develop HTML, Microsoft and Netscape—the two leading Web browser vendors—seem to lead the pack. Some recent improvements to HTML features are as follows:

▼ Scripts can automatically access related Web pages, thus taking strain off the Web server.

■ Dynamic HTML describes a combination of HTML, style sheets, and scripts that allow documents to be animated. The W3C (more on that below) is working to make sure vendor solutions are interoperable.

■ HTML Math displays complex mathematical and technical notations.

■ Web pages can be customized. With proper access, users can edit Web pages and save them on the original Web server.

▲ There is now support for international alphabets and multilingual Web pages.

Both companies have also developed their own proprietary "dynamic HTML." This extension of HTML combines scripts, style sheets, and *document animations*. The World Wide Web Consortium (also known as the W3C) is a standards body working to ensure that both companies' dynamic HTML solutions are interoperable. To that end, the W3C has developed and put forth what it calls the Document Object Model platform. This allows scripts and routines to access and update the content and structure of documents automatically. It will also let these routines process information in the Web page and incorporate the results into the original page.

As you can see, these improvements will make HTML more functional, but may very well put more stress on your network as more and different types of multimedia objects are more easily available to Web pages. Therefore, it's important to stress that Web servers—especially popular ones—must be connected with the highest-capacity network links possible.

# Hypertext Transfer Protocol (HTTP)

As we said earlier, intranets use Web technologies like the TCP/IP protocol to transport information between clients and servers. Intranet servers are repositories for HTML documents that can contain hyperlinks to other places in the same document, to other documents in the same directory, or to documents located on other servers. The protocol that lets a Web browser access a server to request HTML documents is known as *Hypertext Transfer Protocol (HTTP)*. In short, HTML is the document formatting language for intranets, and HTTP is the command and control protocol that sets up communication between a client and a server and passes commands between.

To be more specific, HTTP processes hypermedia links among HTML documents and provides client/server communications on the intranet and on the Web. When a client points a Web browser to an IP address or server, the browser finds the address on the intranet and makes a connection to the designated Web server. First a lookup is performed at a domain name server (DNS) that knows the server name and its IP address. This address is then returned to the browser, which then makes a connection to the server.

RFC 1945, which describes HTTP, sings its praises: " . . .the Hypertext Transfer Protocol (HTTP) is an application-level protocol with the . . .speed necessary for distributed, collaborative, hypermedia information systems. It is a generic, stateless, object-oriented protocol which can be used for many tasks, such as name servers and distributed object management system, through extension of its request methods (commands)."

Figure 18-3 shows how this works. When an intranet client requests information from a server, the server responds by sending HTML information to the client. When the information arrives at the client, its Web browser reads, formats, and displays the data. The connection between client and server is established by HTTP.

For heightened security, HTTP may establish the connection through Secure Sockets Layer (SSL), Secure HTTP (S-HTTP) protocol, or some other secure protocol. S-HTTP is a secure version of HTTP that provides more secure transactions between intranet clients and servers. For further security, the client and server can exchange encrypted information over a secure channel. We'll talk more about security, encryption, and secure channels later in this chapter.

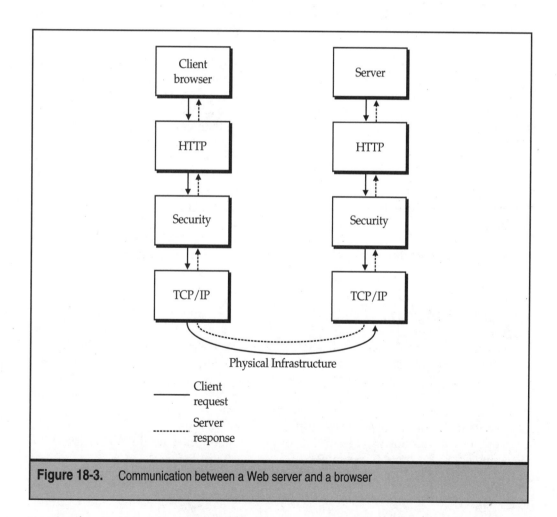

**Figure 18-3.**   Communication between a Web server and a browser

## The Evolution of HTTP

HTTP has evolved over the years. This is good news for intranet users, but can be bad news for network managers who have to keep response times low. We'll show you what we mean.

The original version of HTTP, first deployed in 1990, was called HTTP/0.9. It was a lean client/server protocol that provided basic data transfer functions. It was later replaced by version 1.0. Essentially, HTTP 1.0 supported MIME message formats, which could provide more information about the data being transferred between client and server. More data meant more traffic, and intranets started slowing down.

**HTTP1.1 AND S-HTTP (SECURE HTTP)**    Web browsers and servers don't maintain persistent links during a session. This means that once the text of a page is transmitted from the server to the browser, the link is terminated. If the browser requests another object from the Web page, that object is downloaded as a separate transmission. In other words, each mouse click initiates a new, separate transmission. This means a lot of overhead in setting up and taking down links, which means a lot of traffic clogging up the intranet.

HTTP version 1.1 helps solve some of this by providing the capability for persistent connections and pipelining. This makes the connections between browsers and servers more streamlined and efficient. With HTTP 1.1, servers can transmit multiple objects to a client over a single TCP connection using larger packets. This reduces overhead. Furthermore, HTTP 1.1 allows a server to send more than one object in the course of a single connection.

This new version of HTTP also reduces network traffic by adding cache management to browsers. Under HTTP 1.0, when a browser refreshed a Web page, it downloaded the entire page. With HTTP 1.1, the browser compares the server page to the page it holds in cache. It identifies those items that have changed, and only downloads those items.

All these efficiency features reduce network traffic. In fact, HTTP 1.1 can improve network performance, in terms of number of packets and download times, by as much as 50 percent. Therefore, HTTP 1.1 is the choice for optimal intranet performance.

# Component Technology

*Component technology* is *the* applications environment on intranets. In fact, a distributed computing environment such as an intranet is an ideal place to deploy component technology. In a component application environment, applications are split up into smaller components (also known as *objects* or *applets*), which are then distributed to users. These smaller components are easy to download and updated as needed. They also have an interface that allows programmers to combine them with one another to build complete applications. They are kept in sync with each other by *object request brokers* that coordinate the components throughout the network.

Component technology has a lot of advantages over traditional application development technology. For example:

▼ **Ease of enhancement** You can add new components any time to enhance and expand application functions and features.

■ **Ease of updating** Rather than updating an entire application, you can update only individual components.

■ **Shorter development cycles** You can reuse existing to build new applications, reducing development time.

▲ **Efficient use of resources** Users don't have to install an entire application. They can install only the components they need. As well, by using standard languages like Java, you can combine components from different vendors to make new applications.

Component software has changed the face of most corporate intranets as well as the Internet. You can get components from Web sites to expand the functionality of enterprise applications and utilities, making it quick and easy to get the latest technology. More important, component technology makes it possible to design multitiered environments in which applications are broken up into different pieces that run on different computers and operating environments. For example, application services such as information retrieval, transaction monitoring, and application logic can run on different computing platforms, yet communicate across the network to present a unified application interface.

## Component Development Languages

The two common development languages for component technology are Java, from Sun Microsystems, and ActiveX from Microsoft. The Web is chock full of components available for download for both languages. Some are simple components, such as three-dimensional spinning logo components. Others are more complex, such as financial or scientific calculation components. When you download a component to your Web browser, the component stays on your computer. It executes when you access the server containing the information it was designed to process. If the component ever needs to be updated, the new components are downloaded automatically the next time you access that server.

## How the Pieces Fit Together

The component software development model consists of five pieces:

▼ Components

■ Containers

■ Scripts

■ Transaction monitors

▲ Object Request Brokers (ORBs)

**COMPONENTS**   Components are pieces of applications. More specifically, they are the programming code that makes up a piece of an application.

**CONTAINERS**   *Containers* are programming "shells" where components are assembled. The most popular containers are ActiveX for the ActiveX component development language, and JavaBeans for the Java component development language. When a component is placed in a container, the component registers its interfaces so that other components within the same system know about it. Then the component publishes its interfaces so that other objects know how to interact with it.

**SCRIPTING LANGUAGES**   Scripts are the languages in which component programmers write instructions that make components interact in a particular way. Again, the most popular scripting languages are ActiveX Script for the ActiveX component development environment and JavaScript for the Java component development environment.

**TRANSACTION MONITORS**   In transaction-based applications, such as financial applications, it's critical that the components are coordinated to ensure that the transaction is completed successfully. For example, transferring money from one account to another is a two-step transaction. First, funds are withdrawn from one account. Second, funds are deposited in the other account. Suppose that the first step is completed, but due to a network error the second is not. Unless the first step is "rolled back," there is no money in either account. Transaction monitoring systems keep track of such multipart transactions and ensure that failed transactions are returned to their original state.

An example of a transaction monitoring system is Microsoft's Transaction Server. It both processes and monitors transactions in a component application environment. Therefore, it operates as a transaction-based *object request broker*.

**OBJECT REQUEST BROKERS (ORBS)**   Components communicate with one another in object environments through *object request brokers* (ORBs). ORBs coordinate the registration, publishing, and execution of components, keeping them synchronized with one another across the network. An example of a common ORB is the one used in *Common Object Request Broker Architecture* (CORBA). CORBA is a cross-platform architecture that allows components written for different operating environments to work together.

## Push

Push technologies deliver information to network users without their specifically asking for it. This is a key technology for intranets, in which software must routinely be distributed to users' computers, or in which network users must regularly be informed of events.

**NOTE:**  Traditional data transfer that takes place when a client requests information from another computer is called pull.

In the beginning, push was the means by which one computer sent information to a known network address even though no request for the information had come from that network address. Software distribution or regular data updates are examples of this original push technique. Now, however, push is best known as a Web technology that advertisers and news services use to provide information to their subscribers automatically without a specific request for that information.

## Not All That Delivers Is Push

Here's how push technology works. Suppose a user, known as a *push client*, subscribes to a sports news service that employs push technology. This user wants an update every half-hour on the halftime and final scores of every basketball game being played in the United States. The sports news service will automatically send these scores to the user every 30 minutes.

But what appears to be push technology may not actually be so. Rather than having a push server initiate an update as server content changes and new information becomes available, these services have client software that actually initiates the communication by calling in unattended and requesting updated information in the users' specified areas of interest.

## Getting Pushy

Real push uses a technology called *IP multicast* to deliver information to subscribers. IP multicast assigns an IP Class D address, called a *multicast address*, to packets being sent out over the network. A Class D multicast address is 32 bits in length. The first 4 bits of the address identify it as a Class D address. The other 28 bits identify multicast groups.

Each multicast address defines a *channel* for broadcasting packets. A Class D address is something like a TV channel. When a host computer is assigned a Class D address, it is like selecting a particular channel on a TV set. The host computer receives packets being multicast by a particular source system or systems, just like a TV set receives signals from a particular TV station.

**NOTE:** Because there are over 250 million Class D addresses, there are potentially that many channels for multicasting information.

Host computers for subscribers that want to receive the information being broadcast are all assigned the same multicast address in conjunction with their regular, unique IP address. Once the multicast address is assigned to a computer, that computer has access to the multicast channel and can receive the information being sent over it. Host computers can be assigned more than one class D multicast address, so they can therefore receive information from multiple channels. Host computers can join or leave multicast channels at any time. As well, any host computer can send to multicast channels by sending packets addressed to a multicast group.

## Internet Group Management Protocol (IGMP)

Host computers subscribe to a multicast channel using the *Internet Group Management Protocol (IGMP)*. This is a protocol that manages communication between subscribing host computers and their local multicast routers. Subscribing host computers use IGMP to tell local multicast routers that they want to subscribe to or leave a particular multicast group. If the subscribing host computer is the last device on that local network that is a member of the multicast group, it will remove itself from the multicast group, thus reducing network traffic.

Another traffic-reducing feature of IGMP is the *host membership report*. A multicast router periodically broadcasts a query to its local network asking if any nodes still want to receive multicast transmissions. Subscribing host computers respond to this query with a host membership report stating to which multicast groups it belongs. If no subscribing host computers respond for a particular group, that group is dropped.

## More Ways That Push Reduces Traffic

Note that multicast sends only one copy of the information being pushed, which all subscribing host computers receive. These packets only travel through routers that are connected to subscribers or to other routers that are designated to receive a particular multicast. Remember, routers must support *the Internet Group Management Protocol* (IGMP) to transmit multicast packets. When a host computer transmits a multicast packet, the host computer's local router forwards the packet to multicast-enabled routers with attached networks that include members of the multicast group. This differs from broadcast technology, which sends a separate copy of the information to every host on the network. Clearly multicast reduces traffic over the intranet.

Push also reduces intranet traffic because the traffic resulting from requesting information is also eliminated. This is far more efficient than regular Web browsing, in which users cruise from Web site to Web site downloading pages. There is a flip side to this, however. As more users request frequent, regular delivery of information, network traffic will increase.

To avoid network resource crunches, you should carefully monitor how push technology uses your network's resources. Does everyone need to have football scores delivered every hour on the hour? How much of this pushed information is subsequently being stored on server or client hard drives? And is a steady flow of pushed information coming through the corporate firewall, choking out critical business traffic? Compression techniques can alleviate some of the traffic congestion. You can also configure push services to deliver only information that has changed, rather than entire Web pages. As well, whenever feasible you may want to schedule push updates to take place during low-traffic periods.

# EXTRANETS

Now that we've taken the mystery out of intranets and given you some pointers on how to keep their traffic running smoothly, let's move on to the next mysterious "net": *extranets*.

An extranet is basically an intranet connected to the intranet of another organization. The two (or more) intranets may be connected via the Internet or a private network. That's it—again, there's no magic here.

But there *is* a lot of work. Building an extranet requires a lot of planning coordination between the companies involved. Both partners must determine which data they will share, among which work groups, how they will share the data, and which applications they will use. Then the companies must establish security to enforce these decisions.

There are two defining characteristics of extranets:

▼   Standard data exchange formats

▲   Security

# Standard Data Exchange Formats

A *data exchange format* is simply a structured way of exchanging information. For example, companies that do business together need a standard means of exchanging order and billing information. To make sure that information flows smoothly between these companies, the format and structure of data such as purchase orders and invoices should adhere to mutually agreed upon standards. *Electronic data interchange (EDI)* is a widely used way of doing this, and it has been extended to work with Web technologies.

Another standard data exchange format is *Lightweight Directory Access Protocol* (LDAP). In practice, LDAP enables companies to exchange directory information in a standard manner. It is a directory service protocol designed on a client/server architecture that runs over Transport Control Protocol/Internet Protocol (TCP/IP). LDAP organizes information about a network object, called an attribute, into records called entries. Attributes all have a type, which identifies what kind of object it is—such as an e-mail address or a compressed video file—and at least one value. In the example of an e-mail address, the value would be the actual e-mail address of the object. Each entry is identified by its *distinguished name* (DN).

All of this information is arranged in a hierarchical tree. The tree is built to represent geographical as well as organizational structure. For example, the object at the top of the LDAP tree is the country in which the object resides. Below that would be the state or enterprise in which the object resides. Below that might be the department or functional area. Below that would be the individual entry for the objects.

Because it is designed to run on a client/server model, the actual LDAP database can be located on one or more servers. When an LDAP client wants to find information on an object in the LDAP directory, it connects to an LDAP server and queries it. The server either replies by sending the client the requested information or it sends the client a pointer to another server on which the requested data resides.

## *Security*

After you have established the types of data you will share and the means by which you will share it, the workflow of your extranet is complete. But it is far from being complete. Probably the most important as well as the most complicated task of building an extranet is designing and implementing its security. The rest of this chapter is devoted to exploring the ways and means of extranet security, starting with *virtual private networks (VPNs)*.

## Extranet Security: Virtual Private Networks

Virtual private networks (VPNs) sneaked quietly onto the networking scene a few years back, apparently while no one was looking. Since their inception, VPNs have become the "Next Big Thing" in remote access, but figuring out if you need one, which one to use, and how to go about implementing your own VPN has largely remained a poorly understood exercise in confusion.

So what is a VPN? A VPN is simply a way to use the Internet instead of private leased lines or POTS dial-up lines to extend network connectivity or remote access. While this has historically been done with standard ftp and telnet sessions, a VPN adds a few new and important elements to the mix: authentication, encryption, and tunneling (the encapsulation of data from any source or protocol within a TCP/IP data stream). This way, an e-mail transaction, data transfer, or remote session can be secure from prying eyes, something that isn't possible with standard ftp and telnet protocols.

Many firewall vendors, and all the major ones, were the first to jump on the VPN bandwagon, and with good reason. As the gatekeeper of your LAN, the firewall is the logical point on your network to perform encryption and authentication procedures so insecure traffic never leaves the network. Firewall vendors also saw this as an excellent way to extend the functionality of what was then a rapidly maturing market with no place to go.

While this has forced the VPN market to mature rapidly, it has also confused the issue of when you need a firewall vs. when you need a VPN. To generate sales, vendors will automatically say you need both. While it's true that almost every VPN installation needs a firewall, the reverse is not always the case—even though your firewall may already have VPN features ready for you to activate.

## Do You Need a VPN?

It's not as simple a question as it sounds. Deciding whether you need a VPN is a function of several things, which we'll address in turn.

**SECURITY REQUIREMENTS**    VPN security is a double-edged sword. As opposed to a typical leased line, which is part of your private network, any Internet-based traffic will, by necessity, be less secure, no matter how good the encryption and authentication schemes you put into place are. Compared to POP3 e-mail over the Internet or a modem-to-modem dial-up connection that can be easily tampered with, though, a VPN will be much more secure due to the VPN's encryption.

It's safe to say that a defense contractor is unlikely to use a VPN to transfer highly classified military secrets, because the security drawbacks, however minor, are still there. In fact, that defense contractor will probably use VPN-class encryption to secure documents at all times, even on a private network with leased lines. Clearly, for some applications, there is no such thing as a "reasonable security risk."

At the other extreme is a casual user who uses the company network to jot off a few quick e-mails to colleagues and friends, doesn't access confidential files, and isn't privy to company secrets. In this case, a VPN is too much. Any unsecured Internet service, like using a POP3-enabled e-mail server or a local dial-up connection, will do. The following drawbacks may also make VPNs downright unappealing:

**SPEED REQUIREMENTS**   You now know that the added security of authentication and encryption services comes at the expense of your network's speed. With a VPN, *everything* is authenticated and encrypted, and if your traffic doesn't start out as IP-based, it's encapsulated and tunneled, to boot. All of this stuff will be responsible for making your network quickly slow down, with typical performance degradation in the general range of 50 percent, based on our personal experiences. A 128Kbps ISDN connection becomes 64Kbps. A 28.8Kbps modem connection becomes 14.4Kbps. Is substantially better security worth dropping half your available bandwidth? In many cases, it's not.

**NETWORK PROTOCOLS**   Running an all-NetWare network and want to use the Internet as a transaction medium? If so, you've got little choice but to install some kind of VPN that can translate NetWare's IPX-based traffic into TCP/IP traffic and then undo it at the other end. Your other choice, of course, is probably what you're already doing: Use leased lines to connect sites and let remote users dial in to centrally managed modem banks.

**EXISTING INFRASTRUCTURE**   Take the previous example a step further. Suppose your company has 300 users in five sites around the country, each of which is connected with a frame-relay T1 connection to the local RBOC. Routers and CSU/DSUs are installed at each site, and you also have three dial-up modem banks for remote access users, all of which are scattered across the country.

This is a fairly small network, but ripping out this existing, and probably quite stable, infrastructure to replace it with a virtual private network is going to be a nightmare, involving the wholesale gutting of your network. It will all have to be done at once, too, and it will likely involve a long period of adaptation and frustration for your users.

With VPNs nowhere close to maturity, jumping headfirst into a network redesign in order to use them may not make sense. Then again, if you've got an investment in the aforementioned equipment and services that's probably running in the five figures-per-month range, the final benefit of VPNs may be the deciding factor.

**MONEY**   When you get down to brass tacks, the VPN exists for one real reason: It's cheap. If it wasn't, people would be content with the fully secure, full-speed leased lines they've had for decades. While installing a VPN can be a pain, and it may entail some hefty up-front charges, once you've got the system running, there are no recurring expenses aside from your connection to the Internet—an expense you're probably already paying. This way, all those PVC charges and router maintenance fees can go out the window, and you can use the cash for something else (like doubling your bandwidth!).

## VPN Paradigms

There are several different models for building a VPN. We'll discuss some of the most popular below.

The VPN makes a lot of sense, and causes the fewest headaches, when applied in a site-to-site implementation.

In a site-to-site implementation, you install two or more gateways that serve as VPN way stations. Often, as mentioned earlier, this is the same device as your firewall, although it does not have to be.

A typical network diagram is shown in Figure 18-4.

This diagram works best in situations where both offices are relatively large and have substantial traffic flowing between each site. For example, San Francisco may house the corporate accounting database, and the Austin site uses it for generating invoices. Or, Austin houses the corporate quality documentation and procedural manuals, which need to be accessed by all users at both locations.

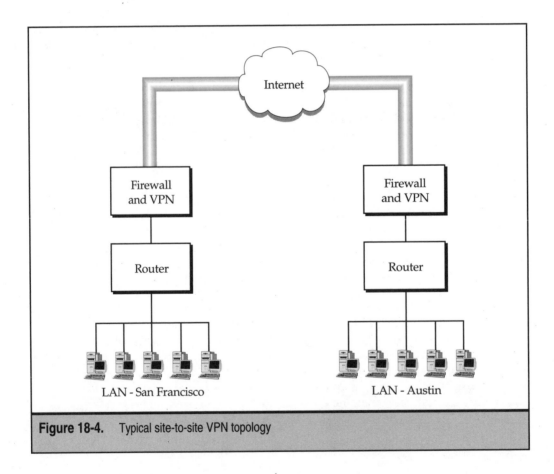

**Figure 18-4.** Typical site-to-site VPN topology

If the WAN is used less intensively—for example, if users are only checking e-mail at a centrally located server, or if just a few users in Austin need access to files in San Francisco—a version of the site-to-user implementation (described and outlined below) can be used and will be less costly.

**SITE-TO-USER**    Replacing modem concentrators and other remote access devices, along with getting rid of long-distance charges, is another benefit of using VPNs, this time, in a remote user-to-central LAN implementation.

In this implementation, the firewall usually is not responsible for encrypting and tunneling. Instead, a dedicated server running some kind of tunneling service (we'll cover the various flavors in a moment) sits on your LAN and does that for you. A typical network topology is shown in Figure 18-5.

A VPN installation like this is generally much easier to implement because it minimizes disruption to your existing network. The only real change involved is switching off your remote access devices and setting up the new tunnel server properly. Client-side changes involve simply installing a few new protocols, services, and/or small applications and configuring them properly.

**MULTIFUNCTION VPNS**    With multiple sites and remote users, you may need some combination of topologies. As the number of sites and users grows, and the reach of your network spreads, this can get substantially more complex, and may involve multiple and varied VPNs for different classes of users and remote sites.

One of the benefits of a VPN is that, even though a 20-site network in four countries with 500 remote users sounds difficult to manage, it's far easier to set up with a VPN than with a traditional WAN-and-modem combination. Adding a site involves obtaining an IP address for your new location and updating your routing tables—no waiting three months for the phone company to set up a leased line and straighten out the billing. It may not be plug and play, but it does beat the alternative.

## Proper VPN Deployment

It is critical to keep in mind that you should only employ a VPN—or a WAN, for that matter—where you absolutely need it.

Do your sites maintain their own servers, sharing nothing but e-mail among them? If so, you don't really need a VPN. You can use an Internet connection to swap e-mail messages and save the headache of maintaining a VPN. If you have a few users at remote sites that report to a central location, you can set these people up with a site-to-user VPN connection and minimize your investment in additional equipment.

The same rules apply to remote or work-at-home users. For each user, ask yourself, does this person *need* all of his or her transactions with the office encrypted? If your CFO works at home, maybe he or she does, but does a technical writer, working on help documentation? How about a graphic designer? Probably not.

Also, if the VPN is going to be used solely for e-mail, consider installing a simple, POP3-enabled mail server that can be accessed through the Internet regardless of location. If encryption is needed, you can implement a PKI for S/MIME secure messaging on a user-by-user basis.

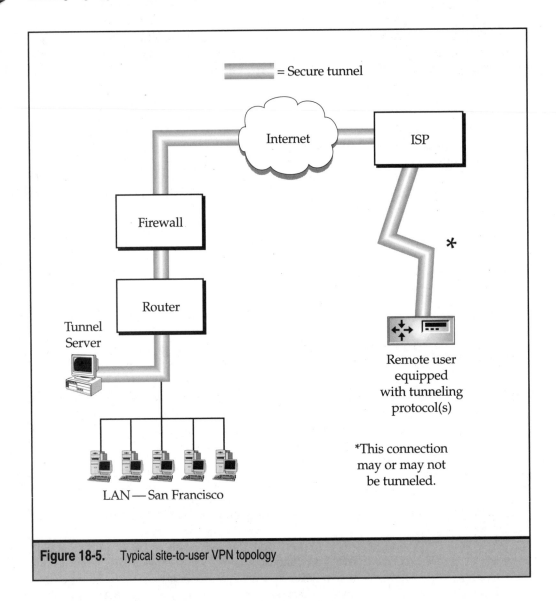

**Figure 18-5.** Typical site-to-user VPN topology

The bottom line is that VPN may be a hot buzzword, but it doesn't mean you need one on every PC and laptop in the office.

## Introducing Tunneling

In VPN brochures, you'll often read of tunneling as a glorious feature of VPNs. If you think about it, tunneling is actually a required component to make the Internet-based VPNs work. It's not a feature at all; it's a necessity that no VPN will work without, and the bottom line is that it slows you down.

Tunneling is simply the encapsulation of any form of data stream encoded with any protocol (IP, IPX, AppleTalk, SNA, or NetBEUI...it doesn't matter) into IP-based traffic that can be routed over the strictly-IP Internet. Figure 18-6 briefly outlines how this works.

Historically, there have been three widely used tunneling protocols in VPN installations: PPTP, AltaVista Tunnel, and L2F. We'll cover each in turn, along with the emerging tunneling protocols.

## VPNs and Tunneling Protocols in Practice

The defining characteristic of any VPN is the protocol that underlies it. Whether it's a free and open protocol like Microsoft's PPTP or a proprietary one like AltaVista Tunnel, the tunneling protocol defines what you can and cannot do, and what your network design will look like when you get finished.

**MICROSOFT PPTP**    One of the earliest and most pervasive VPN implementations, Microsoft's Point-to-Point Tunneling Protocol (PPTP), was designed to be an extension to the PPP protocol, the standard service used for remote access on Windows machines.

PPTP was designed and is best suited for site-to-user implementations, and as you can probably guess, the Windows NT platform is the best one to work with. PPTP is built in to Remote Access Services (RAS) on Windows NT Server 4.0. It is also enabled on the Windows NT Workstation and Windows 98 clients and can be obtained for Windows 95 with the Dial-Up Networking (DUN) 1.2 upgrade, freely available at http://www.microsoft.com/windows/downloads/contents/updates/w95dial-upnetw/default.asp.

To enable a VPN on a Windows NT network, you simply configure the server and client components, connect both to the Internet, and you're through. The connection is encrypted with 40-bit RC4 or DES in most implementations. (A 128-bit version can be enabled with the latest Windows NT Service Pack if you are only using the VPN domestically.) Authentication is performed with Challenge Handshake Authentication Protocol (CHAP), MS-CHAP (Microsoft's version of CHAP), or Password Authentication Protocol, (PAP), a clear-text password transmission. Each of these will be discussed in a later section.

**Figure 18-6.**    Data encapsulation with L2F. L2F and other encapsulation and tunneling protocols serve as a middle ground between IP and other protocols like IPX

You can also obtain third-party remote access servers that support PPTP if you don't want to use Windows NT's RAS to do it. Ascend, Extended Systems, and 3Com/U.S. Robotics all offer PPTP-enabled remote access products.

While PPTP is an excellent and extremely cheap solution for providing secure remote access, there are some limitations you should keep in mind. First, if you aren't running a Windows NT network, PPTP is not for you. PPTP also supports only the major client/server protocols of IP, IPX, and NetBEUI. If you have AppleTalk clients or need mainframe connectivity, PPTP will not do the job.

**ALTAVISTA TUNNEL**    Digital Equipment Corp.'s AltaVista Tunnel 98 is the latest in a line of proprietary VPN products from this security leader. AltaVista Tunnel has been around for a few years, and it has proven to be a stable and relatively inexpensive solution, although it is a proprietary one that will have to adapt or be displaced by emerging standards-based solutions. This is an important point to remember if you're looking to invest in VPNs for the long term.

AltaVista Tunnel runs on Windows NT, BSD UNIX, or Digital UNIX. Its distinguishing feature is that it uses user-based authentication, as opposed to IP-based authentication, to initialize secure connections. This means that a user can roam from place to place and ISP to ISP without changing his or her dial-up settings. AltaVista Tunnel can also be used to build site-to-site tunnels, because each server component can also be used to connect to another server component (unlike Windows NT RAS).

AltaVista Tunnel uses 40- to 128-bit RC4 for encryption, and uses MD5 to hash data for verification that it has not been corrupted or tampered with. Unfortunately, because AltaVista Tunnel uses user-based authentication to verify its connections and open tunnels, it is regarded as somewhat less secure than other VPN solutions. Because security is the prime objective of a VPN in the first place, it certainly bears consideration.

**L2F**    L2F, or Layer 2 Forwarding, was pioneered by router king Cisco Systems, which should tip you off to its primary feature: It's ghastly expensive to implement.

Cisco has L2F built into its internetwork operating system (IOS), so a VPN can be built largely using an existing Cisco environment, so you don't actually have to invest in a lot of additional equipment, provided you already have a Cisco infrastructure. Of course, if you haven't, it's going to cost you—a lot. The Cisco PIX firewall/router costs about $20,000. If you are building a secure network from scratch and don't have routers, firewalls, or VPNs, this isn't that extreme. On the other hand, if you are simply looking for a VPN solution to add to an existing, non-Cisco network, you'll probably want to look elsewhere.

While Cisco is the leader in L2F technology, it is also in use by other companies in remote access products, most notably Nortel and Shiva.

L2F works for site-to-site and site-to-user implementations. It is also one of the more robust encapsulation protocols, tunneling IP, IPX, AppleTalk, SNA, and more. For multiprotocol networks, an encompassing tunneling protocol like L2F may be your only choice.

In addition to CHAP and PAP authentication, L2F supports Terminal Access Controller Access Control System Plus (TACACS+) and Remote Authentication Dial-In User Service (RADIUS). Encryption is handled with IPSec (to be discussed below). L2F also works with dynamic or static IP addresses, making its flexibility in deployment virtually limitless. Of course, you'd expect that for the price you'll pay.

**L2TP**   When both PPTP and L2F were submitted as standards to the IETF, what arose from the ashes was Layer 2 Tunneling Protocol (L2TP), a new specification that would support both prior standards. L2TP is supported by Cisco, Microsoft, Ascend, and 3Com/U.S. Robotics, and it provides the best of both worlds: full multiprotocol support that does not require preregistered IP addresses. It is, however, geared toward dial-up connectivity, not site-to-site implementations. L2TP will be included with Windows NT 5.0 and may replace PPTP. The standard should be finalized by the time you read this.

Encryption and authentication are handled at the PPP level, before tunneling takes place. However, IPSec has been proposed as a means of providing end-to-end authentication and encryption to L2TP tunnels.

Expect to see a massive shift to L2TP as the standard underlying tunneling protocol over the coming months and years. Even without the final standard, implementations are already beginning to show up.

**IPSEC**   IPSec, or IP Security, is an ambitious set of standards emerging alongside L2TP, and it is particularly well suited toward site-to-site VPN implementations.

Besides being a tunneling protocol (sometimes called Layer 3 tunneling), IPSec includes an authentication, encryption, and key management scheme as well. IPSec will work with current IPv4 networks or with the upcoming IPv6 networks, as well. Even more importantly, IPSec authentication and encryption will work with L2TP if you want to use L2TP for remote access purposes, and IPSec will be deployed along with that protocol in Windows NT 5.0. Within the next 12 to 24 months, expect to see IPSec become the standard for secure wide area communications.

IPSec's final barrier is using multiple certificate authorities (CAs) for key management schemes. Currently, IPSec only works if sender and receiver have been issued certificates by the same CA, although the protocol is fully X.509-compliant. This should be resolved before IPSec is widely released, when the PKIX (Public Key Infrastructure Exchange) protocol is finalized.

IPSec uses MD5 or SHA-1 to hash messages and ensure their validity. The encryption scheme is done using Encapsulating Security Payload (ESP), a protocol that allows for the session to be encrypted in tunnel mode (where the entire IP packet is encrypted and encapsulated within a second IP packet) or transport mode (where only the payload of the packet is encrypted). The encryption algorithm can be set by the user or security administrator and includes most major algorithms. IPSec is already showing up in VPN products currently available on the market, including VPNs from AXENT, Check Point, Network Associates, Secure Computing, and RADGUARD. It seems to be working remarkably well, and should find even greater acceptance in the marketplace once Windows NT 5.0 is released.

**SSL AND SOCKSV5**   SSL has also been used with SOCKSv5 authentication to build proprietary VPN solutions like the one offered by Aventail. This scheme works much like any SSL Web session and can include things like virus scanning and content screening because it works at the Session layer. Implementations like this are really only appropriate for remote users, not site-to-site implementations, mainly because of performance problems with SSL. It seems unlikely that proprietary VPN implementations like this will gain popularity in the face of emerging solutions like L2TP and IPSec.

## Authentication with VPNs

When we talk about VPN authentication, we're discussing something different than messaging authentication. Authentication on VPNs deals with the issue of how you determine who to open a tunnel to and who not to. Because users or other sites are remote and not connected to your LAN, this is typically more problematic than a simple password prompt.

Then again, sometimes it isn't. A few VPNs, like those offered by Novell and Aventail, allow you to use your NetWare directory or Windows NT domain information to validate users, thus sparing you from having to set up special accounts just to access the VPN. Using a Windows 95 client with PPTP to connect to a Windows NT 4.0 remote access server works along the same lines. The real trick comes when you need to securely transmit user and password information without fear of interception.

**PAP**  PAP, or Password Authentication Protocol, has a very misleading name. It's one of the most widely supported authentication protocols, but it is rarely used. That's because PAP authentication consists of sending password information in clear text, which really provides no security at all. It should certainly be avoided.

**CHAP AND MS-CHAP**  Challenge Handshake Authentication Protocol comes in two flavors: CHAP and MS-CHAP, Microsoft's version of the protocol. CHAP is one of the most common authentication protocols and is built in to most VPN products, including Windows NT. CHAP works by performing an MD4 hash on the password and using that as part of the authentication and encryption session key. Because CHAP and MS-CHAP rely on passwords to authenticate a user, they are not as secure as key-based authentication schemes.

**SKIP**  SKIP is Simple Key Management for IP and has typically been used with IPSec to perform key management functions. SKIP was quickly displaced by other key management schemes, although you'll still find lingering support for it in current VPN products. Because it is certainly nearing its imminent death, you should look to other key management authentication protocols.

**ISAKMP/IKE/IKMP**  These three key management protocols—Internet Security Association Key Management Protocol (ISAKMP), Internet Key Exchange (IKE), and Internet Key Management Protocol (IKMP)—are all intertwined and are now hopelessly indistinguishable unless you really dig into the protocol specifications. Essentially, when you hear about any of these, you can assume they are referring to the same thing. IKMP is the latest version of the protocol, and we'll refer to it thusly.

IKMP is a framework for key exchange. It is used during the establishment of a secure tunnel to determine which authentication, hashing, and encryption algorithms are used, key length, time until key expiration, and the actual keys to be used during the communication. IKMP is a solid protocol and is the preferred method of key management for IPSec interoperation.

Currently, vendors offering IKMP support with their VPNs include the software of the preferred CA provider with the product or simply build their own CA right into the VPN. When PKIX is finalized, this should become a much more elegant solution, allowing full CA interoperability.

You should find wide and growing support for IKMP as IPSec and PKIX continue to take hold.

**RADIUS**    Remote Access Dial-In User Services (RADIUS) is a very well-established and well-supported standard protocol, especially useful for tracking accounting information on a per-session basis. RADIUS is supported by virtually all site-to-user VPN implementations due to its excellent abilities at providing reports with which scaling decisions can be made. You'll find a RADIUS server used to authenticate most users who dial in to an ISP.

RADIUS support is generally only important if you are considering using your users' ISP to authenticate that user back to your own corporate server for added security. This type of arrangement can get messy, quickly, due to interoperability issues between RADIUS servers from different vendors. If you want to implement some kind of authentication scheme involving RADIUS, you'll likely need to seek the aid of a professional.

**TACACS+**    Terminal Access Controller Access Control System Plus (TACAS+) is an old standby of Cisco. The protocol is built in to Cisco's IOS and can be used much like RADIUS to authenticate users during the establishment of a VPN tunnel. TACAS+ is integrated with L2F in Cisco routers and remote access servers, and it has fairly wide support among other VPN vendors. The protocol is mainly distinguished by maintaining its own internal access list for use after a user is authenticated so the remote access server can assign rights to network resources appropriately. The future of TACACS+ is unclear with the rise of IPSec.

**SOCKS**    SOCKS (the latest version is called SOCKSv5), a cute contraction of "Sockets," is a Session layer protocol typically used for authentication services. Typically it is implemented with firewall products that are integrating authentication into a proxy server, but it has also been used with SSL, as described above, to build VPNs.

Support for SOCKS had been largely nonexistent until the version 5 release, when a flurry of promotion by its originator, NEC, led to its adoption by several companies. Its proponents now include Aventail (SOCKS' original licensee), Attachmate, Bay Networks, IBM, Netscape, Oracle, and Intel, all of whom aim to implement SOCKSv5 in upcoming security and WAN products.

Because SOCKS operates at a higher level in the OSI model, it is easier to manage. This necessarily affects performance, however, and higher-level protocols are generally less likely to be secure due to the many layers that lie beneath them.

Whether SOCKS will mature into a companion to IPSec alongside L2TP remains to be seen, but it's a developing segment of the security market that bears keeping an eye on.

## Encryption with VPNs

As with most security products and implementations, VPN encryption is nowhere close to standardized. Virtually all of the major algorithms are supported by one VPN product or another, although Triple-DES is the most prevalent algorithm you'll find in use today.

**IPSEC/ESP**    Even emerging security standards like IPSec's ESP do not specify what algorithm is to be used during encryption routines. ESP can support any secret key cryptography algorithm, including DES, Triple-DES, IDEA, Blowfish, RC5, and CAST. ESP's default algorithm is 56-bit DES, due to potential export restrictions.

**MPPE**    Microsoft Point-to-Point Encryption (MPPE) is the encryption standard for PPTP. MPPE uses 40-bit RC4 (again, due to export restrictions) and works slightly different than normal RC4 encryption (hence the new name for the process), but the routine is essentially the same. Expect to see MPPE evolve to provide better performance and support for cryptographic accelerators with the release of Windows NT 5.0.

## Another Option: Outsourcing Your VPN

Like a PKI and certificate authority implementation, a VPN can be outsourced to one of any number of telecommunications providers looking to profit by aiding network managers who may not have the time, inclination, experience, or funds to set up their own VPNs within the organization. The thinking is, apparently, if you aren't going to lease a line from them, you might as well pay them for something.

## Service-Level Agreements

As with most other wide area networking services, VPNs are typically covered by service-level agreements (SLAs). Most national service providers guarantee about 99.6 percent availability (under 10 minutes of downtime per year) before refunds or credits are offered.

Unfortunately, what SLAs do not currently guarantee is performance. While the network may be up, it may still be very slow due to the vagaries of Internet-based communications. Performance is rarely, if ever, guaranteed, because there's nothing that can feasibly be done about the problem. Bandwidth is limited, encryption slows things down, and network congestion enters too many variables; all of this is responsible for general uncertainty that makes quality of service SLAs a distant reality, at best.

## The Future of Remote Access

So, where does all of this leave us?

As digital convergence takes hold, high-speed dial-up access will become increasingly prevalent, making remote access less of the pain it currently is. The same goes for operating system sophistication; Windows 98 and NT 5.0 are much more sophisticated in the way remote access is handled. As L2TP and IPSec continue to spread through industry, standards-based remote networking will make it easier for everyone to communicate.

It's not a bed of roses, though. The road to seamless remote connectivity is filled with potholes, and remote access—specifically, remote access *security*—has not been traditionally at the top of anyone's development list. Still, an increasingly roaming and telecommuting workforce will demand this kind of progress. As such, the next few years should be extremely interesting ones on the VPN front.

# AND MORE SECURITY

If you walk into a grocery store to buy a nice bottle of cabernet, any number of authentication processes occur, maybe without your knowledge. If you pay with an ATM or debit card, you'll enter your PIN code at the terminal. The PIN and card information is then wired to the bank, where the PIN's accuracy is verified and your available balance is checked.

Pay by a credit card, and the cashier may check your signature on the receipt against the one on the back of the card. The credit card processing company will also be contacted to ensure the card hasn't been reported stolen and that your credit line hasn't been exceeded.

If you write a check, the cashier will probably ask to see your driver's license to verify it matches the address printed on it. He or she will likely record your license number as a safeguard, too, and may use a computerized check verification service to ensure you aren't committing fraud.

If you're fortunate enough to appear under 21 years of age, the cashier will want proof of age as well. The authentication process doesn't stop there—you can also authenticate the merchant, checking its various business licenses. You can even authenticate the bottle of wine, by making sure it hasn't been tampered with, and later that night, by making sure the vineyard and/or year printed on the cork corresponds to that on the bottle.

In a nutshell, unless you're gray on the head and carrying a lot of cash, you'll go through four or five simple authentication transactions in the space of a minute's time.

Authentication is something we do every day. Whether through a policeman's badge, a credit card number, a secret handshake, your business card, or the password you use to access your computer at work, authentication is a vital part of every business, and even daily life.

## The Evolution of Computer Authentication

Even in the early days of computing, authentication was basic and commonplace in commerce and government, particularly after the two World Wars and the dawn of the Red Menace. It thus remains a bit of a puzzle as to why authentication was never of real concern during the advent of computers.

Obviously, networked computers, and especially a beast like the Internet, had not been conceived of. If a computer was purchased, it was only going to be usable by a highly skilled individual with keys to the building and a specific purpose. Computers of the day weren't particularly useful, anyway. Perhaps they performed calculations too tough for the slide rule, or calibrated a telescope. Either way, it was nothing anyone was going to go out of his or her way to *steal*.

Those days are long since gone, of course, but only in the last five to ten years have computer security and user authentication reached any semblance of being modern. Even now, authentication is a substantially advanced computing concept, and understanding the vagaries of digital certificates, hashing algorithms, certificate revocation, and hardware tokens can be daunting.

Still, we'll try our best within.

## Passwords

Beyond locking a computer behind a thick door, passwords were the first real manifestation of computer security. And while a password is better than nothing, in most cases, it's not better by much. Still, many people place full faith in the ability of a password like "Julie" to protect their most sensitive personal and business information.

Cracking passwords is one of the simplest tools in the hacker's toolkit, and it's often the first avenue any hacker will try in attempting to break in to a system.

If simple guessing doesn't do the trick, or if accounts without passwords are not found, "brute force" (going letter by letter through the alphabet) often does the trick, and could crack a simple password like "Julie" in a few minutes. Even long and apparently obscure passwords like "persimmon" can be cracked quickly using a "dictionary attack," where a list of commonly used passwords in a text file is used to expedite the cracking process. (As it turns out, "persimmon" is often on that list.)

Many modern operating systems can be configured to store dictionary files like these locally, and prevent users from ever using the passwords contained in them in the first place. Many administrators also enforce minimum password lengths, as well, but many more system administrators are not so strict, and on most networks, anything goes.

Even if an administrator is perfect in his or her job of preventing obvious passwords and requiring a sufficient minimum length and frequent changes, problems still remain. The more complex a password gets, the more help a user needs to remember it. How many times have you seen a password scribbled on a note and taped to a computer monitor? Or how often does one user share his or her password with another, not having time to go through the tedious logout-and-login procedure just to switch computers? As well, passwords can be easily coerced from unsuspecting users over the phone.

While the password problem will never be resolved, remember this: A good password is a long password. It also includes numbers, spaces, and nonalphanumeric characters. And of course, you should be able to remember it without having to write it down. Some good examples are listed here:

▼   4score&7YEARS

■   BornOnThe18th!

▲   CalLicense295/XJG

It's not likely that a brute force or dictionary attack will ever come close to cracking these passwords. (Then again, you may still be stymied because older systems will not accept many passwords like these!)

For protecting user information in public key cryptography and digital certificate applications, which we will cover shortly, passwords should be even more complex than those listed above. For these applications, a random line from a book is commonly used. For example, "He blooped across the used car lot now."—the first line on page 96 of Kurt Vonnegut's *Breakfast of Champions*.

Just don't underline the passage.

## IP Address Authentication

While they are not altogether secure, passwords are generally sufficient security on closed networks.

When you connect your LAN to the Internet, that's a different story altogether.

The topic bears repeating here. In a simple firewall configuration, you allow and deny access to your network based, in part, on the IP address of the computer requesting access.

If you network consists of the IP range 220.220.220.0 to 220.220.220.255, your authentication policy is simple: allow anyone in the 220.220.220.* range in, and keep everyone else out. You can further add remote, trusted users to the allowed range, thus building an access policy that can be applied both inside your organization and outside it.

## IP Spoofing

"IP spoofing" is a commonly talked about hack that involves a hostile computer masquerading as a trusted machine on your network. It essentially involves forging the address of the target machine (which is generally crashed or busied out with a DoS attack) and behaving as the target would in its stead. The result is bypassing a firewall and gaining full access. Figure 18-7 shows how such an attack is waged.

A hacker uses a Trojan horse, virus, or DoS attack to crash Server 2, then masquerades as IP address 220.220.220.2 to Server 1, acting as if nothing had happened. The hacker now has Server 2's access rights on Server 1. The hacker could just as easily attach the three user machines to have preferred access.

While this attack has been known about since at least 1985, it is still a very difficult hack to pull off, and it is extremely rare in its occurrence. Most firewalls can now be configured to thwart spoofing attacks, but it often requires a savvy network administrator to do it (or at least a helpful manual).

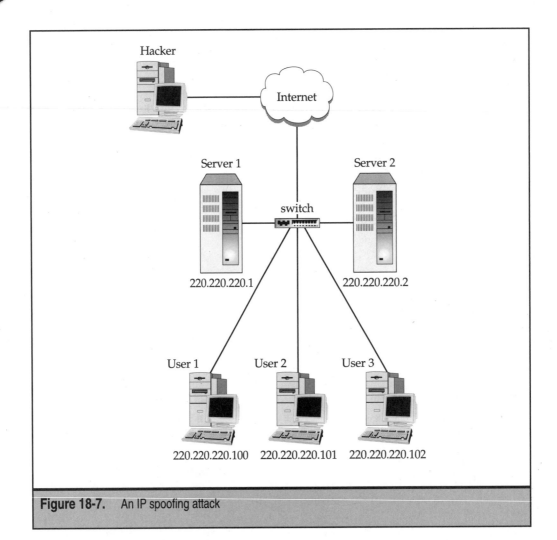

**Figure 18-7.** An IP spoofing attack

## Secret Key Cryptography

A major problem exists with IP-based authentication that often makes it inappropriate. First, any address-based security is only useful if you are attempting to authenticate the use of a shared resource. If you are trying to verify the identity of the sender of an e-mail message or ensure that message is complete, IP-based solutions are useless. For messaging purposes and file content validation, only a key system will work.

Key-based cryptography was designed to mitigate some of the weaknesses of password security and provide a new level of protection for secure messaging. Secret key cryptography was the first manifestation of a key-based cryptosystem.

Secret key cryptography is very simple in its application. The sender and receiver of a message or file simply agree on a key beforehand. A key is an alphanumeric expression that an encryption or decryption algorithm uses as the variable in scrambling or signing the message or file.

The size and content of the key are irrelevant. The important thing is that it is *secret*, and is known only by the two parties who desire secure communication. A message is signed or encrypted using a secret key, is transmitted to the recipient, and is then verified or decrypted, also using the same key. Figure 18-8 shows the anatomy of a secret key transaction.

There's nothing inherently wrong with this procedure. In fact, if you can guarantee that the secret key is known only by the two parties and the key is used once and only once, this is one of the most perfect cryptosystems known, similar to the use of a "one-time pad."

The problem arises in exchanging that secret key. You can't very well send it in plaintext e-mail, read it over the phone, or even drop it in the mailbox. The problem is further compounded when you involve more than two people who want to communicate. If you consider, for example, a company of 50 people who want secure communications, and one is fired, a new key must be generated quickly and transmitted to the remaining employees. Managing this kind of system quickly becomes messy.

Authentication (as opposed to encryption) poses its own problems for secret key cryptography. Part of the point of authentication is to be able to prove—not only to your

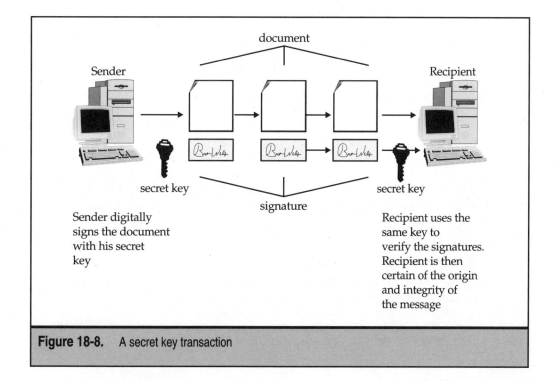

**Figure 18-8.**   A secret key transaction

intended recipient, but also to an independent third party—that a message is genuinely yours. A message signed with a secret key can only be verified by the intended recipient. And conversely, how do you authenticate a message sent to you from someone outside the organization?

## Public Key Cryptography

These limitations led to the advent of public key cryptography in 1976, when Whitfield Diffie and Martin Hellman (of Diffie-Hellman fame) described the concept. It's a very clever idea.

The critical difference between public key cryptography and secret key cryptography is that it uses two different keys for encryption and decryption. In public key cryptography, keys are paired up as "public" and "private"—a matched set that are usable only as a pair. The public key, which is made freely available to the world, can be used to encrypt a message. Only the bearer of the corresponding private key can decrypt the message. This private key is kept by its owner on a machine to which only he or she has access. This way, a secure e-mail can be sent from one person to another, without the two ever having corresponded before, simply by the former looking up the latter's public key.

Authentication works along a similar line. Using your private key, you use a "hashing algorithm" to generate a unique digital signature for an electronic message. Using your public key, the recipient can verify that the message is intact and that you indeed are the authentic author of the message.

The critical point to remember is that, in both an encryption and an authentication scenario, the transaction is one-way and cannot be reversed. Because the nature of the underlying cryptographic algorithms makes them unidirectional, a public key cannot be used to derive the private key upon which it is based. Once the private key is generated through a suitably random procedure, the public key is of minimal value in trying to determine the private key through brute force. But at the same time, the public key can absolutely prove the authenticity of a user or a message!

Public key cryptography solves many of the key management issues associated with the distribution of keys under a secret key infrastructure. Still, despite over 20 years in the making, public key cryptography is far from mature, and it has a number of remaining challenges before it becomes a fully proven and stable technology. Regardless, for the time being, public key cryptography presents the best option for authentication and encryption in any environment.

# Public Key Cryptography and Authentication

What are the real functions of authentication?

Sure, it's important to be able to verify that Steve is the true sender of the message, but what else is authentication good for? Actually, more than you might think. Here's a rundown:

▼ **Verification of identity**   Robert (the receiver) can verify that Steve (the sender) indeed sent the message.

- ■ **Ensuring the integrity of the message** Steve's message was not altered in transit (intentionally or accidentally). Robert cannot subsequently alter it after receipt, either.

- ▲ **Nonrepudiation of the message** Steve cannot later claim he did not send Robert the message.

E-mail is notorious as having none of these three traits, so how do you go about adding these features to something as insecure as electronic messaging? It starts with obtaining a digital certificate.

## Digital Certificates

In order to generate keys, whether secret or public/private, a user needs a digital identity. This is established through obtaining a digital certificate (VeriSign calls it a digital ID). In full standards-compliant public key cryptography, these certificates are called X.509 public key certificates.

The analogy to a passport is commonly made with such a certificate. Like a passport, a digital certificate proves your identity and is issued and verified by a recognized authority. In cryptography, this authority is known as a certificate authority (CA), which we'll discuss in depth later in this chapter.

## Digital Certificate Structure

Every time you digitally sign a message, you attach a copy of your digital certificate to it. Your digital certificate contains all the information a recipient would need to verify the authenticity of the message. A VeriSign Digital ID is described below in Figure 18-9. (You can get more information about VeriSign, a leader in cryptography, which we will use as a reference repeatedly in this chapter, at its Web site at http://www.verisign.com.)

Essentially, Figure 18-9 summarizes the X.509 certificate structure, a standardized way of organizing certificates.

Note that the digital certificate not only contains information about you, but it is also certified as genuine by a third party, usually the MIS or security manager of your company, or an outside security solution provider like VeriSign or Entrust.

## Where Do You Get a Digital Certificate?

Again, digital certificates are issued by certificate authorities. If you're looking for a digital certificate for personal use, you can obtain an ID through a company like VeriSign or Entrust. The cost is about $10 a year. If your company is rolling out digital certificates to many or all of its users, you may want to build a CA on company grounds.

The CA simply provides a way for other users to verify your identity, and you can also use the CA to verify the authenticity of those who send messages to you. More on the intricacies of CAs follows later in this chapter.

So now we get down to the nitty-gritty details on public key cryptography. To fully explain the process of authentication, we'll follow the creation of a digital identity and an

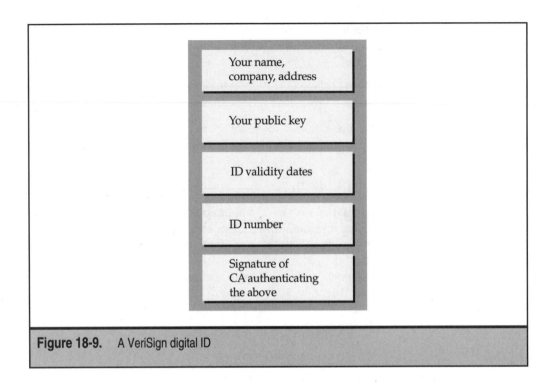

**Figure 18-9.**    A VeriSign digital ID

authenticated message from start to finish. We'll start with the backbone of public key cryptography: the certificate authority.

## Certificate Authorities

A certificate authority (CA) is the central authority that issues digital certificates to a defined body of users, systems, or other components of a computer network. By digitally signing each of the certificates it issues, the CA implicitly connects the identity of the certificate's owner to a public key inside the certificate. This way, the authenticity of the digital certificate cannot be questioned. Figure 18-9 illustrates this concept.

The CA doesn't just issue certificates, it verifies them as well. Users on the network can use the CA's own public key certificate (sometimes called the root key) to verify the certificates of other users on the network. This way, users can be assured that the credentials other users present are legitimate, because the CA vouches for their authenticity.

Without a CA in the mix, public key cryptography would be prohibitively difficult. This is the very problem that PGP, a public key cryptography system discussed later in this chapter, faces today. Because a user's—and a company's—web of trust can grow infinitely large and complex, mainly due to the Internet, it would be infeasible for each user to try to manage the additions, deletions, and changes of all of his or her contacts' digital certificates. A third party is required to centrally manage these services, and the services in question quickly become more complex than you may realize.

## The Roles of the CA

A certificate authority performs a number of services for its "CA domain," the population of users and systems over which it has responsibility.

▼  **Issuing Digital Certificates**    The CA is responsible for creating certificates according to the specifications of the security officer. The CA can generate keys, or the user can generate his or her own keys and present them to the CA. We'll discuss certificate issuance in depth in the following section.

■  **Publishing Digital Certificates**    The CA has to allow access to the public keys of users in its CA domain for use in verifying messages and providing encryption services. Typically, these keys are stored in an LDAP directory.

■  **Revoking Digital Certificates**    If an employee is fired or a private key is compromised, that digital certificate must be invalidated. The management of this information requires a certificate revocation list (CRL), and will be discussed later as one of the problems of public key cryptography.

■  **Updating Digital Certificates**    Certificates expire after a predetermined time in order to prevent a brute force factoring attack against a public key from being successful. A new certificate must be subsequently issued, and the CA must be updated accordingly.

▲  **Digital Certificate Backup**    If a private key is lost, a good CA must have some means of recovering that key. Keeping copies of private keys is also part of a Key Escrow scheme, a controversial requirement for some exported cryptography products.

## Digital Certificate Issuance

As we've outlined above, digital certificates are issued by a certificate authority, be it centralized within your company, provided as a service by your school, or outsourced to a third-party provider like VeriSign.

If you intend to use your digital certificate outside the user base of the company or school that issued it to you (and who wouldn't want to?), then your CA must in turn have an authenticated identity. This is done by giving the CA a digital certificate of its own, and that digital certificate must be publicly verifiable. Usually, the CA simply obtains its digital certificate from one of the above well-known and reliable certificate providers, thus ensuring its public key is a matter of public record.

If you build your own CA in-house, you can set up restrictions and regulations over obtaining a digital certificate. You can require users to meet you in person, provide proof of identity in the form of a driver's license or a passport, obtain fingerprints and photographs, and even run a background check. The point is that the underlying technology doesn't really matter: you can be as stringent or as lax as you'd like, because you are a *person* actually issuing the certificate. (Yes, a computer performs all the technology behind it, but you are the one in control.)

If you obtain a personal digital certificate from VeriSign, you can obtain an ID in two classes. A Class 1 ID authenticates your e-mail address only and is placed in the publicly available VeriSign directory so it can be easily looked up by anyone on the Internet. For better authentication services, you can obtain a Class 2 ID, which authenticates your name and personal identity as well. A Class 2 ID is not really any harder to obtain (and because the transaction is not face to face, it's impossible to be sure who is really requesting the ID in the first place). The cost is $9.95 a year for a Class 1 ID and $19.95 a year for Class 2. Entrust offers a certificate similar to a VeriSign Class 1 ID for free.

What this all means is that your decision over whether to develop your own CA or outsource CA functions will depend, in part, on how much control you want over the certificate issuance procedure. We'll further discuss the in-house/outsource debate later in this chapter.

## Key Management

Although securely issuing digital certificates is a certificate authority's most visible task, the management of those certificates and the keys they maintain is of paramount importance. Key management services are essential for building and maintaining a web of trust, because unless the CA has some means of identifying trusted and untrusted certificates, not to mention revoking trusted certificates that have gone sour, its services are useless. Once a public key has been issued, tracking and monitoring that key are essential.

Key management entails a number of services, outlined below:

▼ Specifying and tracking of untrusted certificates

■ Generation of random public key pairs

■ Secure storage and backup of private keys

■ Revocation and reissuance of new key pairs as they expire

■ Distribution of the CA's public key to publicly available directories

▲ Cross-certification with other CAs

But key management isn't just the job of the CA. Try as we might to entirely unload the burden of managing security from the user, it is still the user's job to keep his or her private key secure on his or her local machine. The user must also be able to securely obtain his or her key pair to start with, as well as transfer public keys with users outside the organization. This is especially true if CA activities are outsourced, or if cryptography services are limited to a handful of users who need it.

If a user's key is lost, corrupted, or compromised by an outsider, it is the user's responsibility to inform the rest of the world before any damage occurs. Again, this burden must be placed on the shoulders of the user alone.

As you can likely imagine, this is all a substantial amount of work, not only for the user, but especially for the CA. A CA has to be managed perfectly; there is no room for error, or else the entire infrastructure could crumble. And managing all of this is no small feat, especially considering the newness of the technology and its underlying theories to most network administrators.

These issues and others are the primary forces that drive the decision of implementing a public key infrastructure inside the organization or outsourcing it altogether.

## Internal vs. External CAs

If authentication services will be a fringe feature for many of your users, if only a few actually need the services that advanced cryptography provides, or if your company's e-mail traffic doesn't consist of much financial or trade secret information, the decision about whether or not to outsource your CA is a simple one. If this describes your company, without a doubt, you should outsource your CA.

Cryptography is undoubtedly one of the most abstract and difficult-to-grasp concepts in modern computing. Furthermore, setting up and managing a certificate authority within your own walls is the most abstract and difficult part of cryptography, and it's not a task that you should embark upon lightly.

Still, for many companies, especially those heavily invested in e-commerce, providing in-house CA services is a critical part of establishing themselves as a legitimate purveyor of goods and services on the Internet. If you can fully manage your company's cryptography needs on your own—and provide related services to your employees, customers, and suppliers—you'll go a long way toward building the elusive web of trust that we so often talk about.

## The Internal CA

There are some substantial advantages to having your CA on the premises. They revolve around the issue of control.

An in-house CA gives you, as the security officer, control over who has access to anything and everything. You set the standards for who can and who cannot obtain a digital certificate. You can require potential users stand before you as proof of who they say they are, submit proper identification, undergo drug and polygraph testing—whatever you desire! The point isn't *what* you do, it's that *you* are the one doing it.

This type of due diligence will give you (as well as your customers, suppliers, and boss) enormous faith that the users who are signing documents with their digital certificate are genuine, and haven't somehow subverted the issuance authentication process (not an altogether difficult feat in many cases). Therefore, if you need or want absolute control over the issuance of certificates (for example, if you allow customers Web-based access to your intranet to directly place their own orders into production), an in-house CA is really your only option.

Sounds great, huh? Well, building your own CA isn't exactly a picnic.

The problem is that the underlying technology of CAs is so new and immature, and not many people have much experience in this area, so the possibilities for making a mistake somewhere during the process are literally endless, despite the vehement claims of the vendors of CA software. And making a mistake on your CA is not like making a typo on the corporate home page: If you do it wrong, you may let the entire world have complete access to your most sensitive documents.

Then there are cost considerations. If you build your own CA, you won't have to pay per-user charges for each digital certificate you issue, like you will with most outsourced CAs. On the other hand, you *will* have to pay a small fortune for the hardware, software, staff, and added physical security you will need just to get the CA up and running. CA software generally requires some big iron to run, and the server application itself doesn't come cheap. You'll also need someone, perhaps full-time, to manage your Public Key Infrastructure (PKI), and while you may be able to find someone with limited experience in this area, they aren't exactly going to work for minimum wage.

Finally, electronic security hinges on physical security. You can't exactly let everyone have physical access to the CA itself, lest you risk a brilliant and accidental DoS attack by someone turning the CA off. At the same time, the CA must be fully available for your users and outsiders to verify a digital signature's authenticity or obtain a public key for one of your employees. This is not an altogether simple thing to do.

## The External CA

Is the prospect of the in-house CA driving you to insanity? You're not alone. Many large and well-known companies have opted out of the "build it here" strategy and, instead, have chosen to let a seasoned company like VeriSign perform CA services for them.

The benefits of the external CA can be significant. A major benefit is that, by outsourcing your CA services, you virtually eliminate the headache of managing it internally. Instead, that management is done by an admitted—and verifiable—expert in the field of public key cryptography. What if your CA crashes? What if your CA is the target of a DoS attack? What if a user has a problem at 3 A.M. on a Sunday morning? Have you thought about these issues and how to resolve them? Probably not, but you can be sure that your CA provider has. Or at least you can check.

Outsourcing the CA also lets you implement a PKI much more quickly and at a substantially lower cost. Because the software is already installed, debugged, and managed by experts, adding your company to the already existing PKI is a matter of adding a few users. Outside of some setup fees, monthly or per-user charges are the only real costs involved, and in the short run, these will invariably be far less than building your own CA from square one. These issues are typically what drive companies to outsource their CAs during a PKI pilot program. Often, they are so happy with the service they never build their own CA in-house.

Another major benefit to outsourcing your CA is that your customers and suppliers may already have a relationship with the same company to which you outsource your CA operations. In this instance, setting up a cross-certification relationship is a snap; just tell your CA provider what other companies you trust, and you're finished. We'll see shortly why this is not so simple for in-house CAs.

Of course, there's a drawback to all of these cost savings and manageability boons, and it's the same thing that makes the in-house CA so appealing: control. By outsourcing your CA, you are, in essence, outsourcing an important security function for your company.

Why is this a problem? It's like asking a stranger off the street to watch a pile of cash for you—permanently. You don't know a thing about the stranger, but perhaps he or she claims to be a well-known security authority. Should you trust that person?

It's not as bad as it sounds. You probably outsource the physical security to your building, in the form of an alarm system or a security guard. You trust your bank not to lose or steal your deposits, too. What's the big deal about another link in the security chain? Well, companies like VeriSign are quite new, and they don't have the complete faith of the industry just yet. While VeriSign certainly has a regal lineage, coming from RSA Data Security (one of the pioneers of cryptography), it isn't exactly AT&T. You don't know who VeriSign hires, and you don't know what its physical security is like. But by outsourcing your CA, you still have to hand over your security policies to the company and indirectly give it access to all of your trade secrets.

Is this a problem for you? If you are a military defense contractor, you bet it is. If you're a gas station, it probably isn't. If you're somewhere in between, well, you'll have to decide for yourself.

A potentially bigger concern is the issuance of digital certificates. If a company 2,000 miles away is issuing certificates on your behalf, how do you know they aren't giving the certificates to charlatans, competitors, or criminals? In a nutshell, you don't. You are once again at the mercy of your provider to do the right thing.

One final concern is that of legal liability. If you perform all cryptographic functions in house, you are responsible for any security breaches—for example, if a supplier's financial information is compromised on your system, the company can sue you over it. Giving control of your CA to an outside source complicates this situation by making the CA provider liable as well. The full legal ramifications of outsourcing a CA is beyond the scope of this book, but it may be a consideration of yours and merits further research. Be aware that companies like VeriSign are working toward mitigating these risks by providing "insurance" in the event of security breaches.

## Hybrid Solutions

If neither of these options is perfect for you, you can also consider a hybrid solution like VeriSign OnSite, where administration and key issuance are performed within your company, but back-end processing, disaster recovery, and support are done outside the organization by the provider. This solution can also be much cheaper than building a full-blown PKI in-house, as it involves a much lower up-front commitment.

Many companies are finding hybrid solutions like these to provide the right mix of security, ease of administration, and cost. They are certainly worth examining if you're investigating a PKI solution.

# Public and Private Keys

Now that you understand public key cryptography in the abstract as well as the form and function of certificate authorities, it's time to turn to a more in-depth analysis of public key cryptosystems and how they work.

As we've said earlier, the central idea behind public key cryptography is that a different key is used for each side of an encryption or authentication transaction. Public key cryptography begins, at the user level, by obtaining a key pair.

## Obtaining a Key Pair

So, where do you get a pair of keys? It starts by simply setting up your digital certificate. Your certificate authority will generally be responsible for generating your private key and its corresponding public key. When your Certificate is generated, a private key of the appropriate length is transmitted to you, and your public key is stored on the CA's publicly available directories.

Some PKI implementations generate key pairs at the client level, so the private key is never transmitted over the network. Obviously, in some security-intensive environments, this option is quite appealing and necessary. Of course, this creates a problem by eliminating the ability for the CA to properly manage and back up key pairs. This is a much greater problem for outsourced CA environments, where a private key may have to be transmitted over the Web.

Either way, once your certificate is generated, your public key is embedded within it, and your private key is stored on your local hard drive. Your private key is then protected by a password of your choosing.

## Public Key Derivation

Your private key and public key are irrevocably linked. Without delving too deeply into number theory, the idea is as follows.

Your private key is a randomly generated number: Generally, it is a binary number between 40 and 255 bits in length. (We'll discuss key lengths in the following section.) A one-way mathematical translation involving what is called a "superincreasing knapsack sequence" is then performed (the underlying algorithms vary depending on the implementation), and the resulting answer is your new public key. The public key size will likely be between 512 and 2,048 bits.

Again, your public key is placed on the CA and your private key is stored locally.

## Key Length

Much ado has been made about key lengths in the trade press of late, and with good reason. As the length of your private key grows, the difficulty of breaking it through a brute force attack also grows, exponentially. The longer your private key, the far more difficult it is to hack. Because of U.S. government trade restrictions, only cryptographic products with shorter keys are permitted for export outside the United States.

Table 18-1 outlines the comparative strengths of commonly used key pair lengths.

| Strength | Public Key Length | Private Key Length |
|----------|-------------------|--------------------|
| Minimal  | 512               | 40                 |
| Moderate | 768               | 56                 |
| Strong   | 1,024             | 128                |
| Military | 2,048             | 255                |

**Table 18-1.**   Comparative Strengths of Key Pairs

When you choose a key length, either for yourself or for your organization, it's important to remember that the added security of longer keys comes at the price of much slower performance. Hashing and encryption algorithms are notoriously slow, and while even a slow server can keep up with the demands of numerous 40-bit digital signature operations, a flurry of 255-bit signatures is a different story. This level of security requires more advanced hardware and probably some form of cryptographic acceleration product.

Currently, 128 bits is the generally accepted key length for "unbreakable" security. For smaller organizations, 128-bit keys should not put too great a strain on server operations, either, so it is a good compromise. We'll further discuss cryptographic speed concerns later in this chapter.

## Personal Key Management

If you tape your network login password to your monitor, you're not engaging in good security practices. If you opt not to protect your private key with a good password, or if physical security is lax in your organization, you run the same risks with a public key cryptosystem, no matter how good the underlying technology, the infrastructure, and the algorithms are.

Keeping your private key secure and out of the hands of outsiders is what makes public key cryptography work, and, as with any security scheme, it's the human element that is the weakest link in the chain.

Coming up with unique and unguessable passphrases that you can still remember is a painful, arduous task. It's so much easier to use your husband's name, your birthday, or your phone number instead of taking the time to come up with a better passphrase.

Your private key is stored on your computer's hard drive. If you use multiple computers, you'll have to store a copy on each of those systems. If an intruder gains access to one of those machines, what's to stop that person from simply copying your private key to a floppy disk, taking it home, and using it? Only a password.

We covered good password practices earlier in this chapter, but it bears repeating. If someone is going to attack your PKI, it is not likely they'll try to figure out your private key through brute force. Much more likely is that he or she will try to steal your private key, and attack the much easier password that safeguards it through a dictionary attack.

No matter how good your password is, this method will always be much simpler for a hacker to do. The best you can do is stymie the process by making that task much more difficult.

So, what do you do if your password is compromised, or if you find evidence of a physical break-in? Notify your security officer immediately. A crack security administrator can invalidate your digital certificate in seconds and quickly issue you a new one. Your old certificate will find itself on the certificate revocation list, and that information will have to also be replicated to any CAs that trust your organization's CA.

Key pairs also expire, in order to further foil the brute force attack we said would never happen. When your key expires, it is your responsibility to securely obtain a new one, much as you did when you obtained your original digital certificate.

Good personal habits in managing your private key are crucial to the success of any public key infrastructure.

## Public Key Authentication in Practice

Now you know everything that leads up to the actual use of a key pair in an authentication transaction. We'll now walk through the authentication procedure from start to finish.

Once your digital certificate is in place on your computer, you are ready to compose your message. Your message can consist of anything, and it can include attachments as well. Once it is complete, it is treated as an unalterable work until it is received at its destination. If the attachment is stripped or garbled along the way, the signature will not confirm the integrity of the message.

Regardless, you're now ready to hit that send button to get the message on its way.

## Hashing

The next step is hashing the message.

Rather than computing a digital signature for the entire message, a shortcut is typically used to boil the message down to its essential parts. This is especially valuable for large messages, which would take a considerably long time to sign. This shortcut is called hashing (or digesting).

A hash function is a one-way mathematical computation that takes an input of any size and returns a fixed-size string, called the "hash value." These functions are called one-way because they are very difficult to reverse. That is, it's simple to get a hash value for a given string, but it's almost impossible to reconstruct the string given only the hash value. For a good hash function, it is also infeasible to find two different messages to hash to the same value—although, statistically speaking, they must exist. This is known as the algorithm being "collision-free."

Most secure messaging systems will let you choose the algorithm you want to use to hash messages with. Without guidance, this can be an exercise in picking a random cryptic acronym from a list. Here's a guide to what's what:

▼ **MD2 – Message-Digest 2**   Ron Rivest developed MD2 in 1989, and it is suitable for older (8-bit) computers. Note that because it is an 8-bit operation, MD2 is very slow. MD2 produces a 128-bit hash value, as do MD4 and MD5.

■ **MD4 – Message-Digest 4**   A next-generation hashing algorithm, developed by Rivest in 1990. MD4 uses iterative hashing operations and was architected for 32-bit machines, so it is very fast. It was soon found that MD4 had certain cryptanalytic weaknesses, and is commonly regarded as a broken cryptosystem among the cryptographic community. It should really not be used at all, but it is nonetheless still supported by many PKI systems, mainly due to its impressive speed. (Note that MD3 never made it out of the lab due to flaws.)

■ **MD5 – Message-Digest 5**   Rivest fixed MD4 in 1991 with MD5. It is quite similar to its predecessor, but is much more secure. This security comes at the expense of about 25 percent of the speed of MD4, unfortunately. Still, MD5 is one of the leading hashing algorithms for 32-bit machines. It is an excellent choice if you are choosing your own hashing algorithm within a security application.

■ **SHA – Secure Hash Algorithm**   SHA was developed by NIST and NSA in 1991 as part of their Digital Signature Standard (DSS)—developed to be the authentication standard for the U.S. government. SHA produces a 160-bit hash, using a system similar to MD4. Messages must be less than $2^{64}$ bits in length. It is considerably slower than MD5 (about half MD5's speed—what did you expect from a government project?) because of its longer hash length. It is regarded as fully secure. It is commonly supported by most crypto software packages.

■ **SHA-1**   SHA was tinkered with in 1994 to correct an unpublished flaw. Otherwise, SHA-1 is essentially identical to its predecessor.

■ **RIPE-MD**   RIPE-MD is a European-developed algorithm similar to MD4. It has not been implemented in the United States in any widespread applications that we've seen.

■ **HAVAL**   HAVAL is a hardened version of MD5 that lets you produce hash values of 128, 160, 192, 224, or 256 bits. It is, by its nature, even more secure than MD5, and much slower as well (but faster than SHA). There is very little support for HAVAL in today's cryptographic software.

▲ **Davies-Meyer, and many other symmetric block algorithms**   Many lesser-known hash functions use modified encryption algorithms to perform hash functions as well, the idea being that if the encryption function is secure, then the hashing version of it will be secure, too. There are dozens of these hash functions, and most are painfully slow (MD5 is 20 times faster than Davies-Meyer). Some are secure and some are not, and none are widely supported. Avoid, if for no other reason than compatibility.

The bottom line on which function to choose? MD5 or SHA-1 give the best combination of speed and security.

## Encrypting the Hash Value

Regardless of which hashing function you choose, after the message has been hashed, the hash value and your private key are used to create a digital signature. This is done by encrypting the hash value with your private key. The resulting signature is appended to the message and sent on its way.

## Examining the Signature

Once the recipient has the message in hand, it's time to take it apart.

First, he or she takes the reputedly intact message, and uses the same hash function that you did to get a hash value.

Second, the recipient obtains your public key from a central certificate authority. He then decrypts the digital signature appended to the e-mail he has just received. If this is successful, the signature will decrypt to reveal the hash value that you received when you hashed the message in the first place. If this value (the value you sent) matches the value that the recipient obtained by hashing the message himself, then the message has come through intact.

As you can see in Figure 18-10, if any information—either the message itself or the signature—has been altered in transmission (intentionally or not), the signature will not decrypt to the proper hash value and the message will not be authenticated. Further, if your public key has somehow been altered, the digital signature will not decrypt to the proper hash value. Thus, if any link along the chain is compromised, the operation will fail, ensuring authenticity.

## Key Expiration

Now that you know how to use your key pairs, there will come a time when, inevitably, they expire. Again, this is done to protect the keys against a long-term brute force attack, just like passwords should frequently be changed to thwart dictionary attacks.

The time until expiration is set by the CA. Six months to a year is typical before renewal is required. The idea is to make the time to expiration much shorter than the time it would take to derive the private key for a given public key through a brute force factoring attack. For 128-bit keys, this time can be on the order of centuries, given the state of today's hardware.

When your key does expire, you simply apply for a new one, the same way you did when you initially obtained your digital certificate. Then, you're ready to start the process again.

# Advanced Authentication Tools

Public key cryptography not good enough for you? Perhaps you traffic in military intelligence, or are the chief developer of Microsoft's next operating system. If you have

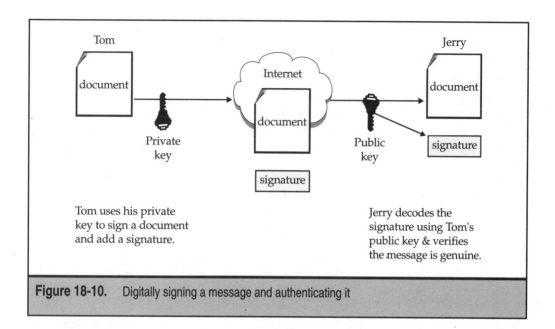

**Figure 18-10.**   Digitally signing a message and authenticating it

extreme cryptography needs, there are devices out there to help you obtain the security you need.

## Cryptographic Tokens

Despite its confusing name, a cryptographic token is simply any hardware device that stores your private key, in lieu of your hard drive. The idea behind a cryptographic token is to let you separate your computer and your private key, in the event the former is stolen or compromised. Since cryptographic tokens are generally small, they can be locked in safes or carried on your person.

Cryptographic tokens can be as simple as a floppy disk: just insert your floppy into your system when you need access to the key. While this is a very cheap method of building a physical layer of security, it is certainly not recommended. The general instability of floppy disks and the ease with which anyone else would be able to use it if it was stolen make storing your key on a floppy a bad idea. Still, it's a simple example of a token.

More advanced are PC Card tokens like the Luna from Chrysalis-ITS. These tokens are PCMCIA card-based devices that store your key for you in flash memory. The Luna also has a built-in cryptographic accelerator to speed up crypto algorithms. Just like a floppy, you can remove the Luna altogether when you aren't using your system, and because it's based on a PC Card instead of a standard like a disk, it is considerably more difficult for a thief to read its contents. These cards cost about $200 to $300 each.

Other cryptographic token implementations get even more interesting. Datakey has designed a token embedded within a plastic key that you put on your key chain. When you need cryptographic services, you insert the key into a base unit that connects to your machine. It's a clever way to instill good security habits into your users, as they won't likely go home without their keys...for cryptography or their car!

## Smartcards

Note that the unfortunately similar terms "smartcards" and "smart cards" are often used interchangeably, but are completely different concepts. *Smart cards* are chip-enabled cards like credit cards that work as electronic cash. *Smartcards* are simply magnetic cards that contain user information—in most cases, a digital certificate and private key. Although this usage is nowhere near standardized, and you'll usually have to figure out which is which by context, we'll try to keep the two terms straight within the confines of this book.

Smartcards work exactly like other tokens, although their low cost often makes them much more attractive to implement. Smartcards are finding acceptance in a number of implementations, although they are still relatively new on the scene. Smartcards are especially popular for use in containing the root key for certificate authorities—a critical private key that, if compromised, can create much more trouble than any one user's key.

## Biometrics

Now we get into the James Bond stuff: thumbprint scanners, radio badges, voiceprint identifiers, retinal scanners, and their ilk. Commenting on biometric devices like these is difficult without sounding alternately paranoid and condescending. The problem with most biometric devices is that they are limited to enhancing physical security. Most thumbprint readers simply allow and deny access to a computer as a whole. If a crook can bypass the device, he or she can often gain complete access to the compromised system. Even though they seem high tech and very secure, many biometric devices may lull you into a false sense of security.

Regardless, if your organization needs something like a retinal scanner, *you already know it*, and you don't need us telling you otherwise. In situations where security is critical and money is no object, these devices can be indispensable. For everyone else, try investing in some user training as a first step toward advanced security.

# Encryption

Authentication is an obvious requirement for most computer users and definitely for any business. The need for encryption is a bit different, and as such, encryption tools have a slightly different audience.

The key distinction is this: With authentication, the goal is to simply prove that people communicating across electronic links are who they claim to be. With encryption, you have to assume that that electronic link is vulnerable to tampering or compromise by malicious outsiders. Encryption is designed solely to foil that tampering.

## The Origins of Encryption

The first well-known implementation of encryption dates back to Julius Caesar, who reportedly used a simple substitution cipher to communicate with his friends and generals on the battlefield.

You're probably already familiar with the Caesar cipher, where the alphabet is rotated some arbitrary number of letters in one direction in order to scramble a message. One simple example involves rotating one letter to the right, thus:

**Plaintext:**    A   B   C   D   E...
**Ciphertext:**   B   C   D   E   F...

A message encoded with a Caesar cipher would look like:

**Plaintext:**    The monkey flies at midnight.
**Ciphertext:**   Uif npolfz gmjft bu njeojhiu.

While the "security" that a Caesar cipher gives you is largely nonexistent, Caesar ciphers are still around today. Their major implementation is known as "ROT13," a cryptosystem in which the alphabet is rotated 13 places either way such that A=N, B=O, C=P, and so on. As a bonus, with ROT13, the same algorithm can encrypt and decrypt the plaintext.

ROT13 is used in many situations where the recipient will want to avoid seeing the plaintext until later: mainly, puzzle answers and movie or video game "spoilers." Most newsreaders and many e-mail clients have ROT13 built in (in Netscape Messenger, this feature is under View > Unscramble).

## Encryption Today

Not to do any disservice to the ancient Romans, but ROT13 as a secure encryption algorithm is simply not going to cut it today. Today's encryption environment is a high-stakes, mission-critical market.

The search for a secure cryptosystem began in earnest in the 1800s, and became more and more involved with the two World Wars. The successful Polish/British cryptanalysis of the Enigma, a German encryption device used during World War II is legendary in the crypto community.

Today, the search is not so much for a secure cryptosystem (there are dozens that have never been broken), but rather on how to keep these cryptosystems out of the hands of terrorists and other nefarious sorts. An answer has not exactly been forthcoming.

## Encryption in Practice

The same issues surround encryption that surround authentication. Early implementations of encryption solutions were built upon secret keys. With the advent of public key cryptography, public key–based encryption applications are now the preferred method of secure electronic communications.

As with authentication, secure messaging is the primary use for encryption tools. Client-based applications like Netscape Messenger, WorldTalk WorldSecure Client, and Entrust/Express extend the functionality of an individual's e-mail reader by allowing the use of digital signatures and encrypted messages. You can also obtain personal encryption tools like Symantec Norton Your Eyes Only, SecureWin Technologies SecureWin, Entrust/ICE, and WinMagic SecureDoc, each of which allow you to encrypt files stored on your hard drive. Then there's secure Web browsing: protocols like SSL and S-HTTP, which are used on Web servers (and are built in to your Web browser) to provide secure communications over the Internet. We'll discuss each of these applications in turn.

You'll find that authentication and encryption products are almost always one and the same. Your e-mail application or plug-in can authenticate a message through a digital signature, encrypt it with a secure algorithm, or do both. In fact, it's very rare for a user to send an encrypted message without also authenticating it. The added benefits of verifying the sender's identity and the integrity of the message are considerable. And, since the bulk of the processing burden is consumed by the much more involved encryption algorithm, the addition of a small hash-and-sign operation after encryption is finished is usually insignificant when compared to the speed of the encryption operation.

**BUILDING THE ENCRYPTED MESSAGE**   Let's assume you have successfully obtained a digital certificate from your certificate authority (local or off-site), and your public and private keys have been successfully installed on your local machine.

Your next step, as with authentication, is to compose a message and include any attachments you'd like. With encryption, the use of attachments is commonplace, as messages that need encrypting are much more likely to be composed of large, ongoing document projects like strategic business plans, corporate financials, or project development specs.

Regardless of the message content, you simply instruct your messaging system to encrypt the message, and digitally sign it if you'd like.

**THE ENCRYPTION PROCESS**   After you choose to send the message, your client will encrypt it for you using your recipient's public key. You can obtain your recipient's public key through a common CA that you are both a member of, or your recipient can directly mail his or her key to you (though this is less secure).

If you have elected to digitally sign your message, it will be hashed, and then the hash value will also be encrypted with your private key. This differs from the encryption algorithm, where the recipient's public key is used to encrypt the message. Figure 18-11 outlines how these two functions work together in one transaction.

Without delving too deeply into the theoretical arcana of encryption, the idea is to apply a one-way algorithm against the digital contents of your message and convert that message into garbage that can only be decoded by the intended recipient.

In order to do that, you will likely have to choose an algorithm to perform the encryption, and as with everything in computing, there is substantial debate as to which

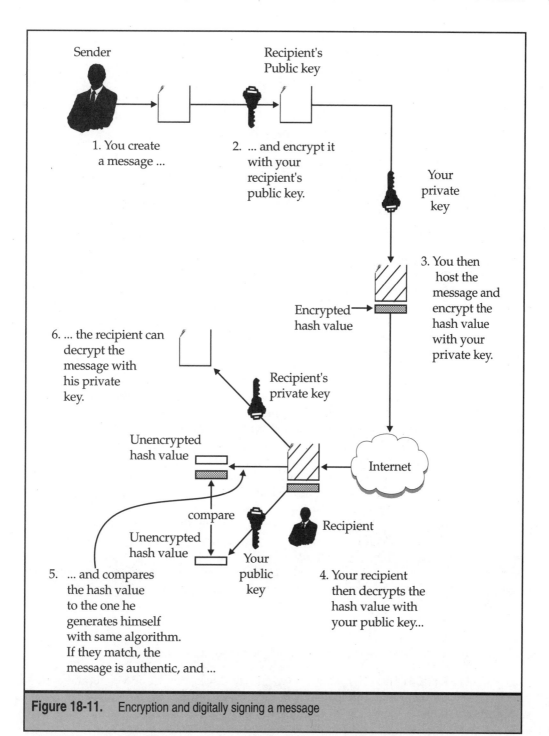

Sender

Recipient's
Public key

1. You create
a message ...

2. ... and encrypt it
with your
recipient's
public key.

Your
private
key

3. You then
host the
message and
encrypt the
hash value
with your
private key.

Encrypted
hash value

6. ... the recipient can
decrypt the
message with
his private
key.

Recipient's
private key

Unencrypted
hash value

Internet

compare

Recipient

Unencrypted
hash value

5. ... and compares
the hash value
to the one he
generates himself
with same algorithm.
If they match, the
message is authentic, and ...

Your
public
key

4. Your recipient
then decrypts the
hash value with
your public key...

**Figure 18-11.**   Encryption and digitally signing a message algorithm is best. Here is our take on the messy state of today's encryption algorithms and which one you should use.

**ENCRYPTION ALGORITHMS**   If you thought choosing from the field of hashing algorithms was a mess, wait until you see the state of encryption algorithms, with RSA, DES, and DSA the best known (although each has a different application). Be advised that both public and secret key algorithms are discussed below.

**RSA**   RSA is the grandfather of cryptographic algorithms, and it is widely regarded as the most secure encryption algorithm on the market in wide use. It is also the only real choice for a public key cryptography algorithm (most of the algorithms below are secret key algorithms). Invented by (and named for) Ron Rivest (of MD5 fame), Adi Shamir, and Leonard Adleman in 1977, RSA uses two large prime numbers and some essentially one-way mathematics to generate a public and private key pair. To encrypt, the plaintext is subjected to an exponential function involving the recipient's public key. It can only be decrypted with the corresponding private key. RSA is widely implemented today, and is, in fact, in wider use than any other public key cryptosystem.

Recently, RSA sponsored a challenge to break a 56-bit private key, and the attack was successful in 39 days of brute force number crunching. On the whole, RSA has stood up extremely well to attacks and is regarded as secure. The algorithm is patented (and subject to licensing) and expires in the year 2000.

**DSA – DIGITAL SIGNATURE ALGORITHM**   DSA is part of the NIST's Digital Signature Standard (DSS), proposed for use in 1991. For all intents and purposes, when you hear about DSA and DSS, they are both part of the same thing: a standardized algorithm for performing digital signature calculations. DSA's introduction sent shock waves through the crypto community, with many of its members assuming a conspiracy was afoot to do away with RSA in favor of a government-developed standard.

Unlike RSA, DSA is only good for digital signature functions. It is not designed for encryption at all. As such, it is more limited in its application (in fact, the NIST has no public key cryptography standard at all, although DES is certified as a secret key standard). Much of DSA's criticism focuses on its functionality (limited), its speed (slightly slower than RSA; although with RSA, the signature takes longer, and with DSA, the verification takes longer), and its origins (the NSA, which many feared had embedded a trap door into the code). After complaints that the key length was too short and the security of DSA was called into question, the length was doubled.

We're getting up on a decade later, and the battle between DSA and RSA still rages on. Lawsuits are pending, patent infringements have been alleged, and DSA is slowly starting to show up in some applications. With the force of the government behind it, it's only a matter of time before the field becomes interminably muddied.

**DES – DEFENSE ENCRYPTION STANDARD**   Originally developed by IBM, DES (aka DEA and DEA-1) is another much-maligned cousin of RSA. Contrary to common belief, DES is *not* part of a public key cryptosystem at all. Rather, it is a simple and not entirely secure secret key cryptosystem based on an algorithm called a block cipher. DES is the officially certified cryptosystem of the U.S. government, much to the chagrin of cryptographers everywhere.

DES keys have been broken through brute force and through an attack called linear cryptanalysis, although these attacks are not altogether feasible. Of greater concern is the problem of secure key exchange. So, with all these drawbacks, why is DES accepted as a standard? It is 100 to 10,000 times faster than RSA because of its simplicity. It's also just as secure as any other secret key algorithm on the market.

**TRIPLE-DES**    To mitigate some of the problems with DES, Triple-DES (often abbreviated as 3DES) was developed. Triple-DES, in its widest implementation, uses two keys to strengthen the security of DES-encrypted plaintext. In standard Triple-DES, the plaintext is encrypted with key #1, decrypted with key #2, and reencrypted with key #1. This makes cryptanalysis much more difficult than standard DES. Triple-DES is a widely implemented standard for secret key cryptosystems, although it is not approved as a government standard.

**KEY EXCHANGE WITH DIFFIE-HELLMAN**    Diffie-Hellman (invented in 1976) was the first public key algorithm ever devised, although it cannot be used for encryption. Instead, Diffie-Hellman is used to solve the key exchange problem of secret key algorithms like DES. Diffie-Hellman uses a simple formula to take two random numbers generated by the sender and receiver and use them to generate a secret key that only the two of them can know, even if the entire transmission between the two parties has been overheard. Diffie-Hellman can also be extended to work with more than two parties.

If you choose to employ DES, you'll need some way of exchanging the secret key. This can be done with a key exchange algorithm like Diffie-Hellman, or you can simply generate a secret key, then use a public key algorithm like RSA to encrypt the secret key, and then send that encrypted message to the recipient. Using Diffie-Hellman instead of RSA in this situation allows you to avoid two problems: first, using RSA means setting up some form of PKI, which can be a pain; second, Diffie-Hellman's patent has expired, so it's free, unlike RSA.

Then again, if you opt to use RSA to encrypt DES keys, you're going to have to set up a public key infrastructure anyway, so why not just use the more secure RSA algorithm for all your cryptography needs, instead of having RSA and DES together? That's a question no one will be able to answer for you (although there are thousands who would like to try).

**THE ENDLESS LIST OF OTHER SECRET KEY BLOCK CIPHERS**    Most cryptographic algorithms you'll hear about are block ciphers like DES. They are designed for use with secret key cryptosystems, and you'll have to come up with another way of exchanging keys (like Diffie-Hellman or RSA for encrypting the key, as described above). Block ciphers are called this because they work on fixed-size chunks, or blocks, of plaintext data at a time. Typically, this is 64 bits. A block cipher will encrypt the first 64 bits of your message, then move on to the next 64 bits, and so on, until the end is reached. Each block is treated separately and independently. This often causes block ciphers to be slow in comparison to stream ciphers, which we'll cover in a moment.

▼ **RC2 – Rivest Cipher 2**  aka "Ron's Code 2." RC2 is another Ron Rivest job, a proprietary block cipher built for RSA Data Security as a secret key alternative to DES. The code remains a secret and is not patented. It's also two or three times faster than DES and can be made as secure or as weak as you'd like through longer or shorter key lengths. RC2 has another thing going for it in that software manufacturers can gain speedy export approval if their security products use 40-bit keys and RC2 algorithms; DES is rarely approved for export at all regardless of key length. RC2 is no more vulnerable to attack than DES and is an excellent (and free) alternative.

■ **RC5 – Rivest Cipher 5**  RC5 is a fast block cipher with multiple routines (like Triple-DES) designed to heighten security. Keys can be up to 2,048 bits in length. RSA is patenting RC5, which means it will require a license to use. There is currently minimal support for RC5 in the real world.

■ **IDEA – International Data Encryption Algorithm**  IDEA is a 128-bit secret key algorithm that has considerable popularity as an alternative to DES. Its speed is also comparable to DES, and even though $2^{51}$ of the $2^{128}$ possible keys are regarded as weak, IDEA is considered fairly strong. (It sounds like a lot at first, but those weak keys are extremely unlikely to be chosen, statistically speaking.) IDEA is patented, and is the algorithm behind the encryption functions of PGP. Otherwise, IDEA has found only moderate acceptance.

■ **Skipjack**  Skipjack (completed in 1990) is the algorithm behind the highly controversial Clipper chip, the NSA's hardware solution for providing encryption services with a catch: the secret key is escrowed and can be used by the government for "backdoor" access to otherwise secret communications. Skipjack itself uses 80-bit keys and its details are classified, but small groups of cryptographers with limited access to the algorithm have found it to be secure. The key escrow issues behind Clipper, however, are the main concerns that Skipjack has found itself embroiled in. Skipjack can only be implemented in government-authorized hardware, not in software.

■ **CAST**  CAST is a 64-bit algorithm designed by Canadians Carlisle Adams and Stafford Tavares. CAST was named for its inventors and as a homage to its strength (as in "cast iron") and its randomness (as in "cast dice"). The inventors were right: CAST has stood up remarkably well to all sorts of attacks, and it is widely implemented in software today. It may also become a standard for the Canadian government, and it is patent pending.

■ **Blowfish**  Blowfish is crypto expert Bruce Schneier's take on a block cipher. It was designed to be fast and simple, and use keys up to 448 bits for extra security. Schneier's experiment was a grand success. The algorithm is in the public domain, and it has found wide acceptance in real-world applications.

- **SAFER – Secure And Fast Encryption Routine**   SAFER is a block cipher developed in 1993 by James Massey for Cylink Corp. It has implementations with 64-bit keys and 128-bit keys and is freely available. It is considered to be secure, but has not found wide implementation in the real world, although support for it appears to be growing.

- **GOST**   GOST is a Soviet block algorithm used for unclear purposes during the Cold War. GOST uses 256-bit keys and is extremely secure. There is also a GOST digital signature algorithm like DSA. As a Russian algorithm, you are unlikely to run into it in any commercial application.

- **Lucifer**   Lucifer is a 128-bit block cipher dating back to the early 1970s. It has been broken by several different cryptanalytic attacks and is essentially a dead algorithm.

- ▲ **FEAL**   FEAL is a Japanese block cipher with 64-bit keys. It was intended to be a faster alternative to DES, but turned out to be ridiculously simple to break, and is now one of the laughingstocks of the cryptography community and has virtually no support outside of theoretical applications.

**SECRET KEY STREAM CIPHERS**   Stream Ciphers are algorithms belonging to a different family of secret key ciphers than the above algorithms. Stream ciphers are designed to work on small units of data (usually one bit at a time), rather than large blocks as block ciphers do. Thus, a stream cipher is generally much faster than any block cipher. Much of the research into stream ciphers is still theoretical, though, and real-world applications are currently limited to a handful of algorithms, outlined below:

- ▼ **RC4 – Rivest Cipher 4**   RC4 is the leading stream cipher, and it is officially a trade secret of RSA Data Security, although the code has been leaked through the Internet. Still, it is subject to license from RSA. RC4 has been shown to be quite secure, and if key length is kept at 40 bits, developers can quickly gain export approval. RC4 can be found in many cryptographic software applications and is part of the Cellular Digital Packet Data specification.

- **SEAL – Software-optimized Encryption ALgorithm**   SEAL is a pseudostream cipher completed in 1993 and optimized for 32-bit processors. SEAL is very fast, but it is also very new and has not been subject to many cryptanalytic attacks. A patent is pending.

- **PKZIP**   Roger Schlafly's compression algorithm also includes encryption if you choose it. An early stream cipher, PKZIP encryption can be hacked in a matter of a few hours on any PC. If you want security on your compressed files, you should not use PKZIP's built-in encryption.

- ▲ **WAKE – Word Auto Key Encryption**   WAKE is another stream cipher that is very fast, although this algorithm has been found susceptible to some attacks. It has waning support in the industry, but can still be found in a few applications.

**OTHER PUBLIC KEY CIPHERS**    There are several other public key ciphers. Some of them are described here:

▼ **Pohlig-Hellman**    Pohlig-Hellman is a simple, proprietary public key cryptography algorithm that is surprisingly similar to RSA. It is rarely implemented in the real world, but it is available for license.

■ **ElGamal**    ElGamal is currently the only public key cryptography algorithm (there are literally thousands of versions) that can be implemented without obtaining licenses and paying royalties. It is similar in design to the Diffie-Hellman algorithm, is comparable in security to RSA, and is only slightly slower than RSA. Has there been a mad rush to ElGamal? No. Will you find it supported in any software application? Perhaps, but RSA currently remains infinitely more popular in use.

▲ **Elliptic Curve Cryptography**    Expect to hear a lot more about elliptic curve cryptography in the coming years. Elliptic curves are geometric and mathematical constructs that can be used in place of the modular multiplication operations in traditional public key cryptosystems. Elliptic curve mathematics was originally touted to be superior in its ability to hold up against cryptanalytic attacks, but that claim has been debated and is questionable. Outside of one implementation by NeXT Computer, elliptic curve cryptography has yet to really find any wide implementation. However, it has become something of a buzzword in the cryptography field, so expect to see implementations popping up over time, along with a more official word about its security.

**SO WHICH ONE DO I USE?**    Choosing from this mess is no simple task, although there are some guidelines you can follow:

▼ If you want a genuine public key cryptography solution for internal use, RSA will serve all your needs admirably.

■ If you are developing software for a government entity or need to communicate with government employees, you may be stuck with a secret key encryption scheme (DES) and DSA for digital signatures. Key exchange can be done through RSA or Diffie-Hellman.

▲ If you need simple, secret key cryptography (for personal or limited use), Triple-DES, RC2, CAST, and Blowfish are all excellent choices and will provide plenty of speed.

## Other Functions of Encryption

We've focused our discussion of encryption on secure messaging, as that is its most prevalent implementation. Of course, encryption has many additional functions outside of sending secure e-mail.

**PERSONAL ENCRYPTION TOOLS**   The most obvious use for encryption is for protecting sensitive data on your computer, whether or not you intend to share this data with anyone else. If physical access to your computer is a possibility (and really, where isn't it?), then a personal encryption tool is a great way to protect your data.

Do a Web search for these types of systems and you'll find hundreds. That's because while designing a full-fledged PKI system is extremely difficult, building a one-shot, stand-alone personal encryption application is pretty simple. In fact, any decent programmer can put together an encryption tool in a manner of minutes, and source code for most of the common algorithms is freely available.

Still, it's probably best to leave cryptography to the experts. Encryption software is very affordable, and it could easily earn back its value by discouraging data theft attempts. Look at packages like Network Associates' PGP for Personal Privacy or Symantec's Norton Your Eyes Only for a couple of mainstream encryption tools, both of which are bristling with advanced features.

With personal encryption tools, the algorithm is not as important as it is in secure messaging. For example, if you encrypt a file on your hard drive, you can implement DES without fear that your private key is going to be compromised, because you never transmit the key to anyone else.

You can protect your key any way you see fit: on a floppy disk, on a cryptographic token, or just leave it on the hard drive. The other side to this coin is that you absolutely need a stellar password to protect access to your key. Remember: If someone can gain physical access to your system, your private key will be easily obtainable. Only a very strong password will be able to prevent them from making your encryption scheme completely transparent.

**FILE- OR DISK-BASED ENCRYPTION?**   There is some debate over which is better, applications like Norton Your Eyes Only, which encrypt on a file-by-file (or directory-by-directory) basis, or programs like WinMagic SecureDoc, which encrypt at the block level of your disk drive, generally encrypting the entire contents of the drive. While file-based encryption tools let you have more control over the encryption process, disk-based tools are faster and more secure because they encrypt everything on the drive—including temporary and swap files that may unwittingly hold remnants of confidential information.

The jury is still out, and both kinds of personal encryption tools have their uses. If your cryptography needs are limited, with only a few files needing protection, a file-based tool will probably suit you just fine. For mission-critical security or heavy encryption usage, a disk-based tool with the private key stored on a floppy disk or cryptographic token is your best bet.

**ENCRYPTED WEB BROWSING**   Secure Internet services will become more and more important over the coming years, and secure browsing protocols are already in wide use.

**S-HTTP**   As we mentioned earlier in this chapter, S-HTTP is the Secure Hypertext Transfer Protocol, and it is also known as HTTPS or https. S-HTTP is an Application layer extension to the standard HTTP Web protocol, designed to support encryption during an HTTP session. Because it is application dependent, S-HTTP is limited in its deployability. It can also be implemented without the use of public key cryptography.

**SSL**    SSL, or Secure Sockets Layer Handshake Protocol, was developed by Netscape and is the current public key cryptography standard for secure Web browsing and transaction processing. SSL is built-in to Netscape and Microsoft browsers and most Web servers, and it operates on TCP port 443. Unlike S-HTTP, SSL is a Transport layer service and is therefore application independent, so whether you are using HTTP, ftp, telnet, or even gopher during your Internet session, the encryption process will occur transparently on the client system. This makes it preferable to S-HTTP for the major encryption need on the Internet: e-commerce.

As a Web site designer, you simply configure SSL on the server and then specify which pages require an SSL connection for access. CGI and other API routines can also be written to work with SSL.

When a client tries to access an SSL-enabled page, the server sends the client its certificate and algorithm preferences to the client. The client then generates a secret key, which it encrypts with the server's public key and sends back to the server. The server decrypts the secret key and authenticates it by sending an acknowledgement back to the client, encrypted with the secret key. The client then verifies that everything is kosher by returning the acknowledgement with the client's digital signature. The secure Web session is now enabled. This is illustrated in Figure 18-12.

SSL supports a number of cryptographic algorithms. RSA is used during the initial handshaking steps. For the secret key–encrypted acknowledgement, RC2, RC4, IDEA, DES, and Triple-DES are all used, based on configured preferences. MD5 is used as a message hashing algorithm.

**SET**    SET, or Secure Electronic Transaction, is an emerging protocol for e-commerce developed by Visa and MasterCard. It works much like SSL does, only it adds a bank or credit card company to the loop. Eventually, it should displace SSL for e-commerce transactions, as Internet purchasing continues to grow in popularity.

## Speed Considerations

Let's face it. Cryptographic security comes at the expense of speed.

As key lengths get longer, so does the time it takes to encrypt a file. In fact, encrypting 2MB worth of files on a 400MHz dual Pentium II system takes over three minutes with Triple-DES and a 2,048-bit key. That's on a fast system; imagine how long it takes on an average PC.

As data storage formats and the e-mail that contains them grow larger and larger, this problem isn't going to get any better. Also, because necessary key lengths continue to grow, the problem of slow cryptography will continue to worsen.

Keep in mind that for a stand-alone e-mail client, where encryption tools are used on an occasional case-by-case basis, the few extra seconds an encryption routine adds to the task of sending a message is of little consequence. Because encrypted files are only

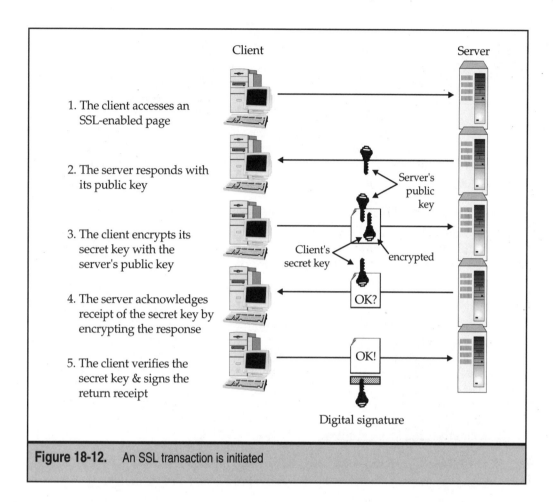

1. The client accesses an SSL-enabled page

2. The server responds with its public key

3. The client encrypts its secret key with the server's public key

4. The server acknowledges receipt of the secret key by encrypting the response

5. The client verifies the secret key & signs the return receipt

**Figure 18-12.**    An SSL transaction is initiated

slightly larger than their nonencrypted counterparts, network performance should not be affected by implementing cryptography on your network.

On the other hand, if you are running a Web server that serves up a substantial number of SSL-enabled pages for e-commerce or another secure application, the toll of performing numerous encryption tasks might become a difficulty.

**CRYPTOGRAPHIC ACCELERATORS**    In order to combat this problem, vendors are starting to enter the market with cryptographic acceleration hardware, PCI cards or SCSI devices that have dedicated cryptographic processing chips for increasing the throughput of encryption and digital signatures operations. Rainbow Technologies' CryptoSwift series and nCipher's nFast products are among the market leaders.

Of course, there's a catch. Cryptographic accelerators like the ones mentioned are very specialized devices. Currently, CryptoSwift only supports SSL transactions for

Netscape and Microsoft Web servers. nFast only supports SSL on Netscape. If you use S-HTTP, you're out of luck. And if SSL is displaced by SET or another emerging e-commerce protocol (which is very likely), these devices will suddenly be useless.

And they aren't cheap. nCipher's high-end accelerator costs over $10,000. That might be more than the server you connect it to. Before you invest in a crypto accelerator, make absolutely sure you need it. Make sure you aren't using SSL on pages where encryption isn't needed, and make sure the cryptographic processes are the bottleneck. Even busy e-commerce sites rarely perform more than one or two transactions per second. The top nFast box can crunch out 300 RSA signings per second, which may be much more than you'll ever need.

## Problems in Public Key Cryptography

Problems? In an emerging field like public key cryptography? It's probably stating the obvious, but public key cryptography is littered with problems that are going to take at least a decade to solve. Speed, which we touched on above, is a big one. Here are several more to get you thinking.

**CRYPTANALYSIS** Whenever a new algorithm or cryptographic implementation is introduced, cryptanalysis is sure to follow, and that's a good thing. Cryptanalysis is the science of discovering the original plaintext of an encrypted message, or recovering the private or secret key without prior knowledge.

Cryptanalysis ensures that algorithms are safe and that key lengths are long enough. RSA Data Security is perpetually sponsoring challenges (with prize money) to break its codes and recover private keys, and every few years an attack is successful. We've discussed weak algorithms and vulnerable key lengths in the section on algorithms above.

Cryptanalysis can be accomplished in a number of ways:

▼ **Ciphertext-only attacks** Given the encrypted text of several messages, the attacker attempts to deduce the plaintext and/or the encryption key.

■ **Known-plaintext attacks** Given the encrypted text and plaintext of several messages (obtainable through any number of ways), the attacker attempts to deduce the key. Obviously, this makes the attack easier than a ciphertext-only attack.

■ **Chosen-plaintext attacks** Given the encrypted text and plaintext of several messages, the attacker also gets to choose the plaintext that gets run through the algorithm. This is more powerful than both previous attacks, because certain blocks of plaintext may reveal weaknesses in the key used to encrypt it.

▲ **Adaptive-chosen-plaintext attacks** The same scenario as a chosen-plaintext attack, but the attacker can alter the plaintext for encryption at will. This is the most powerful form of attack that's widely known.

Several other less widely used attacks exist, as well. Other forms of attack, like the so-called "rubber hose attack" that involves extortion, bribery, or torture, are not classified among cryptanalytic attacks, even though they are probably the most effective!

The problem with cryptanalysis arises with algorithms and key lengths that have not been widely studied and tested yet are held up as secure. It's conceivable that a way to successfully reverse any algorithm has been discovered and not publicized. This is a common fear over government-sanctioned algorithms like Skipjack, but it's equally possible for any given encryption algorithm.

Over time, as computers becomes faster and cheaper, cryptanalytic attacks will become easier and easier to accomplish. In the minds of many, this is not a big concern, as key lengths can always be extended. In the minds of a few, a successful cryptanalytic attack is just a matter of time, no matter how secure you believe your algorithm and private key to be.

**POOR PASSWORD SELECTION**    This problem goes hand in hand with poor physical security. If your computer is stolen or someone breaks into the building, the key is in an attacker's hands and is protected only by a password of your choosing. Many of us have bad password selection habits: using a spouse's name, a phone number, or a simple word that we believe only to have meaning to us. So we think.

Password crackers have become extremely sophisticated pieces of software that can often make short work of your key protection in a matter of hours. Forget advanced cryptanalysis—it's much easier to determine someone's private key by simply hacking the password that's used to encrypt it.

Therefore, it's critical that you and your users utilize well-thought-out passwords that are long enough to defy brute force character-based attacks and are not composed of a single, simple word. It's also important to change your password often: Every 60 to 90 days is a good figure that shouldn't cause too many headaches.

While this is undoubtedly good advice, we are creatures of habit. Even worse, we're lazy when it comes to typing in passwords, and the shorter it is, the easier it is to remember. Instilling good password habits into your users isn't simple, but it can certainly pay off in the long run.

**ATTACKS ON CERTIFICATE AUTHORITIES**    Let's assume your public key algorithms are secure, your key lengths are long enough, and your passwords are steel-reinforced. Your building is secure, and you use cryptographic tokens and smartcards where necessary. You've basically done everything you can to build a secure environment. You're safe, right?

A potential weak link in the chain is the certificate authority, which you wouldn't normally think of as a place to attack. Of course, it makes perfect sense: Attack the PKI at its central nervous system and gain access to the entire chain.

**MASQUERADING**    The simplest attack is one where an outsider simply presents himself or herself as a trusted member of the organization and applies for a digital certificate. This will only work if the trusted member the attacker is masquerading as does not already have a digital certificate; this may be quite common in implementations where the system is not used very often or where some less technical users rarely use e-mail at all.

In any case, when the attacker receives the certificate of the trusted member, he or she simply presents himself or herself as that person, and can then work his or her way into receiving sensitive communications. If your initial authentication process is secure, this kind of attack shouldn't be a problem. However, it is something you'll need to watch for if you outsource your CA operations.

**CERTIFICATE THEFT**   A more sophisticated attack involves actually stealing the digital certificate of an existing user. The attacker absconds with the certificate of a legitimate user on the system, then presents himself or herself as that user. The certificate can be stolen in any number of ways: through a request for a lost ID, or copied directly from a user's computer, either in person or through a remote attack. Proper configuration of the CA and management of the key reissuance process is key to avoiding certificate theft, as is physical security and network firewalling.

**CERTIFICATE AUTHORITY PRIVATE KEY COMPROMISE**   The CA has its own private key, the master key that is used to issue, validate, and revoke all the certificates in the PKI. If a hacker obtains the private key of the CA, he or she can begin to perform these functions himself or herself—a frightening thought! It is therefore critical to ensure that the private key of the CA is exceptionally well protected. It should be as long as possible, and should usually involve some form of cryptographic token or smartcard security to protect it. The CA's private key should also be changed regularly—at least once a month.

**NEFARIOUS DEEDS**   Then there's bribery and other nefarious deeds intended to coerce a legitimate ID out of one of your security officers. There's not much you can do to prevent this outside of careful employee screening and random auditing.

**KEY REVOCATION**   People quit. People get fired. Keys and passwords are compromised. These are the realities of business. What do you do if any of these things happens?

Revoked digital certificates are placed on what's known as a certificate revocation list (CRL). This is simply a list of certificates that have been revoked before their scheduled expiration.

In a perfect world, every time a signature is checked, the CRL should be consulted. Unfortunately, key revocation was not heavy on the minds of the original PKI designers, and CRL implementations are currently iffy at best. The problem is that, in order to be thorough, the CRL must be nearly endless. New entries can be added, but old ones cannot be removed until they would normally have expired (this can be a matter of years). This means that a CRL will typically begin to stretch into hundreds, thousands, or tens of thousands of entries for large organizations, and if complete authenticity is desired, this CRL must be checked every time a digitally signed message is received. This can take a very long time.

In order to mitigate the speed issue, many authentication clients simply don't check CRLs during signature authentication, leaving a gaping hole in the overall security of the process. Furthermore, many CRLs are only updated once a day or even once a week, leaving a time lag when the CRL's work is most critical: immediately after a firing or the discovery of the theft of a certificate.

Even worse is the interaction between multiple CAs and the distribution of these increasingly lengthy CRLs. How do you securely manage multiple CRLs for multiple organizations? No one has really figured out a method that works well, and there should be substantial research into improving the CRL process, probably through the implementation of a tree-based CRL standard, over the next few years.

**CROSS-CERTIFICATION** Cross-certification is the process wherein two certificate authorities exchange key information and generate a trust relationship between each other. Cross-certification is particularly important if, for example, your company and your top customer want to build a web of trust but each of you has your own in-house PKI.

It sounds simple, but this is certainly not a trivial task. First, you'll have to be absolutely comfortable with the security policies of the other company. How are IDs issued? How is the CA protected from attack? What algorithms does the company use? If you're satisfied with the answers, then you have achieved an important first step.

Even then, the secure transmission of key information between two CAs is difficult enough, but as both organizations grow larger, the trust relationship becomes progressively more difficult to manage. The key revocation issues we discussed in the previous section are compounded when multiple CAs must be updated.

Take all of these concerns and add a third company to the mix. And a fourth. And a tenth. As the number of CAs in the web of trust grows linearly, the complexity of managing the web grows geometrically. With 10 companies, there are 45 trust relationships that may be required. And all of these companies may not trust each other. In fact, if two of them are your customers, some will likely be competitors who specifically do *not* trust each other. As you can see, the trust problems get complicated, quickly.

This is one of the major arguments for outsourcing your CA: Let someone else deal with this mess. Still, it's a difficult problem that is going to remain difficult for some time. While some PKI solutions do address cross-certification agreements, there is considerable confusion and skepticism over their security. This is an area that will have to be watched over the next few years, as the procedure for cross-certifying CAs is streamlined and secured.

**MULTINATIONAL ISSUES** If you want to use encryption products in a foreign office, build a web of trust with a foreign company, or export a software product with encryption features built-in, you're staring at a huge mess.

Thanks to Cold War treaties, cryptography products are covered under U.S. munitions laws, alongside guns and tanks. This means that if you sell an encryption product overseas without a license, you can be convicted for foreign arms dealing!

The government takes this very seriously, and numerous inventors (even cryptography hobbyists) of encryption products who post their applications on the Internet have found themselves visited by men in black who abscond with all the computer equipment in the house. Even presenting material *about* cryptography in public has been subject to government scrutiny, although, thankfully, this has lessened considerably.

Still, if you want to implement encryption off of American soil, you'll need to make sure the product you purchase is approved for overseas use. Typically, 40-bit cryptographic products are allowed anywhere, since these keys can be cracked through brute force in a matter of hours or days. Some 56-bit products have been allowed to be exported, although the government typically requires the purchaser to present proof that some kind of key escrow plan is in the works.

Subsidiaries of U.S. companies and their foreign offices can typically obtain 128-bit encryption products, but 255-bit products are not allowed for export. Also, if you are a bank or some other financial company, you'll typically find it easier to get better encryption products for e-commerce usage (meaning, you won't necessarily be able to also use the system for secure e-mail).

On the other hand, the United States has no import restrictions on foreign cryptography products, so you can implement, for example, a full-blown 255-bit encryption system between a U.S. office and an Irish subsidiary using a PKI from Baltimore Technologies, an Irish company. Of course, if you have offices in other countries, you'll be subject to their import restrictions as well, and this can get complicated pretty fast.

Managing a multinational encryption network is currently a mess, but this should get better over the next few years, as post-Cold War hysteria continues to lessen, as Europe unites to become the ECC, and as cryptography products continue to gain popularity domestically.

**KEY ESCROW**    Key escrow is simply the practice of backing up private keys. It is a vehemently controversial topic.

Key escrow, as a technology, is not necessarily a bad idea. If you are the security officer of a company and one of your users forgets his or her password or crashes his or her hard disk, key escrow saves you the trouble of revoking the old digital certificate and creating a new one. Instead, you can simply restore his or her private key from a secure backup, and he or she will be up and running as if nothing had happened. Provided there is no possible way for an outsider to obtain these key backups, key escrow can be a great thing.

Key escrow, as a government initiative, scares the pants off of most people. As part of the NSA's Capstone project, the government has been trying to mandate that encryption products contain key escrow features, ostensibly so that if cryptography products fall into the hands of drug dealers and arms traders, the government can read their e-mail.

With the exception of the Clipper chip, the government's key escrow initiatives have failed. To most, the idea reeks of Big Brother. There is also the issue of the security of the key escrow agent. Would any sane person trust the government to safely store all the private keys in the world without fear of the database being compromised? Government computers are subject to more hacking attempts than any others, and many of these attempts are successful. What about a third party to store the escrowed keys? Wouldn't that be an inviting target to hackers? And how are all of these keys going to be transmitted to the escrow agent without fear of compromise along the way?

These serious questions and others have stalled the key escrow initiative, perhaps permanently. Still, the idea is constantly kicking around, but unless businesses are required to implement escrow services, don't expect to see off-site key escrow services implemented any time soon.

**LIMITATIONS OF PUBLIC KEY CRYPTOGRAPHY**    There are also some built-in problems with public-key cryptography that make it difficult to implement. One of the major issues is, how do you encrypt files for numerous recipients? Because encryption is done with the recipient's public key, only one person can be the recipient of an encrypted transmission. To anyone else on the CC: list, the file will be unreadable. If 100 people need the file, do you encrypt the file 100 different times? In truth, a secret key encryption system works much better in this situation.

What if keys are corrupted or lost, and there's no quick way to authenticate that the request for key reissuance is genuine? During initial setup of a digital identity, this is usually not a problem, but if a key is corrupted in the middle of a busy work week, how do you take care of the situation without disrupting business?

Entrust and its brethren have been working on hybrid public/secret key cryptography systems to address issues like these, but with each change made to a cryptosystem, the more potential it has to be broken open. While public key cryptography is still in its infancy, it's issues like these that are slowing its deployment.

**USER TRAINING**    If you've made it this far, you've done better than most. While we've done our best to keep the text at a real-world level, the concepts contained herein are still exceptionally heavy on theory.

Introducing something with the complexity of a PKI into your organization is going to leave you wondering how you teach the foundations of cryptography to your user base.

The sobering realization is that you can't.

The average manager simply wants the e-mail to work, be fast, and be secure. That's it. They're not interested in the opposing merits of DES and RSA, or concerned with key escrow debates. And to them, hashing means something completely different.

How do you train a user like this about the importance of verifying the certificates of users outside the company, using a long enough key, or protecting the key with an appropriate password? It isn't easy.

In user training, stay away from heavy technical details and work on real-world applications of the technology. This goes for any new technology, but it's especially appropriate for encryption and authentication. Explain the benefits of proper use of the tools—how they are properly used so as not to defy company policy—walk them through the signing and encryption procedures, and warn them of the consequences of improper use. And keep your door open for questions. There will be many.

## Additional Resources

It's hard to squeeze everything you need to know about cryptography into a single chapter. If you want in-depth details about algorithms, cryptographic theory, large number factoring, cryptanalysis, and government initiatives, we can recommend two excellent references.

First is Bruce Schneier's book, *Applied Cryptography*, the avowed bible of the cryptographic industry, which contains just about everything you could possibly want to know about encryption and authentication. It's very heavy on mathematical theory, but it's an invaluable reference, even including C source code for implementing cryptographic algorithms yourself.

Another good reference is RSA Data Security's "Answers to Frequently Asked Questions About Today's Cryptography." This reference is currently in version 3.0 and has the added benefit of being free for download from RSA's Web site at http://www.rsa.com/rsalabs/newfaq. You will probably notice that, because the FAQ is kept up by RSA itself, it is heavily slanted in support of its own products and proprietary algorithms. As RSA is the undisputed industry leader in cryptographic services, this isn't as bad as it sounds, but it is important to keep in mind while you're browsing its pages.

# CHAPTER 19

# Management Systems for High-Speed Networks

An essential part of planning your network infrastructure is designing and implementing methods for managing it. "Network management" is certainly a broad term, which can and does encompass everything from determining the amount of traffic on a particular segment to monitoring how an application uses memory on a network client to tracking whether certain devices are functioning properly.

In this chapter we will take a look at three very broad areas of network management and the various management systems used for each. The areas of management are as follows:

▼ Traffic management

■ Application management

▲ Device management

# TRAFFIC MANAGEMENT

When most people talk about "network management," they are really talking about *traffic management*. The purpose of traffic management is to determine how much of what type of data traffic is traveling over your network infrastructure at any given time. Upon determining this, you can decide whether your network infrastructure can handle that amount of traffic, and make changes in the bandwidth or access method or protocol type to ensure optimum throughput.

Traffic management systems fall generally into three categories:

▼ Packet generators

■ Network analyzers

▲ Application testers

## Packet Generators

*Packet generators* operate at the Network and Data-Link layers of the OSI model. They load a network with "synthetic traffic." Synthetic traffic is composed of packets that the packet generator created (rather than packets from real network production traffic). These packets are sent in huge volume from a central location on the network. The goal of packet generators is to "stress test" a network, or find its maximum traffic limits. Packet generators are able to flood a network, while normal production traffic is rarely able to do so.

The downside of packet generators is that the traffic patterns they produce aren't real. Ordinary network traffic doesn't come as fast, as constant, or as uniformly shaped and directed as the traffic produced by packet generators. Therefore, while packet generators are great for determining the maximum theoretical limits of traffic that your network can handle, they don't tell you much about how your network will perform under day-to-day traffic loads. A well-known packet generator is SmartBits from Netcom Systems, Inc.

## Network Analyzers

*Network analyzers* monitor actual network traffic. They allow you to take a sample of traffic and analyze its content and composition. For example, if you are getting a slow response time on a particular segment of your network, you could place a network analyzer on that segment to monitor it for several hours—or even several days. The network analyzer would record the type of traffic (10Base-T, token ring, etc.), the network protocol (IP, IPX, router protocols, and others), how much of the available bandwidth is being used, and information about collisions, incomplete packets, and packet retransmissions. This information can help you locate "chattering" cards (cards that are malfunctioning and flooding the network with bad packets), overloaded segments, and "top talkers"—users who take up most of the network's traffic resources.

Some examples of network analyzers are Internet Advisor from Hewlett-Packard and Sniffer from Network General.

## Application Testers

*Application testers* model and measure node-to-node traffic patterns from the Application layer. They simulate real-world traffic associated with using specific types of distributed network applications such as databases and document preparation packages. The packages allow you to test the impact that adding a given application would have on your network so that you can plan infrastructure changes accordingly. Some examples of application testers are Chariot from Ganymede Software, Inc., and Dynameasure from Bluecurve, Inc.

# APPLICATION MANAGEMENT

While traffic management devices are great for helping you locate problems and bottlenecks in the infrastructure, they don't tell you anything about the resources that are being used by network applications, nor the resulting availability and response time of those applications. This is the venue of application management systems, which have arrived fairly recently on the scene.

In fact, application management systems are so new that at the time of this writing, there are no standards for application management. Right now, application vendors are using proprietary technology to implement management and monitoring systems. For example, Oracle Corporation has enabled SNMP support for its database, and has developed its own proprietary management console. This works well in a single-vendor situation, but in reality, most enterprise environments will have multiple mission-critical applications from a variety of vendors. Each of these applications should be monitored—and a separate management system for each critical application simply isn't workable. The ideal application management product should be able to monitor a wide range of applications with an open and scalable architecture.

Therefore, the Desktop Management Task Force (DMTF) is working on developing such standards. Currently the Distributed Application Performance (DAP) Working Group of the DMTF has been charged with defining a standard model for the behavior of distributed applications. This model will define the runtime behavior for applications for *each unit of work*. A unit of work could be a transaction, a database query, or even an input/output event.

The stated goals of the DAP working group are as follows:

▼ Extend the core/meta schema, if necessary, to model runtime performance and incorporate quality of service objects

■ Relate these models to the common schemas of the other management domains: Systems/Devices, Network, Applications, Service, Support, and User

▲ Evolve standard methods to populate the model developed independent of operating system or performance agent availability

For more information on the DMTF Distributed Application Performance (DAP) WG, please contact the chairperson at chair-dap@dmtf.org.

# DEVICE MANAGEMENT

One of the most widespread needs in network management is to monitor devices to determine whether they are functioning properly. This is called *device management*.

Most device management packages gather information from devices by using *agents* to collect information from devices all over the network, then send it back to a centralized *management console*. At the management console, the network manager can use the information to create reports on the health of the network.

Device management systems also use agents to send alerts about trouble on the network such as device failures or performance problems. Agents reside throughout the network on servers, routers, switches, and client computers. Agents gather information about the device on which they are installed and send it back to the management console. Management console functions include network topology mapping, event reporting, traffic monitoring, network diagnostic functions, trend analysis, and report generation.

The most widely used management applications that employ agents use the *Simple Network Management Protocol* (SNMP). SNMP is a management protocol for TCP/IP networks. Due most likely to the UNIX roots of TCP/IP networks, most SNMP management systems are UNIX based, although Windows NT systems are becoming more popular. In any event, SNMP was developed by the Internet community, and it defines how agents and management consoles interact through request and response messaging.

# Simple Network Management Protocol (SNMP)

SNMP is a communication protocol for gathering information from network devices. Each network device hosts an agent that gathers information about the performance of the device, then sends that information to a management console. Each piece of information gathered about a device is defined by a *managed object*. A managed object is a logical representation of a real physical entity on the network. Each managed object gathers some information from the device hosting it. The managed object then maintains that information for use by the management system.

All of these managed objects are organized as a management information base (MIB). A *MIB* is just a hierarchical database of managed objects. There are both generic and vendor-specific MIBs. Individual vendors must design managed objects for each piece of information they want to monitor on their devices. The vendors must provide these managed objects in the form of a MIB that adheres to SNMP standards.

## How SNMP Works

Figure 19-1 shows the components of a typical SNMP management environment and how these components work together. The components are as follows

▼  **Devices**   Network devices such as hubs, switches, and routers hosting agents that gather information about the devices and send it to the management console.

■  **Proxy agent**   In devices that aren't able to host an agent, a proxy agent can be run by another device on behalf of the SNMP-incapable device.

■  **Management systems**   The application that assembles the information gathered by agents.

▲  **SNMP**   The protocol that provides both the query language for gathering information from—as well as the transport protocol for sending the information to—the agents that run in the devices.

Most SNMP management systems discover the topology of the network automatically, then display the network topology in the form of a graphic. Administrators can choose a particular segment to view in more detail. They can then select a particular device to monitor, and view all information collected from it.

The agents running on the managed devices constantly collect information. Each agent collects only that information it is specifically charged with collecting. For example, an agent on a switch may count each packet received on each port. Collecting this information and sending it to the management system is the sole job of the SNMP agent.

Back at the central collection point, the management system continuously contacts the various agents to obtain the information they have collected. SNMP uses UDP, which is part of the TCP/IP suite, to carry its messages across the network. Because SNMP uses

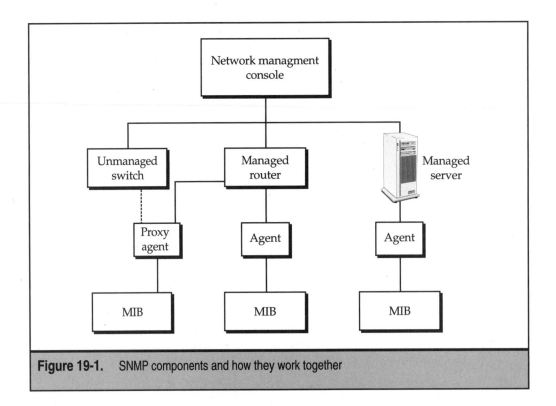

**Figure 19-1.**    SNMP components and how they work together

this connectionless transport protocol and a simple command set, it is fairly efficient and can usually operate over the busiest networks without causing noticeable stress. The agents send this information to the management system upon request.

**NOTE:**    The management system knows only about those pieces of information listed in its MIBs for the managed object. Therefore, it's important that the management system's MIBs be updated to include all the pieces of information that the agent running on the device can collect every time a new device is added to the network.

## SNMP Alarms

Network administrators can set alarms to alert them to device failures or other problem spots on the network. Alarms are triggered when predefined *events* occur on the network. Events occur when limits specified in MIBs are exceeded—for example, when the number of bad packets received on a switch port exceeds a fixed amount. When an event occurs, the device that identifies the event "traps" the event, then sends a report to all management consoles.

SNMP is simple, robust, and—most important—it does its job well. However, it's not without its shortcomings. For example, an SNMP management console constantly polls agents to gather information. This both increases network traffic to some degree and places all management burden on a central point: the console.

## RMON to the Rescue

To alleviate some of this stress, the Internet Engineering Task Force developed RMON—*remote monitoring*—to let agents collect information only about their own network segments. Actually, RMON is a MIB extension that collects information about entire network segments rather than just about individual devices.

Like SNMP, RMON uses agents, called *probes*, which are software processes—running on devices—that collect data. However, with RMON, the collected information is stored in a local MIB rather than at the central management console.

Figure 19-2 shows how this works. Probes located in network devices such as hubs and switches collect and maintain historical information in a MIB located on the same segment as the device. The network management console does not need to constantly poll probes and receive information from them to ensure that historical management information is properly collected. In fact, in RMON, the relationship between probes and

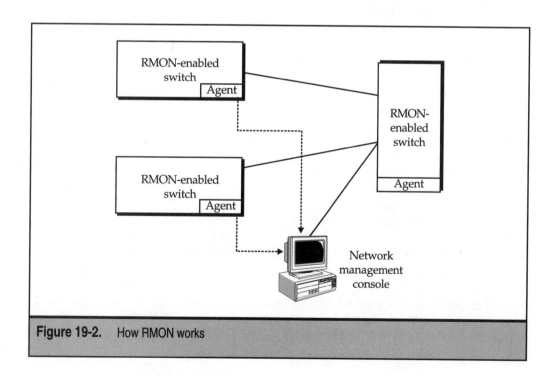

**Figure 19-2.**   How RMON works

the management console is reversed. The probes function as servers and the management console acts as a client in a client/server relationship.

Just like SNMP, RMON can send alarms when events occur. When a manager receives an alarm, he or she can assess network conditions by analyzing the information provided in the nine RMON *groups*:

▼ **Statistics**   Gathers and maintains traffic statistics and errors

■ **History**   Collects statistics at specified intervals for historical analysis

■ **Alarms**   Sends alerts when events occur

■ **Hosts**   Gathers information and calculates statistics based on MAC addresses

■ **HostTopN**   Gathers data about which hosts are generating the most traffic

■ **Matrix**   Gathers data about which devices are communicating with each other

■ **Events**   Triggers actions based on alarms

■ **Packet capture**   Lets you capture packets by type

▲ **Filter**   Lets you view only selected packets

For example, a manager receives an alarm informing her of excessive traffic. She could then collect information from the HostTopN and Matrix groups to find out which nodes are transmitting the most information and to whom they are talking. Once the busiest transmitters are located, the manager can analyze traffic from those transmitters to see whether there are errors—indicating a device that needs to be repaired—or whether more bandwidth can be added to that segment to accommodate the traffic.

RMON is not a replacement for SNMP, but rather an extension of it. SNMP, via UDP, still provides the communication mechanism for transmitting data from the RMON probes to the management consoles.

Basing RMON's architecture on that of network analyzers, the IETF's goal in developing the RMON standard was to allow open monitoring of all networks from any vendor's network management system. It also provides network analyzer functionality on remote networks. For example, RMON also supports packet filtering and capturing on specific network segments. It also lets network managers remotely analyze traffic at all seven layers of the protocol stack. This means that running RMON on a remote network will obviate traveling to a network site to attach a network analyzer.

## Son of RMON: Merging with Application Management

At the time of this writing, the current RMON RFC is 1757. This RFC was released in 1995, which means that an update is both inevitable and imminent. The current RMON RFC has two Ethernet-specific monitoring groups and seven monitoring groups that apply to both token ring and Ethernet. The next RMON standard is RFC 1513, which defines additional token ring extensions. In addition, RMON 2 provides monitoring support all the way up to the Application layer. It will allow managers to monitor the amount of traffic that is generated by applications running in workstations and servers. This should be a big boost to the application management initiative, because it gives information about the actual usage of the network, not just traffic flows. RMON 2 also provides information about end-to-end traffic flows.

## Evolving SNMP

Nothing stays the same, and SNMP is no exception. The IETF began work on SNMPv2 in 1992. The goal of the next incarnation of SNMP was better security, enhanced management features, and more efficient information retrieval. Unfortunately, the developers of SNMPv2 soon found that adding security would make it incompatible with the original SNMP. As a result, SNMPv2 development ground to a halt, and the IETF disbanded the SNMPv2 group in 1996. Later, however, the SNMP revision group reemerged and development soon began on SNMPv3.

While a new official version of SNMP was trying to develop, a trend emerged that used the HTTP protocol to transport management information, making each managed device into a Web server of sorts. This makes management information available via Web browsers modified to function as management consoles. This takes us into the world of *Web-based network management*.

# Web-Based Network Management

As mentioned above, Web-based network management lets network managers monitor their networks using Web technologies like browsers and HTTP. It lets administrators monitor devices remotely, in real time, and collect information about systems. It also lets them troubleshoot systems and create reports about network problems or trends. Web-based network management uses the TCP/IP protocols, which are the coins of the realm on the Internet and corporate intranets. Therefore, the same Web management tools can be used to manage a switch in the same room or anywhere in the world via the worldwide Internet. This trend is becoming so popular that many vendors of network management systems have already added Web browser interfaces to their management systems.

## Web-Based Enterprise Management (WBEM)

In July of 1996, five companies formed the Web-Based Enterprise Management (WBEM) Consortium with the express goal of integrating disparate management protocols, management information, and management systems. The five companies are

▼ BMC Software

■ Cisco Systems

■ Microsoft

■ Intel

▲ Compaq

While WBEM was founded by these five companies, its initiative is now supported by over 50 vendors. So, what is the WBEM initiative all about? While SNMP is still the most widely used management protocol, WBEM would like to see new Internet standards such as Hypermedia Management Protocol (HMMP) and Common Information Model (CIM) take the forefront in network management. The HMMP advantage, says the WBEM Consortium, is that it lets network management system vendors build systems that use all the same protocols and provide access through the same user interface. As well, the WBEM Consortium is interested in developing a common data structure to facilitate easier, more uniform access to corporate data.

**HYPERMEDIA MANAGEMENT PROTOCOL (HMMP)**  Hypermedia Management Protocol (HMMP) is an Internet protocol used to access and publish data across the Internet, as well as to exchange management and control messages between HMMP nodes. As a client/server protocol, it is similar to Hypertext Transfer Protocol (HTTP). HMMP clients request data from HMMP servers. However, unlike HTTP, HMMP clients can be management processes running in standard Web browsers or management and monitoring processes that are hosted by managed devices. When HMMP servers receive requests from clients, they either respond to those requests with information or pass the request on to another server. In the latter instance, the requesting server is now a client of the server to which it is passing the request. As you can see, HMMP doesn't require that every client know how to manage every device it needs to use directly. Instead, clients can make requests to servers that manage groups of devices. The devices it manages may in fact use proprietary management mechanisms and protocols unknown to the client. This doesn't affect the client making the request, because the servers always respond to the clients' requests for information using HMMP.

**COMMON INFORMATION MODEL (CIM)**  Common Information Model (CIM) is also part of the WBEM initiative. CIM is a data structure that uses HMMP to access and manipulate data held by HMMP management hosts. The CIM structure is a set of standard classes and types that represent hardware devices and other such managed objects in the network management environment.

## Where Is WBEM?

WBEM really hadn't made much headway at the time of this writing. Two years after its inception, the WBEM Consortium was still developing its initiatives and garnering support for them. Will WBEM ever become the Internet-wide force for uniform management that its founders hoped? That remains to be seen.

## Java Management API

As an alternative to WBEM, Sun Microsystems and some 15 other companies developed and presented the Java Management API (JMAPI). JMAPI is an environment for developing Web-based management applications using the Java programming language. JMAPI uses a simple ODBC database to store collected management information. To access and analyze the management data, developers can write applets that will run on any system that has a Java-enabled operating system. Any Java-enabled browser can then access the management information. It supports SNMP, so JMAPI applications can access information collected by SNMP agents.

While JMAPI sounds like an elegant and much-needed solution for IP network management, we're not sure that it will ultimately succeed. Unfortunately, at the time of this writing we haven't seen any JMAPI applications, so it is difficult to know whether this far-reaching solution will actually take hold.

# MANAGEMENT PLATFORMS

All of the various types of network management systems we have discussed represent a substantial investment in money, time, and staff. So much of an investment, in fact, that running separate management systems for each type of system is prohibitively expensive. With limited resources, you may feel you must select which one of the management systems to implement, and therefore have to choose which of the types of systems is most crucial to your network.

Fortunately, this isn't the case. All of these systems can be integrated into one of several comprehensive network management platforms that act as a framework for building, operating, and—yes—*managing* network management systems. The seven major network management platforms are listed in Table 19-1, along with the Web site addresses of the manufacturers.

The networking world refers to these products as "platforms" because they have extensive features, they can manage entire enterprise networks, and they have the ability to manage other network management systems.

| Company | Product | URL |
|---|---|---|
| Cabletron | Spectrum | ctron.com/spectrum |
| Computer Associates | Unicenter TNG | cai.com/products.htm |
| Hewlett-Packard | OpenView | hp.com/openview |
| Microsoft | Systems Management Server | microsoft.com/smsmgmt |
| Novell | ManageWise | novell.com/managewise |
| Sun Microsystems | Solstice | sun.com/soltice |

**Table 19-1.**   Network Management Tools

# IETF NETWORK MANAGEMENT DEVELOPMENTS

As you may have guessed from the preceding sections, the most influential standards body in developing management system standards is the Internet Engineering Task Force. The IETF has a number of working groups that are developing methods for using SNMP and other protocols to access management information for a wide variety of devices on intranets and the Internet. Its primary goal is to advance management initiatives for Web servers and the HTTP MIB, but the IETF also—at least officially—states an interest in expanding its standards work to include many other devices.

To keep abreast of the IETF and its many RFCs (requests for comment) related to network management, check out the IETF Web site at http://www.ietf.org/html.charters/wg-dir.html.

# CHAPTER 20

## Speed Kills:
## Avoiding a Crash

If this book has met its objectives, you now have a lot to think about. We hope we've given you enough guidance to help you determine where—and whether—you need a high-speed protocol. As well, we hope we've provided enough information about the strengths and weaknesses of each protocol to enable you to choose one, or at least put together a "short list" of suitable high-speed protocols for further investigation. Now the hard part begins: building the high-speed network.

The worksheets in Chapter 6 will help you plan what needs to be done and how much it will cost. They are thorough, so going through them in the context of your organization's network should help you address every detail of the implementation plan. So, what do you do after you have created a project work plan and budget?

## FIRST: TRY BEFORE YOU BUY

I can't stress this enough. All the vendor promises in the world notwithstanding, before you make your final selection of high-speed networking products, get the products into your network and test them under real conditions. I've seen too many products that looked great on the specifications sheets but failed miserably in the real network. Even if the product works out great, you'll probably uncover a detail or two about integrating it into your network that the sales literature didn't mention. For example, you may need to reconfigure the memory of, or even add memory to, your networked PCs to accommodate the high-speed network adapter. Or, you may find that your routers can't be upgraded to be compatible with new protocols, and will have to be replaced altogether. These are things you won't necessarily discover in a vendor's demonstration. In fact, you may never discover them unless you get the products you plan to buy into your shop and put them through real-life testing.

**TIP:** In my experience, any vendor who promises that a network product has "seamless integration" and will be "transparent to the rest of the network"—especially if the vendor has never worked on my network—should be shown the door immediately.

Until you get the network products into your shop and discover all the details of installation, you won't be able to put together a comprehensive budget or schedule. So make this your first priority!

## SECOND: IDENTIFY THE NEXT BOTTLENECK

This is something you can do while you're testing equipment. As you probably know, improving network performance is simply a matter of moving the bottlenecks around. Right now, your network's bottleneck is inadequate bandwidth. When that is eased, where will the bottleneck be? Will it be underpowered servers? Decrepit workstations? At the same time you are making your pitch for a high-speed network, you should tell your management where the next slowdown will be and what will cause it. This will add to your credibility and save you from discussions that begin, "You said if we put in this high-speed network, the network would speed up! What happened?"

# THIRD: MAKE A SCHEDULE

Using the information from the worksheets in Chapter 6, create a schedule for the project. Determine the order in which the upgrades and installations will have to be done in your organization. Be sure to figure in ordering lead times and delivery delays. Then, create a Gantt chart, like the one pictured in Figure 20-1, showing dependencies and which steps have to be completed before others can begin. Assign beginning and ending dates.

*TIP:* You'll probably want to schedule network installation one building or one floor at a time.

## Class Time

Consult with training companies or in-house instructors to create a schedule for training staff and network users. Timing is critical here. Training should take place close to the time of network implementation, or everyone will have forgotten what they learned by the time the network is in place. If you have a lot of people to train, you'll probably want to use outside training specialists even if you have in-house trainers so that everyone can receive training shortly before the new network is put into service.

# FOURTH: GET YOUR BUDGET APPROVED

Now that you know everything you have to do and buy, how much it will cost, and how long it will take, it's time to get your final budget approved. Frequently it's difficult for a network manager to justify to a nontechnical management committee the expense of building a high-speed network. You know it will increase performance, thus saving time and making network users more productive. Productivity, however, is a difficult thing to quantify. Indeed, a high-speed network may be helpful, even vital, to your organization. But given the reluctance of the powers that be to spend money on anything that won't show a tangible economic benefit, how do you convince them to approve the expenditures to build one?

The answer is deceptively simple: Put a price on it. Determine:

▼ How much the system really costs (you've already done this in Chapter 6)

■ How much money it will really save (or make)

▲ If the difference is worth it

| Task | 4/1/99 | 4/15/99 | 5/1/99 | 5/15/99 | 6/1/99 |
|---|---|---|---|---|---|
| Order test components | | | | | |
|    Network adapters | XXXXX | | | | |
|    Switches | XXXXX | | | | |
|    Patch cables | XXXXX | | | | |
|    Hubs | XXXXX | | | | |
|    Router interface cards | XXXXX | | | | |
| | | | | | |
| Build test network | | XXXXX | | | |
| | | | | | |
| Test protocol | | | XXXXX | | |
| | | | | | |
| Final implementation decision | | | | XXXXX | |
| | | | | | |
| Notify users of implementation decision | | | | | XXXXX |
| | | | | | |
| Order components | | | | | |
|    Network adapters | | | | | |
|    Switches | | | | | |
|    Patch cables | | | | | |
|    Hubs | | | | | |
|    Router interface cards | | | | | |
| | | | | | |
| Install router interface cards | | | | | |
| | | | | | |
| Install switches in wiring closets | | | | | |
| | | | | | |
| Notify users of implementation schedule | | | | | |
|    Floor 14 | | | | | |
|    Floor 15 | | | | | |
|    Floor 16 | | | | | |
|    Floor 17 | | | | | |
|    Floor 18 | | | | | |
| Install network adapters | | | | | |
|    Floor 14 | | | | | |
|    Floor 15 | | | | | |
|    Floor 16 | | | | | |
|    Floor 17 | | | | | |
|    Floor 18 | | | | | |
| Cut over to new protocol | | | | | |
|    Floor 14 | | | | | |
|    Floor 15 | | | | | |
|    Floor 16 | | | | | |
|    Floor 17 | | | | | |
|    Floor 18 | | | | | |

**Figure 20-1.**    A Gantt chart for a network implementation project

| 6/15/99 | 7/1/99 | 7/15/99 | 8/1/99 | 8/15/99 | 9/1/99 | 9/15/99 | 10/1/99 | 10/15/99 |
|---|---|---|---|---|---|---|---|---|
| | | | | | | | | |
| | | | | | | | | |
| | | | | | | | | |
| | | | | | | | | |
| | | | | | | | | |
| | | | | | | | | |
| | | | | | | | | |
| | | | | | | | | |
| | | | | | | | | |
| | | | | | | | | |
| | | | | | | | | |
| | | | | | | | | |
| | | | | | | | | |
| | | | | | | | | |
| XXXXX | | | | | | | | |
| XXXXX | | | | | | | | |
| XXXXX | | | | | | | | |
| XXXXX | | | | | | | | |
| XXXXX | | | | | | | | |
| | XXXXX | | | | | | | |
| | | XXXXX | | | | | | |
| | | | XXXXX | | | | | |
| | | | | XXXXX | | | | |
| | | | | | XXXXX | | | |
| | | | | | | XXXXX | | |
| | | | | | | | XXXXX | |
| | | | XXXXX | | | | | |
| | | | | XXXXX | | | | |
| | | | | | XXXXX | | | |
| | | | | | | XXXXX | | |
| | | | | | | | XXXXX | |
| | | | | | | | | XXXXX |
| | | | | | | | | |
| | | | | | | | | |
| | | | | | | | | |
| | | | | | | | | |

**Figure 20-1.** A Gantt chart for a network implementation project *(continued)*

You'll get a lot more attention when you present a purchase request in terms of money it can make or save your company than when you recommend it for convenience and ease of use. Telling your boss that a high-speed network will improve response time is one thing. Pointing out that having one is like getting an extra workday from each user each year is quite another.

Of course, this answer may be simple, but the means to accomplish it is a little more complicated. The task is to pinpoint the economic benefits of the high-speed network, calculate its exact cost, and determine whether the benefit justifies the cost. This requires not only technical expertise, but also business savvy and creative thinking. Let me give you a few pointers on how to translate benefits and costs into dollars and cents.

## It's a Wonderful Life

The first step to putting a price on the benefit of a high-speed network is to take an objective look at life without the product—past, present, and future. Ask yourself what past problems the high-speed network could have eased. For example, did the network in accounting slow to a standstill during year-end closing last January? Are your remote offices unable to start work on time each morning because the nightly data transfers from headquarters are taking too long to complete? Use these as concrete examples for your management of how the high-speed network will be used in your organization.

Next, ask yourself what will—or won't—happen in the future if you don't build a high-speed network. Then, figure out how that will affect your business. For example, survey your network users to find out how long it takes to complete a print job on a network printer. At the same time, ask them how much they expect their printing to increase over the next few quarters.

As another example, let's say that you manage a network with 2,500 users and you find through your survey that on the average it takes users ten seconds to save a document. According to your research, the same task on a high-speed network would take two seconds. You also find, through your document management system, that the average network user saves 15 documents a day. "Eight seconds?" You say, "Big deal." A little math will show you that this is a very big deal indeed:

8 seconds × 15 documents × 250 workdays = 8.33 hours per year

This means that saving eight seconds per saved document amounts to saving a day's worth of work each year. Your friendly accounting department can help you put a dollar value on this. Suppose you find that the average salary of a network user is $35,000. A day's salary for an average network user would then be $140. Getting an extra day's work each year from all 2,500 users would mean an annual savings of $350,000. That should certainly get your manager's attention!

## Doomsayer

Now that you have a feel for what not having a high-speed network is costing you, take a moment to play Cassandra. Get your known facts together, then conjure up the worst possible scene that could result from this. In our document saving example, for instance, assume that your company is actually paying a day's worth of overtime ($500,000 per year) for work that can't be done during regular business hours.

In another example, determine whether the bandwidth crunch on your network, coupled with increasing network usage, might cause work to slow to the point that important tax or SEC filing deadlines are missed. When you present visions like these to your management, you'll have their attention.

## Considering the Alternative

Now it's time to concede that a high-speed network is not the only solution. There may be other ways to solve the problem. To have a persuasive pitch, you will have to acknowledge that there are alternatives and show that you have considered them. Then you have to reveal their inadequacies—if you can.

One of the problems with the alternatives that we have suggested is that most of them require much more maintenance and management than a high-speed network. Network segmentation in particular requires a great deal of configuration and reconfiguration as users are added and moved. As well, virtual networking requires expertise in the software and concepts of virtual networking, as well as time to maintain the virtual segments.

### Too Much Is Not Enough

The biggest inadequacy of any of the high-speed networking alternatives is that there is never, ever enough bandwidth. Any means of squeezing a little more performance out of 10Mbps is truly a stopgap measure. As more users are added to the network, and PCs gain processing power, and more multimedia applications are put on networks, you will find that even a shared 100Mbps network may not provide sufficient bandwidth for long. One of the driving forces behind this seemingly unstoppable bandwidth drought is user expectations. As users are buying high-powered PCs for home, they will expect their work PCs—despite being networked—to match the response time of their supercharged stand-alone home PCs.

Therefore, giving your budget committee a short history lesson on the growth of networks, application packet sizes, PC processors, user expectations, and bandwidth requirements over the last three years should bring them around to reality.

## The Price Is Right

Now it's time to put a complete price on the high-speed network you want to build. As you are now aware, the cost of a high-speed network is much more than the purchase price. Ask yourself how the new protocol will affect client and server resources. Will additional hardware be required to install and run the system properly? Will you have to purchase annual support contracts? How will implementing the management system affect staffing? Overtime? Training? As we've mentioned, the worksheets in Chapter 6 will help you put together a detailed budget. Be honest with yourself when calculating these costs.

## Benefit Analysis

After you evaluate the costs of the high-speed network, you must assess its benefits. If you do build the network, how will it really benefit you? As we mentioned earlier, making your life easier isn't going to satisfy the budget committee. How is it going to save money? A product that cuts staffing and/or overtime, or that solves a significant operational or customer service problem, is going to get the budget dollars.

In my document-saving example, if the total cost of building the high-speed network is $1,000,000 or less, the system will pay for itself in less than three years in time savings alone. After that, the high-speed network will be giving your company $350,000 worth of time each year.

## Show Time

Now that you've gathered your facts, found the costs and shortcomings in your own solution, addressed the holes in your own logic, and built a case based on economic need and common sense, it's time to prepare your presentation. Start by telling your management how much the high-speed network will save the company. Then, give your example of a past project that would have been done more cost-effectively if the high-speed network had been in place. Next, present the worst-case scenario if the network isn't built, then conclude with a step-by-step explanation of the analysis you used to arrive at these conclusions. Finally, just in case your argument sparks enthusiasm, it's a good idea to have a high-level implementation plan on hand to give your management an idea of what will be involved.

## You Can't Always Get What You Want

Your analysis has either produced a sound, justifiable, and hopefully unassailable case for building a high-speed network, or a reasonable explanation of why the project just isn't feasible. In either instance, you win. Understanding why a purchase doesn't make business sense will build your credibility with your management just as much as knowing when it does. It also makes you aware of the types of systems and pricing that will make sense.

If your analysis shows that building a high-speed network isn't a sound business move, don't give up. Instead, calculate a price at which the network would be a good buy. Then present that figure to your vendor (be fair—vendors have to make money, too). You never know—there may be room for negotiation. Even if there isn't, this will give your vendor information to take back to their manufacturers to let them know their products may be overpriced for their market.

This exercise will also give you more than a business case for building a high-speed network. It will help you gain a broad perspective on how your network fits into your organization. It also encourages constant, close communication with other departments and an understanding of how they use the network and information about the network.

This is the kind of perspective that will not only make you a better network manager, but also serve you well throughout your career.

# FIFTH: SET EXPECTATIONS

As soon as you complete your implementation plan and schedule for your high-speed network, start setting appropriate expectations for your managers, your users, and your staff. Here are some tips:

▼ **Communicate.**   Write a memo, hold meetings, post notices, and talk with everyone you meet in the hall about what you are doing and why. Explain it in excruciating detail. Tell them why it is necessary. Be a walking, talking seminar on building your high-speed network. Even though some people may not understand everything you're saying, they will have an opportunity to grasp the enormity of the undertaking and perhaps be more sympathetic to any difficulties encountered as a result.

■ **Listen to their concerns about "another network project."**   Everyone dreads having the network down, and it often seems that every major network upgrade or conversion is followed by a frustrating period of sporadic downtime while working out the "bugs." Some users may be anxious about the network project because they are about to begin demanding projects of their own. You should be aware of these projects and plan the network implementation accordingly. After talking with your users, you may even want to reschedule so that the network won't be "under construction" during a critical work period such as tax season at an accounting firm or a large trial at a law firm.

■ **Be very candid about how long the project will take.**   You will gain nothing by being overly optimistic. If anything, overestimate the duration of the implementation.

■ **Let all concerned know where and when you are likely to encounter problems or delays.**   At the same time, share your contingency plans for meeting important deadlines and keeping the work flowing even when the project isn't going as well as planned.

■ **Don't oversell the expected performance increases.**   Obviously, you wouldn't be undertaking the project if you didn't think it was worthwhile. However, while you should be positive about the benefits of a high-speed network, don't make anyone expect a miracle.

■ **Prepare your staff for long hours.**   Be sure you have communicated very clearly exactly what this project is going to demand of them. Show them the schedule and the task assignments. Be sure everyone is committed to successful completion of the project. Then, help them prepare for it.

*TIP:*   Giving them some time off before the project begins may help ensure that they are fit, well rested, and in good spirits at the outset. This will help the whole project to go more smoothly, to say the least.

▲    **Be prepared for cranky users.**   No matter how carefully and thoroughly you communicate, there will no doubt be a user or two who becomes frustrated with the progress of the project and lashes out at you and/or your staff. Don't take it personally (no matter how personally it is aimed) and make sure your staff doesn't, either. Tell them that this is likely to happen, and instruct them to listen patiently to angry users, apologize for any inconvenience, tell the users what is being done, and walk away.

*TIP:*   It might be wise to offer your staff an incentive—such as a bonus, a victory party, or some time off—or all of the above—when the project is completed.

# SURVIVING SPEED

This chapter sounds more like you're preparing for war than for a network upgrade. However, it's not meant to scare you away from building a high-speed network. In fact, its aim is to ensure that you come away from the project with a high-performance network and an intact career. The secret to a successful implementation is

▼    Doing your homework and carefully selecting which protocols to implement where

■    Carefully planning and scheduling the tasks and expenditures

▲    Preparing your staff, your users, and your management

Follow the guidelines laid out in this book, and you too can be King—or Queen—of the Network Superhighway!

# PART V

## Appendixes

# APPENDIX A

## Open Systems

Open systems, in broad terms, are computer architectures, computer systems, computer software, and communication systems in which the specifications are published and available to everyone. An open system encourages the development of compatible vendor products. Customers benefit from open systems because they can choose from a wide variety of products that work with the system and, most important, are easily interconnected with other vendors' products. An open environment provides standard communication facilities and protocols, or provides a way to use a variety of protocols. The computer community is putting more pressure on vendors for open systems because there is a need to purchase equipment, under open bid, with the guarantee that equipment will work on existing open systems.

## SPECIFYING OPEN SYSTEMS

Open systems are defined by vendors, consortiums of vendors, government bodies, and worldwide standards organizations. Typically, the sponsoring vendor, consortium, or standards organization controls the specifications but works with other vendors and users at public meetings to define the specifications. Recent trends have moved away from striving for complete openness and more towards acceptance of in-place standards. For example, the Transmission Control Protocol/Internet Protocol (TCP/IP) protocols have proved more popular than the Open Systems Interconnection (OSI) protocols because of the momentum gained as the primary protocol in use by the Internet. Most vendors now support TCP/IP, while few support the OSI protocols.

Several organizations involved in the standards process are listed next, including those that support the use and integration of in-place standards, such as the Open Software Foundation.

▼ The Open Systems Interconnection (OSI) model was developed by the International Organization for Standardization (ISO) in the early 1980s. It defines protocols and standards for the interconnection of computers and network equipment.

■ The Open Software Foundation (OSF) is a membership organization that acquires technologies from other vendors to create computing environments. Its environments include the Distributed Computing Environment (DCE), an open platform that simplifies the development of products in heterogeneous environments. It is also involved with OSF/1, a UNIX-like environment, and OSF/Motif, a graphical user interface.

■ The Common Open Software Environment (COSE) is a consortium of vendors including IBM, Hewlett-Packard, SunSoft, and Novell that are cooperating to deliver a common desktop environment (CDE) to UNIX that can rival Microsoft Windows.

■ The Object Management Group (OMG) develops a suite of object-oriented languages, interfaces, and protocol standards that vendors can use to create applications that operate in multivendor environments. OMG certifies the compliance of products that are designed to the standard.

■ SQL Access Group (SAG) is a group of database management system (DBMS) vendors that have taken on the goal of creating interoperable Structured Query Language (SQL) database standards. SAG consults with the ISO and ANSI (American National Standards Institute) to bring about its goals.

▲ X/Open Ltd. is a group of vendors that promotes open, multivendor environments for the creation of interoperable applications. It publishes information and provides certification services.

Computer vendors such as IBM, DEC (Compaq), Hewlett-Packard, and others have recently supplemented or moved away from the proprietary architectures and systems they advocated in the 1970s and 1980s to new open environments. For example, IBM now supports its existing customer needs for Systems Application Architecture (SAA), Advanced Peer-to-Peer Networking (APPN), and other standards, as well as new customer needs for open environments by defining the Networking Blueprint, which has the following features:

▼ Hides the underlying networking components so customers can use applications of choice. This is accomplished through the use of the OSF DCE and OSI standards.

■ Allows the use of multiple communication protocols, such as APPN, TCP/IP, and OSI.

▲ Uses advanced bandwidth technologies for communication.

Digital Equipment Corporation supports the OSI protocols with DECnet Phase V, which was announced in 1987. It provided full compliance with the OSI model and backward compatibility to Phase IV. However, in 1991, DEC announced ADVANTAGE-NETWORKS, a strategy that adds support for other protocols such as TCP/IP. In doing so, DEC backed away from its total commitment to OSI in Phase V. Most important, DEC provides support for TCP/IP and the ability to build multiprotocol backbones that can transport DECnet, TCP/IP, and OSI data. For example, users can transmit data between TCP/IP applications using OSI transport protocols, or between OSI applications using TCP protocols.

# MOVE TO INTEROPERABILITY

The OSI protocols have served as the model for open systems design for the last decade, although general acceptance of the protocols has been slow. IBM and DEC now fully support OSI. Even the Internet community, which uses the TCP/IP protocols, has been working to integrate OSI protocols. However, with generally sluggish acceptance of OSI, vendors continue to design proprietary products and advocate their own networking architectures. Recently, however, TCP/IP has been one of the driving forces toward interoperability, mainly because of its ability to handle internetworking and its widespread use on the Internet.

The open systems movement has shifted from the need to develop one grand protocol model such as OSI to the acceptance of many different protocols. As companies move to integrate their departmental computers into enterprise systems, there is a requirement to integrate IPX, TCP/IP, AppleTalk, NetBIOS, and many other protocols into the emerging network platform that ties everything together. Advances in processing power, multiprotocol routers, and middleware software have made this multiprotocol support feasible.

Middleware in this case is a generic term that refers to software platforms that hide underlying systems from applications and allow applications to interface with one another. For example, a user running a Windows application on a Novell network can access a traditionally incompatible database on a UNIX computer system attached to a TCP/IP network. The middleware product handles all the communication and interfacing requirements.

The acceptance of many different protocols and the availability of equipment to handle them have brought about an expanding market in interoperable products. Network administrators and users now have more choices, and can use many more of the resources available on their networks. In addition, product vendors can concentrate more on designing unique products and concentrate less on compatibility issues.

# OPEN SYSTEMS INTERCONNECTION (OSI) MODEL

The OSI model is a standard that was created by the International Organization for Standardization (ISO). It defines a layered model for an open systems environment in which a process running in one computer can communicate with a similar process in another computer if they implement the same OSI layer communication protocols. The OSI model is pictured in Figure A-1. During a communication session, processes running in each layer on each computer communicate with one another. The bottom layer defines the actual physical components such as connectors and cable and the electrical transmission of data bits between systems. The layers immediately above define data packaging and addressing methods. Still further up are methods for keeping communication sessions alive. Finally, the uppermost layers describe how applications use the underlying communication systems to interact with applications on other systems.

The OSI model was designed to help developers create applications that are compatible across multivendor product lines, and to promote open, interoperable networking systems. While OSI hasn't caught on as planned, its model is still used to describe and define how various vendors' products communicate. A comparison of the OSI protocol stack to other protocol stacks is pictured in Figure A-2.

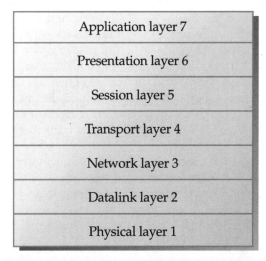

**Figure A-1.**    The Open Systems Interconnection model

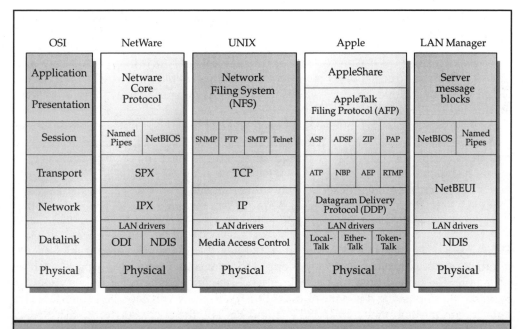

**Figure A-2.**    Protocol model comparison

Protocols are loaded into a computer as software drivers. Each layer of the protocol stack defines a specific set of functions. An application at the uppermost layer interacts with the layer below when it needs to send information to another system on the network. The request is packaged in one layer and passed down to the next layer, which adds information related to functions handled at that layer, creating a new packet within a packet. This package is then passed down to the next layer and the process continues, as shown in Figure A-3. Each layer adds information to the message packet, and this information is read by the corresponding layer in the receiving system's protocol stack. In this way, each protocol layer communicates with its corresponding protocol layer to facilitate communication.

Each layer defines rules and procedures that communication subsystems must follow in order to communicate with peer processes on other systems. Some example processes handled by communication subsystems are listed next:

▼ Interaction and exchanges between applications, as well as translations between differences in syntax and data representations

■ Data exchange management in either full-duplex or half-duplex mode

■ Connection-oriented session management (that is, monitoring and maintenance of a communication channel between two systems)

■ Network routing and addressing procedures

■ Network drivers (that is, framing of data in preparation for transmission)

▲ Network interface card functions (that is, the transmission of electrical, optical, or radio signals over the network media)

Product developers use protocol standards to create products that interoperate with other vendors' products. For example, the bottom layers define hardware interfacing techniques. A developer working at this level designs network hardware and software drivers following the rules defined in the layer.

In an actual communication session, each layer in the protocol stack communicates with its peer layer in the other system, but it does so by adding the information it needs to communicate to a packet that is passed down to the next lower protocol layer, as mentioned previously.

The following sections describe network protocols. You must have the network hardware—the Physical layer—in place before any of the other layers of communication can take place, so the Physical layer is described first.

**THE PHYSICAL LAYER**   The Physical layer defines the physical characteristics of the interface, such as mechanical components and connectors, electrical aspects such as voltage levels representing binary values, and functional aspects such as setting up, maintaining, and taking down the physical link. Well-known Physical layer interfaces for data communication include EIA RS-232 and RS-449, the successor to RS-232. RS-449 allows longer cable distances. Well-known local area network (LAN) systems are Ethernet, token ring, and Fiber Distributed Data Interface (FDDI).

Frame of data

| Layer | Information added |
|---|---|
| Application | Node address added |
| Presentation | Code-set information added |
| Session | Communications information added |
| Transport | Checksum header added |
| Network | Packet quantity/sequence information added |
| Datalink | Packet checksum trailer/message end added |
| Physical | Packet sent as bit-stream |

**Figure A-3.** Information related to the functions of each layer is added to a packet as it passes down the protocol stack

**THE DATALINK LAYER** The Datalink layer defines the rules for sending and receiving information across the physical connection between two systems. This layer encodes and frames data for transmission, in addition to providing error detection and control. Because the Datalink layer can provide error control, higher layers may not need to handle such services. However, when a reliable medium is used, there is a performance advantage by not handling error control in this layer, but in higher layers. Bridges operate at this level in the protocol stack. Here are common protocols occupying the Datalink layer:

▼ High-level Data Link Control (HDLC) and related synchronous, bit-oriented protocols

■ LAN drivers and access methods, such as Ethernet and token ring

■ Fast packet wide area networks, such as frame relay and Asynchronous Transfer Mode (ATM)

■ Microsoft's Network Driver Interface Specification (NDIS)

▲ Novell's Open Datalink Interface (ODI)

**THE NETWORK LAYER** The Network layer defines protocols for opening and maintaining a path on the network between systems. It is concerned with data transmission and switching procedures, and hides such procedures from upper layers. Routers operate at the Network layer. The Network layer can look at packet addresses to determine routing methods. If a packet is addressed to a workstation on the local network, it is sent directly there. If it's addressed to a network on another segment, the packet is sent to a routing device, which forwards it on the network. Here are common protocols occupying the Network layer:

▼ Internet Protocol (IP)

■ X.25 Protocol

■ Novell's Internetwork Packet Exchange (IPX)

▲ Banyan VINES Internet Protocol (VIP)

**THE TRANSPORT LAYER**    The Transport layer provides a high level of control for moving information between systems, including more sophisticated error handling, prioritization, and security features. The Transport layer provides quality service and accurate delivery by providing connection-oriented services between two end systems. It controls the sequence of packets, regulates traffic flow, and recognizes duplicate packets. The Transport layer assigns packetized information a tracking number that is checked at the destination. If data is missing from the packet, the Transport-layer protocol at the receiving end arranges with the Transport layer of the sending system to have packets retransmitted. This layer ensures that all data is received and in the proper order. A logical circuit, which is like a dedicated connection, can be established to provide a reliable transmission between systems. Non-OSI Transport-layer protocols that can provide connection-oriented services include the following:

▼ Internet Transmission Control Protocol (TCP)

■ Internet User Datagram Protocol (UDP)

■ Novell's Sequenced Packet Exchange (SPX)

■ Banyan VINES Interprocess Communication Protocol (VICP)

▲ Microsoft NetBIOS/NetBEUI

**THE SESSION LAYER**    The Session layer coordinates the exchange of information between systems by using conversational techniques, or dialogues. Dialogs are not always required, but some applications may require a way of knowing where to restart the transmission of data if a connection is temporarily lost, or may require a periodic dialog to indicate the end of one data set and the start of a new one.

**THE PRESENTATION LAYER**    Protocols at the Presentation layer are part of the operating system and application the user runs in a workstation. Information is formatted for display or printing in this layer. Codes within the data, such as tabs or special graphics sequences, are interpreted. Data encryption and the translation of other character sets are also handled in this layer.

**THE APPLICATION LAYER**   Applications access the underlying network services using defined procedures in this layer. The Application layer is used to define a range of applications that handle file transfers, terminal sessions, and message exchange (for example, electronic mail). OSI Application layer protocols are listed here:

▼   Virtual Terminal

■   File Transfer Access and Management (FTAM)

■   Distributed Transaction Processing (DTP)

■   Message Handling System (X.400)

▲   Directory Services (X.500)

Figure A-4 shows how data flows through the protocol stack and over the medium from one system to another. Data starts at the Application and Presentation layers, where a user works with a network application, such as an electronic mail program. Requests for services are passed through the Presentation layer to the Session layer, which begins the process of packetizing the information. A connection-oriented communication session may be opened between the two systems to provide reliable transmissions. Once the session is established, protocol layers begin exchanging information as appropriate.

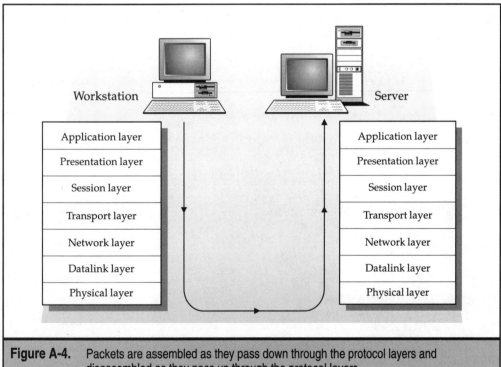

**Figure A-4.**   Packets are assembled as they pass down through the protocol layers and disassembled as they pass up through the protocol layers

# APPENDIX B

## The Standards Organizations

Throughout this book I refer to standards and specifications issued by various national and international standards organizations. To help you understand how these organizations interact—as well as to help you make your way through the "alphabet soup" of these organizations' acronyms—I've listed the names and descriptions of the major standards bodies.

# AMERICAN NATIONAL STANDARDS INSTITUTE (ANSI)

This U.S.-based organization defines coding standards and signaling schemes for the entire nation, as well as functioning as the U.S. representative in the International Standards Organization and the International Telecommunications Union's Consultative Committee for Telegraph and Telephone. You can visit their Web site at http://www.ansi.org, or write to them at

> American National Standards Institute
> 11 West 42nd Street, 13th Floor
> New York, NY 10036
> 212-642-4900

# INTERNATIONAL CONSULTATIVE COMMITTEE FOR TELEGRAPH AND TELEPHONE (CCITT)

The CCITT is a committee of the United Nations organization called the International Telecommunications Union, and is now commonly referred to simply as the ITU. The function of the ITU's CCITT is to study and develop draft technical and procedural standards for international telecommunications. The CCITT forwards its draft standards to the ITU, which votes to adopt or reject the drafts as international standards. The United States is involved with the ITU, as it is with all United Nations organizations, through the U.S. Departments of State and Commerce. You can visit their Web site at http://www.itu.ch. You can also get copies of ITU proposals and recommendations by writing

> U.S. Department of Commerce
> National Technical Information Service
> 5285 Port Royal Road
> Springfield, VA 22161
> 703-487-4650

# INSTITUTE OF ELECTRICAL AND ELECTRONIC ENGINEERS (IEEE)

This is a society based in the United States that develops standards for the electrical and electronics industries. Networking professionals are particularly interested in the work of the IEEE 802 committees, which develop data communications standards for local area networks. The 802 committees focus their efforts on developing standards protocols for the physical interface of local area network connections, which functions on the Physical and Datalink layers of the ISO/OSI Reference Model (see Appendix A). These specifications define how data connections among network devices are made, managed, and terminated, as well as specifying physical connections such as cabling and connectors.

After completing draft standards, the IEEE 802 committees forward them to the American National Standards Institute and/or to the International Standards Organization for finalization and adoption.

The IEEE 802 committees are

802.1   Internetworking
802.2   Logical Link Control
802.3   CSMA/CD Local Area Networks
802.4   Token Bus Local Area Networks
802.5   Token Ring Local Area Networks
802.6   Metropolitan Area Networks
802.7   Broadband Technical Advisory Group
802.8   Fiber-Optic Technical Advisory Group
802.9   Integrated Voice and Data Networks
802.10  Network Security
802.11  Wireless Networks
802.12  Demand Priority Access Local Area Networks

You can contact the IEEE at

Institute of Electrical and Electronics Engineers
445 Hoes Lane
P.O. Box 1331
Piscataway, NJ 08855-1331
908-981-1393
800-678-4333

# INTERNATIONAL STANDARDS ORGANIZATION (ISO)

The International Standards Organization has representatives from important standards organizations all over the world, including the United Nations' Economic and Social Council. Its goal is to develop and adopt standards of all kinds that will facilitate international trade and intercultural exchange. Therefore, the International Standards Institute is involved in developing standards for everything from weights and measures to business practices to networking protocols. The United States is represented in the International Standards Organization by the American National Standards Institute. You can visit their Web site at http://www.iso.ch, or write to them at

International Organization for Standardization
1, rue de Varembé
Case postale 56
CH-1211 Genève 20
SWITZERLAND
41-22-479-0111

# APPENDIX C

## Bibliography

Technical knowledge obviously comes from many places. Mine has come from a variety of sources: testing and working with products, talking to analysts, debating with vendors, pouring through standards documents, and reading everything I can on the subject of high-speed protocols. Although there is no substitute for the knowledge I've gained from my experience working with these technologies and the people who develop and work with them, reading has been an invaluable source of reference material and ideas. The following is a selective bibliography of the works that I have found especially helpful:

Black, Uyless, *ATM: Foundation for Broadband Networks*, Prentice Hall PTR, Englewood Cliffs, NJ, 1995.

Black, Uyless, *Data Link Protocols*, Prentice Hall PTR, Englewood Cliffs, NJ, 1993.

Bryce, James Y., *Using ISDN, Que Corporation*, Indianapolis, IN, 1995.

Handel, R., and Huber, M. N., *Integrated Broadband Networks: An Introduction to ATM-Based Networks*, Addison-Wesley Publishing Company, Reading, MA, 1991.

Held, Gilbert, *Ethernet Networks*, John Wiley & Sons, Inc., New York, NY, 1994.

Hopkins, Gerald L., *The ISDN Literacy Book*, Addison-Wesley Publishing Company, Reading, MA, 1995.

Miller, Mark A., *Managing Internetworks with SNMP*, M&T Books, a subsidiary of Henry Holt and Company, Inc., New York, NY, 1993.

Motorola University Press, *The Basics Book of ISDN*, 2nd edition, Addison-Wesley Publishing Company, Reading, MA, 1992.

Shah, Amit, and Ramakrishnan, G., *FDDI: A High Speed Network*, Prentice Hall PTR, Englewood Cliffs, NJ, 1994.

Sheldon, Tom, *LAN Times Encyclopedia of Networking*, Osborne/McGraw-Hill, Berkeley, CA, 1998.

Sheldon, Tom, *LAN Times Guide to Interoperability*, Osborne/McGraw-Hill, Berkeley, CA, 1994.

Smith, Philip, *Frame Relay: Principles and Applications*, Addison-Wesley Publishing Company, Reading, MA, 1993.

# Index

## G

## H

## M

## N